Making
Music
in

Looking
Glass
Land

Third Edition

A Guide to Survival
and Business Skills
for the Classical Musician

Ellen Highstein

A Concert Artists Guild Publication

Highstein, Ellen.

Making Music in Looking Glass Land:
A Guide to Survival and Business Skills for the Classical Musician.

ISBN 0-9629075-9-6

Concert Artists Guild is a non-profit organization which, since its founding in 1951, has been dedicated to the career development of gifted musical artists. The Guild is a membership organization, offering its members invitations to concerts, special events, a newsletter and other benefits. For further information on Guild programs, write to the address above, or call 212-333-5200.

Ellen Highstein, Executive Director
Robert Besen, Associate Director, Artist Services
Christopher Crowley, Associate, Artist Services
Mary Madigan, Director of Marketing / Manager, Corporate & Individual Giving
Sarah Schwartz, Manager, Foundation and Government Grants
Jessica Stone, Administrative Assistant

08/02

To Virgil, Gus, Nat and Jennie

Contents

Introduction

Concert Artists Guild began producing career development workshops in 1983. Called <u>Career Moves</u>, the workshops — begun modestly, with one self-produced event that season in New York City, growing to eight to ten workshops each year at venues around the country — were a way of being useful to a larger constituency than would be possible by working only with the entrants to and winners of our annual New York Competition.

It seemed to those at the Guild that most musicians, when they emerge from conservatory, are unprepared for the demands they face in the professional world. Though most pre-professional training may be less than adequate in regard to the realities of post-graduation life, musicians face an additional handicap which is, perhaps, unique; they are encouraged, in preparing for a life in music, to specifically <u>avoid</u> thinking about anything but art . . . or technique, of course. Most performers begin to study music when they're extremely young, and are enthusiastically, sometimes lavishly, rewarded for their talent and effort. Until they graduate into the professional arena, the message is, "just keep practicing; your talent is all you need." When reality hits, they find out that it's not all they need, by a long shot. The effect of meeting the field as it is — moving from a world where everyone knows and respects you to one in which no one knows you, or seems to care much — can be like an ice cold bath. Some kind of orientation, addressing subjects rarely covered in the university or conservatory music curriculum, was badly needed.

When I joined the Guild in 1986, and became involved in developing the workshops and the philosophy behind them, I strove to maximize their value and usefulness by making the information included as specific as possible. Featured speakers include those representing the "consumer's" point of view in relation to the performer, and those artists who, having been through it all, have definite points of view about what works and what doesn't.

Concert Artists Guild still produces these workshops. With this book I have sought to provide a more permanent reference for those who attend them, and to pass on much of the information they include — as well as additional tips — for those who can't be with us in person.

The Career Moves Philosophy

Those of us at the Guild believe that there is inestimable value in studying and making music, that highly trained, gifted musicians should be able to survive to work in their field, and that they shouldn't be stopped in this effort by not knowing how to keep afloat.

To survive in a difficult environment requires knowledge and creativity, no less in this field than elsewhere. By encouraging artists to become informed about the field and their possible place in it, we seek to broaden their knowledge; by shaking up the artists' viewpoints, and getting them to look at the world through other eyes, we hope to stimulate their creativity.

We believe that it is not harmful to musicians to think about issues not directly related to how they play. <u>But we also believe they usually don't think enough even about how they play, in the larger sense — that is, whether they're making music in a way which adds a new thought and a new voice to the field.</u> They also may not have considered whether there will be audiences who will hear them. Therefore, the final message of the workshops and the book concerns the artists' relationship to and responsibility for the future of the field.

Who should find this book useful?

This book is aimed most directly at emerging, professional-level performers and composers of classical music. It often concentrates on specific issues faced by artists aspiring to careers as soloists or chamber musicians, or artists who wish to make solo or chamber music performance part of their professional lives - orchestral musicians, for example. Because it includes information that could be described as

Business For Musicians 101, though, it should be useful to anyone trying to break into the music field — or perhaps other fields as well. Switching the focus to another venture within the profession requires some common sense substitutions of names, categories, and the like, but the concepts remain the same.

What this book includes, and what it doesn't

We've chosen here to address topics which are both basic to an understanding of how the field works and which are the ones about which musicians most consistently seem to want information. It would be impossible to convey the breadth of knowledge and wealth of detail (not to mention the anecdotes and entertainment) provided by our expert guest speakers; however, we've tried to maintain the tone of the workshops, which we hope is savvy without being cynical. We've also tried to provide the specific information — names, addresses, phone numbers, and prices — which back up more general guidance, either in the text or in the Resource Sections. If something of this kind has been left out, we would be delighted if our readers would point this out so that we can include it in a future edition. There are many topics which we have not included, and which might be of interest. Please let us know what additional chapters would be useful to you. Your ideas are welcomed.

This is a how-to-survive-as-a-musician book, not a how-to-become-something-else book. It is neither professional training in publicity, audio engineering, graphic design, or anything else, nor is it vocational guidance if your efforts in career building don't succeed. We tell you how to write certain kinds of letters, and how to make some phone calls; however, when we deal with areas that require specific, non-musical technical skill in support of your career efforts, we suggest what you should aim for, how to spot problems and find solutions on a budget, and how to find a professional who will give you value for your money. Should you decide that you want to engineer your own tapes and CDs, produce your own graphics, or do the legal work involved in not-for-profit incorporation, there are other sources, far more complete than we could be here, which will tell you how. As for career alternatives, and day jobs, we've limited ourselves to references to other sources and some remarks interpolated into the text.

A note for composers

Composers' career development needs sometimes require a slightly different way of looking at the field and slightly different support materials. I hope that composers will read the whole book and not just the chapter on composers anyway, since our approach to developing a place in the field is basically the same for performers and for composers, and much of what is stated is therefore equally applicable to anyone in the business. It will require some patience, and some creative substitutions of terms or ideas as you go along. Our apologies for the resulting awkwardness, and our hope that you will find it worth the effort.

How is this book organized?

The order of the chapters very generally corresponds to the order of what is needed when in a developing career. That is, you probably will need a good tape and some decent pictures before you can approach those in the professional world; you may need to amass some credentials — through performances and competition experience for example — before approaching various important individuals who will form a supportive network of associates; you will need this network before you can approach a manager.

There are, however, many exceptions to this order. Chapter IX, "On Stage," should logically be at the beginning but appears near the end of the book, since it serves more as a reminder to take care of this issue rather than as advice and instruction on specifics. The second part of Chapter VI (which deals with self-management) could appear much earlier, perhaps in the section on developing credentials; it appears here to demonstrate how the gulf between management and self-management is more apparent than real. And the section on making CDs appears too early, in Chapter III; but it was simply easier to place this information in a section dealing with audio and recording.

Some ways of organizing all the preceding material appear in the last chapter; here's where the reader will find new sections entitled "It's Never Too Early To ... " and "What You Can't Afford to Graduate Without," both of which should be helpful in personalizing your musical development calendar.

The *Resource Sections* which follow each chapter and Chapter X, "General Resources" contain specific information which backs up much of our advice. The information included in the Resource Sections directly refers to the issues in that chapter; the most general references are listed at the end. The "Topic and Resource Index" provides an easy way of quickly looking up this information without having to go through the chapter topics.

Being very specific does mean running the risk of being quickly outdated. The information included is correct (double and triple-checked) as of 1997, and periodic updates help us to keep the names and numbers current. Our apologies in advance for any inaccuracies.

Why we often use New York City in our examples

Our frequent reference to New York City is not because we believe that this is the only place to be, but rather because, first, we know the field in this city very well, and second, a very large number of aspiring musicians do come here to start their careers. This does not in any way constitute a recommendation that those aspiring to a life in music should be based in New York. Depending on the artist and the goal, our feeling is often quite the contrary.

Acknowledgments

This book is truly the product of the generosity and wisdom of the <u>Career Moves</u> workshop speakers, particularly those who have participated in workshops since 1987. The Guild and I cannot sufficiently express our gratitude to them all.

The author owes a debt as well to all those who generously read, criticized, took apart and put together . . . and generally made great improvements to this third edition. They include, among others, CAG staff members Robert Besen, Mary Madigan, Christopher Crowley, and Sarah Schwartz. Robert Besen is due special, very grateful thanks, as an indefatigable original member of the workshop team, and as the provider of many ideas and much information. Our summer administrative assistant, Charles Bartunek, did much of the exhaustive updating for this third edition, with additional updates researched by Jessica Stone. Ongoing thanks are due to Ray Ring for his design concept for the book. And a final acknowledgment is due for the "Alice" illustrations of John Tenniel, the source of some inspiration and much amusement for the CAG staff, as they hopefully will be for readers.

A note to the third edition

For this new edition of *Making Music*, several sections have been added and all the material has been extensively reviewed and rethought; nonetheless, some things have been left unchanged. When an example or an interview has been left unchanged from previous editions, it is probably because it still seemed to be the best example, or the most illuminating advice, that I could find.

- Ellen Highstein
Executive Director
Concert Artists Guild

I. The Lay of the Land

> *"Now! Now!" cried the*
> *Queen. "Faster! Faster!" And they went so*
> *fast that at last they seemed to skim through*
> *the air, hardly touching the ground with their feet till, suddenly,*
> *just as Alice was getting quite exhausted, they stopped, and she*
> *found herself sitting on the ground, breathless and giddy.*
>
> *The Queen propped her up against a tree, and said kindly,*
> *"You may rest a little now."*
>
> *Alice looked round her in great surprise. "Why, I do believe*
> *we've been under this tree the whole time! Everything's just as it*
> *was!"*
>
> *"Of course it is," said the Queen. "What would you have it?"*
>
> *"Well, in our country," said Alice, still panting a little, "you'd*
> *generally get to somewhere else — if you ran very fast for a long*
> *time, as we've been doing."*
>
> *"A slow sort of country!" said the Queen. "Now, here, you*
> *see, it takes all the running you can do to keep in the same place. If*
> *you want to get somewhere else, you must run at least twice as fast*
> *as that!"*
>
> — Lewis Carroll, <u>Through the Looking Glass</u>

The field of classical music is, for most performers, like Looking Glass Land. There are a very few individuals who, because of circumstance — extreme youth combined with extraordinary ability, acknowledged elder statesman status, or an extra-musical and sensational entry into the field, for example — seem able to leave their career development problems to others: but they are very few and far between. For most musicians, the effort to stay in the same place, to keep working in the field, is constant and endless.

The performer is dependent for the success of this effort on the supportive assistance and good will of an exceptionally large group of people. He or she needs the enthusiasm, interest, confidence and familiarity of presenters, conductors, managers, the press, colleagues and audience. The classical music field is certainly not unique in this; other fields — politics for one — share in the fact that without the support of a large personal constituency one's career efforts are likely to fail. However, classical musicians are perhaps unique in believing the myth that great artistry, and more practicing, are all they need, and that having to go out and work on developing a constituency is proof of artistic failure.

In this fantasy the performer is encouraged by a system of training which, by and large, addresses only the question of how to sound good enough for the job rather than how to get the job. In fairness, since it is very difficult indeed to achieve great proficiency as a performer, the overwhelming amount of the conservatory's and the teacher's attention is necessarily directed to a restricted number of musical issues. Also, a few people seem naturally to have the creative instincts and political savvy which can win them admiration and employment. But working at developing these qualities is often seen within the field as detracting from the main business of playing, and the acquisition of them — if not discouraged — is generally not applauded.

Most musicians want to survive as musicians, though, and are willing to work to make that happen. <u>It is impossible, even with great effort and great talent, to guarantee a major career.</u> Such careers exist as the result of a confluence of factors, many not under the control of either the performer or the performer's advisors. <u>It is probably possible, however, to make a career which allows the performer to keep making music before the public.</u> It does take some changes in most musicians' thinking about the field and their role in it.

To maximize the chance of being in demand as a performer, you, the artist, must:

▪ Know the marketplace

Understand who is listening to music, and when, where, why and how they're listening; who pays for the creation and performance of music, and how music and audiences are brought together; be able to see where flexibility exists in these market conditions, and how they can be influenced by a creative approach.

- ## Know the customer

  See the field from the consumer's point of view, including those of the various groups in your constituency.

- ## Know yourself

  Understand, specifically and precisely, what you have to contribute to the field, what makes you unique as a musician.

Acting on this knowledge does not imply changing to suit a current craze, or creating false relationships with those said to be important and influential. Rather, this understanding must be used to find your own supportive constituency, and to create opportunities for sharing your particular musical vision with others.

The Marketplace

It is important to understand that the field of classical music is a marketplace, with buyers and sellers, consumers and products. The consumers and buyers are a varied bunch, including audiences, concert presenters, musical colleagues (conductors, orchestra managers, artist managers and others), the press and electronic media and patrons. As in any marketplace, there is money being made and spent. Understanding where the money is, and what causes it to move around, is basic to understanding why the field functions as it does. As in any marketplace, there is at any given time more or less interest in a specific item. There are fashions and trends, caused by social, cultural and economic factors.

It is a buyers' market. To demonstrate this in regard to performers, you need only attend one of the big performing arts trade shows, and see the market in action (see Resource Section). Visiting the biggest of these, the annual conference sponsored by the Association of Performing Arts Presenters (APAP), can be an exceptionally unsettling (and perhaps discouraging) experience. Picture the enormous convention rooms of a major New York City hotel, filled with booths manned by managers and artists ranging from the giants (Columbia Artists Management and the like) to individual players. Music, dance, theater and everything else are cheek by jowl, vying for attention. With video monitors, photo and record displays, slogans, dishes of candy and free ice cream cones, the sellers try to attract the attention of the buyers: the concert presenters. Representatives of organizations presenting performers, from Lincoln Center to small arts series in tiny towns across the country, wander among the booths, looking for something new, something different — or perhaps not, perhaps looking for their friends, and for the same tried and true performances that have worked for them in the past.

The sellers far outnumber the buyers. Each of the booths operated by a management represents a roster of artists; simple arithmetic is all that's needed to demonstrate how few opportunities there are relative to the number of artists who want them. Further divide the number of performance slots available by the number that feature music, and then by the few that want classical music. And then remember all those musicians not "on display," competing for the same jobs!

Other conditions have contributed to musicians' marketing difficulties. Among them is the fact that artists are often hired apart from direct experience of them as performers: on the basis of third party recommendations (from managers, critics, colleagues or teachers), or materials such as pictures, flyers and demo tapes. And because of the current state of music education and the complexities of the way the field is administered, even when presenters have the opportunity to actually hear the artist in live performance, they may not be capable of or confident in their own ability to distinguish great from merely good, or even merely competent, music-making.

What all this means is, simply, too few jobs chased by too many good musicians. The artist must therefore define clear, realistic career goals in the field and understand what may be required, both musically and extra-musically, to achieve them.

The Customer

You need people to provide the support which will make it possible for you to work. Among them are:

- **Fans** - audiences who will come to hear you (or hear your music, if you're a composer), pay for tickets, applaud, tell their friends, write to the concert presenter to get you rehired, and come again.

- **Presenters** - people who will hire you to play.

- **Colleagues** - other musicians or people in the field who will often be the primary source of direct employment or referrals for work, and who offer a network of musical and emotional support.

- **Patrons** - individuals who have the wherewithal to provide financial or other support for career development when it's needed.

All of these consumers behave much as consumers of any other product or service do. They tend to think of the familiar and the well-known before the less familiar and the obscure. They operate with a set of restrictions (budgetary, aesthetic, etc.) which affect their choices. And — they tend to like to choose and work with their friends.

Part of successfully working with a constituency, therefore, is developing friendly relationships with these consumers.

Self-knowledge (Musically Speaking)

It stands to reason that in an overcrowded field the person who stands out is the one who has something very special — even unique — to offer. Obviously, you are in the best position to know what you have that is unique. For many artists, defining and articulating what these special qualities are, specifically rather than generally, is very difficult. But it is absolutely essential:

> **If <u>you</u> don't know what about you is special, those who don't know you <u>certainly</u> won't know;**

> **If you don't know, you won't be able to tell anyone;**

> **If you can't tell anyone, then you may not get the opportunity to show what you have to offer to an audience, and they won't get to hear these special qualities for themselves.**

Specifics

Once the principle is accepted that it is not enough to be good, but that you must let others know that you're good, you can follow some quite specific guidelines in moving toward making a consistent and fulfilling life in music. It is useful to keep in mind that starting out in music requires the same investment of time, money and marketing creativity as starting a small business. It also may require the same kind of hard-nosed business decisions; how scarce hours are best spent, how resources — financial and otherwise — can be put to maximum use.

Like any business person, the musician needs:

- **Credentials**

- **Effective communications materials**

- **A supportive network of customers**

- **The ability to deliver the goods when the job has been landed.**

The first sections of this book will deal with both amassing performance and other credentials and assembling the physical materials with which an artist represents him or herself to the world.

Resource Section

Information Source Book

To learn about the marketplace, to learn more about your customers, and to see who's out there trying to do what you're trying to do, an important source of information will be:

Musical America International Directory of the Performing Arts
Published by:
  Musical America Publishing Inc.
  K-III Directory Corporation Publication
  10 Lake Drive
  Hightstown, NJ 08520
  609-371-7700 (phone)

Referred to throughout this book, this is pretty much the bible of the industry. The Directory is published annually in December, and is expensive — the 1997 edition costs $95. However, it is available in most general libraries and almost all music libraries. If you're feeling wealthy, you could buy one at a music store.

Besides being a source of much general news about the business (the Directory annually features their equivalent of the Time Magazine Man of the Year, for example, which is fun), virtually all of the 800 or so pages contain useful information. The advertising and articles cover almost every management, and will give you a feel for who's doing what: the listings include sections on orchestras, performance series, festivals, music schools, competitions, publishers of music, magazines and newspapers, and on and on. Not all listings are equally complete, and you shouldn't use these lists without further research, but it's a good place to start, and as good an overall view of the field as you can get.

Trade Shows

If you should want to attend a trade show (the biggest one is organized by the Association of Performing Arts Presenters, and is held in New York City each January), there are several ways. You can try to hook up with someone who is renting a booth — a manager or whoever — and ask them to buy an extra pass for you, which will cost them $20 each over the number of passes included in their booth rental. You can, similarly, try to find a presenter who will include you in their group, again for the fee imposed per additional badge. You can rent a booth yourself (a "half" booth, 5' X 10', is $790), but you have to be an APAP member, and that's $450. If you are a full-time student, you can attend for free by volunteering to help out, with registration or other needed administration. Call Jane Roxbury at the number below to inquire about this possibility.

Association of Performing Arts Presenters
1112 16th Street N.W., #400
Washington, D.C. 20036
202-833-2787

Alternatively, you could attend one of the regional shows. Though less gigantic, they will give you the feel of the market at its most marketlike. Some of these, with conference times, are:

New England Presenters
Music Dept., Amherst College
Amherst, MA 01002-5000
413-542-2199
September
(NEPAC) Northeastern
Performing Arts Conference

Southern Arts Federation
181 14th Street NE.
Suite 400
Atlanta, GA 30309
404-874-7244
Late September

Western Alliance of Arts Administrators
44 Page St.
#604B
San Francisco, CA 94102
415-621-4400
Early September

Arts Midwest
528 Hennepin Ave.
Suite 310
Minneapolis, MN 55403
612-341-0755
Mid-September

II. Materials

Written and Visual Materials

We live in a visual culture, where much of the time what you see is what you believe. No matter how good your tape is it may not get played unless your supporting materials, both written and pictorial, are intriguing enough to convince someone to listen to it. These materials have to look professional. In our advertising-infused society, your potential customers, whatever their musical background, are almost certainly very visually sophisticated; less than professional looking materials imply less than professional quality artists. Your materials must be both attractive and must convey an arresting, accurate message about you.

On the positive side, with the almost universal availability of computers and laser printers, some of the materials you will need can be produced very cheaply and can be very slick. On the negative side, some materials — notably photos — are expensive, and all require regular updating.

The most basic materials that a musician needs are a biography and a picture. In addition to these, at some point you may want to put together a complete press kit, which would contain reproductions of reviews and other supporting materials and perhaps a flyer, as well as the preceding materials. If you are presenting a concert, you will need some kind of advertising piece (a flyer, postcard, or brochure) which will let the public know about the event. We will discuss each of these in order. The materials which composers use to introduce themselves and their work to the world are specialized, and will be discussed in the chapter specifically directed to them; nonetheless, composers should read the following materials, and note the general principles which apply to everyone. Items such as press releases and pitch letters, which are sent to the press together with these materials, will be discussed in Chapter V.

While reading this section, keep in mind that its aim is not to teach you the technical details of photography, flyer design, proofreading language, printing terms, etc., though you may want to learn something about these from one of the many sources available. Rather we hope to encourage you to think as an informed and discerning consumer, and understand your specific responsibilities in the process, while keeping in mind the point of view of the recipient of your materials. For example, we will describe how to choose a photographer, what you want your pictures to look like, and how to get the resulting pictures reproduced, since that is your responsibility. We won't tell you how to take pictures, or what kind of film a photographer should use.

Biographies

What you need for a) getting performing jobs, and b) sending information on yourself to the press, managers, or others in your potential constituency, is a narrative biography. A resume — that is, a non-narrative listing of credentials and accomplishments that is often arranged in reverse chronological order — is useful for getting academic jobs, applying for arts council grants and the like, and for certain areas in the field which specifically require one (opera companies, for example, will want to see chronologically arranged resumes with lists of roles learned or performed). Should you need a resume, there are books which will tell you how to create an effective one (see Resource Section); if you're still in school, your placement or career development office can certainly help you to put one together.

However, the narrative biography is a basic tool for letting the world know what **you** consider to be your most important professional accomplishments and qualities.

Usually this biography will <u>not</u> be chronological; the fact that you began to play the snare drum at the age of two, and the names of your first teachers, will not, hopefully, be the most interesting things about you to date. Remember who's reading it: to a media person those kinds of facts probably aren't news, and a presenter, for example, is considering hiring you for the professional you are now, not for the talented child you were yesterday. (Obviously if you are extremely young, the fact that you are a prodigy may, for the time being, be most important.) The narrative biography is written much like a news story, in the inverted pyramid form; the most important information — what makes you special — is in the first paragraph, and the information becomes of lesser importance as the reader proceeds through the later paragraphs. The least important or the most general background information should end the biography.

In many cases your biography will be used as is: by presenters in their program booklets and promotional materials, by the press when writing about you or announcing your program in the paper or on the air, and by others who need to distribute information about you. There are several reasons, therefore, for using the narrative format biography:

- You're controlling both the content and the order of the information, and making sure that the things which you think are most important are those that are picked up; when you leave that decision to others, you may not be lucky in their choices.

- You're making it more likely that the press will want to put something in the paper or on the air, since you're saving them valuable time. A busy journalist won't have to extract and create a story out of a resume.

If you are advanced enough in your career to have a substantial amount of material to use for your biography, it is helpful to have several versions of different lengths available, ranging from one paragraph to a full length piece of one to three pages.

Here are examples of biographies Concert Artists Guild uses for several of our artists. All are on Guild letterhead, with our address and phone number clearly included. Your biography, in fact all of your materials, must include this kind of information.

Pianist Mia Chung has done a lot and received considerable recognition, and it's simply a question of finding the right order to put it in. The first paragraph of this biography includes information her winning our competition (we always put this credit up front, as the biography is a source of information about us as well as our artists) as well as the Avery Fisher Career Grant. These two awards serve to legitimize our saying that she "has quickly ascended to the top ranks of America's young pianists."

The second paragraph highlights the praise she has received for her recordings, as well as a reference to a very successful New York debut, including some impressive press quotes; the third paragraph is devoted to her residency activities with three major radio stations in Boston, Washington D.C. and nationally through National Public Radio. The fourth paragraph lists her engagements for the next season and one prior season, and her participation in the Chamber Music Society Two; the fifth, past concert activities; and the last, her educational background and current teaching credentials. Note how this information is left for the end, as it is least relevant to her immediate booking prospects.

Note also the date at the bottom of the second page; it is important for the reader to know how recently the bio has been updated and approved.

MIA CHUNG, piano

Since winning First Prize, the U.S. Trust Award, the Channel Classics Prize, and the ITT Corporation Prize at the Concert Artists Guild Competition in 1993, Mia Chung has quickly ascended to the top ranks of America's young pianists. Most recently, Ms. Chung was recognized with an Avery Fisher Career Grant in April 1997.

Ms. Chung has received the highest praise for her interpretations of Beethoven's sonatas. Her debut recording, as part of Channel Classics' Winning Artists Series, features Beethoven sonatas and bagatelles. Upon selecting this recording as a "Best of the Year" for 1995, *Gramophone* magazine noted: "Chung's performance is inspired ... a totally absorbing musical experience." Of her performances of these same sonatas at her New York debut, *The New York Times* wrote, "Uncommonly insightful, individualistic and lively ... Her playing was dazzling." Channel Classics recently released Ms. Chung's second recording which features the music of Robert Schumann; her third recording, also of works by Beethoven, will be released in 1997.

Ms. Chung has been actively involved in radio since 1995, when she served as the first "Young Artist in Residence" for National Public Radio's Performance Today. After working with her, NPR nominated Ms. Chung for "Debut Artist of the Year." Also in 1995, her performances and commentary aired throughout metropolitan Boston when she was "Artist-in-Radio" at WCRB-FM. As the station's resident artist, she brought classical music to inner-city children through in-school concerts. Ms. Chung is currently "Artist-in-Radio" with WGMS-FM in Washington, D.C.

February 1997 marks Ms. Chung's European debut at the Concertgebouw in Amsterdam. As an artist member of the Chamber Music Society Two, a new project of the Chamber Music Society of Lincoln Center, Ms. Chung and her CMS TWO colleagues perform in their own series, collaborate with members of the Chamber Music Society in performances at Alice Tully Hall and Merkin Concert Hall, and participate in educational outreach programs throughout the New York area. Solo performances during the 1996-97 season included engagements at the Concert Society of Maryland, University of Massachusetts at Amherst, the Terrace Theater at the John F. Kennedy Center for the Performing Arts, with the Corpus Christi Symphony Orchestra, and in recital in Parma, Italy. Highlights of her 1995-96 season included debuts in Japan at the Yokohama International Piano Festival, in Seoul, South Korea, in recital at the Hoam Art Hall, and in Boston at Jordan Hall.

(continued)

850 Seventh Avenue/New York, NY 10019 ♦ Tel: 212-333-5200
Fax: 212-977-7149 ♦ E-mail: CAGuild@aol.com ♦ Web: http://www.concertartists.org

Page 2: Mia Chung, piano

Mia Chung made her debut at age twelve as soloist with the Baltimore Symphony Orchestra, and her highly praised recital debut at age eighteen at the Hall of the Americas in Washington, D.C. She has since performed again with the Baltimore Symphony, as well as with the National Symphony and the New Haven Symphony. She made her New York recital debut in 1994 at Weill Recital Hall at Carnegie Hall. Festival appearances include the Flagstaff Festival in Arizona, the Rockport Chamber Music Festival in Massachusetts, and Concert Artists Guild's San Juan Islands Chamber Music Festival. Chosen as an Artistic Ambassador by the United States Information Agency in 1993, Ms. Chung toured the former Soviet Union, Thailand, Singapore, and Tonga under the agency's auspices, becoming the first American pianist to perform in Kazakhstan, Kirghizstan and Turkmenistan.

Mia Chung was born in Madison, Wisconsin, and grew up in the Washington, D.C. area. She holds a Bachelor's degree from Harvard College, a Master's degree from Yale University and a Doctorate from The Juilliard School. Her teachers have included Peter Serkin, Boris Berman, Raymond and Anne Hanson, and George Manos. Ms. Chung is currently Artist-in-Residence and Assistant Professor of Music at Gordon College in Wenham, Massachusetts. She lives in Cambridge, where she is a resident tutor at Harvard College.

April 1997

850 Seventh Avenue/New York, NY 10019 ♦ Tel: 212-333-5200
Fax: 212-977-7149 ♦ E-mail: CAGuild@aol.com ♦ Web: http://www.concertartists.org

By contrast Joseph Lin is quite young and at the beginning of his performing career, but his credits include some major competition wins. We chose to open the bio with these. The second paragraph includes a very good press quote about his New York debut recital, and goes on to note his recent and future performance experience; the third lists some past performances. The fourth and last paragraph includes information about teachers and educational affiliations.

JOSEPH LIN, violin

Eighteen year old violinist Joseph Lin already has earned broad recognition for his mature artistry since his first international acclaim as the youngest participant in the 1994 Hannover International Violin Competition. Last year, he was a First Prize winner of the Concert Artists Guild Competition, already having won first prizes of the 1994 Seventeen Magazine/General Motors Competition, and the 1996 Arts Recognition and Talent Search, which lead to his selection as a Presidential Scholar in the Arts.

During the 1996-97 season Mr. Lin made his New York debut at Weill Recital Hall at Carnegie Hall, about which *Strings Magazine* said, "Enormously talented, relaxed and dignified, his brilliant technique and big, beautiful tone always at the service of the music, he played with intense emotional concentration and genuine expressiveness." During the same year Mr. Lin made his Boston debut presented by the Longy School of Music. During the 1997-98 season, Mr. Lin will perform again in Boston at the Gardner Museum and at the Fogg Art Museum at Harvard, at the Caramoor Festival, and at the Ravinia Festival.

In prior seasons Mr. Lin has made recital appearances around New York and in Taiwan, and concerto appearances with the Hudson Valley Philharmonic, the Orquesta Filarmonia de Lima, the La Plata Symphony in Buenos Aires, and with orchestras in Michigan, Canada, and Germany. Mr. Lin has also recorded with popular singer/songwriter Lisa Loeb for Geffen Records.

In June 1996, Mr. Lin graduated from The Juilliard School Pre-College Division, where he studied with Shirley Givens, and currently attends Harvard College.

September 1997

850 Seventh Avenue/New York, NY 10019 ♦ Tel: 212-333-5200
Fax: 212-977-7149 ♦ E-mail: CAGuild@aol.com ♦ Web: http://www.concertartists.org

Biographies for ensembles can be difficult to write, but are easier when the group is quite experienced and active — as the New Century Saxophone Quartet, whose biography follows, is now. (They had a fairly short biography in a previous edition of this book; it might be interesting to compare the two.) Given the extent of their activity, we start with a summary of the range of their activity in the first paragraph, and tell how unusual and interesting they are — a statement which we proceed to back up in subsequent paragraphs. The quartet got a very good review for their New York debut recital, so we used a quote from it in paragraph two. The body of the biography lists live engagements and recordings, radio and television, and their commissioning activity.

→

Materials

Concert Artists Guild

NEW CENTURY SAXOPHONE QUARTET
Michael Stephenson, soprano saxophone
James Boatman, alto saxophone
Stephen Pollock, tenor saxophone
Brad Hubbard, baritone saxophone

As the only ensemble of its kind ever to win First Prize of the Concert Artists Guild New York Competition, this pioneering and versatile young group has won new-found enthusiasm for the saxophone quartet and its diverse repertory, ranging from the Baroque to innovative contemporary works. The recipient of grants from the National Endowment for the Arts and Chamber Music America, New Century has been heard in major concert venues around the world, both live and on radio and television; in recordings for the Channel Classics label; and in unusual performance settings, ranging from a Command Performance for President Clinton in the White House to a concerto performance with the United States Navy Band.

New Century's 1993 New York debut at Weill Recital Hall at Carnegie Hall earned the group praise for their "virtuosic display of dexterity and keen ensemble work," in which the "players handled all the music with panache" (*New York Post*). Upon becoming the first saxophone quartet presented at the Ambassador Auditorium in Los Angeles, the *Los Angeles Times* heralded the Quartet's West Coast debut: "Tackling brave new territory in the conservative-leaning realm of classical music takes a unique blend of conviction, refined talent, and a bit of damn-the-torpedos ambition. Those qualities are amply in evidence with the New Century Saxophone Quartet, not to mention a finely honed musicality deserving wider acceptance."

Other engagements have included Chicago's Pick-Staiger Concert Hall, Atlanta's Spivey Concert Hall, Boston's Symphony Hall and Gardner Museum, New York's Merkin Concert Hall, and the Juneau Jazz and Classics Festival in Alaska. New Century was the first saxophone quartet to be presented at La Huaca del Complejo Atlapa in Panama City.

The New Century Saxophone Quartet has appeared on television and radio across the United States in features on National Public Radio's *Performance Today*, the Voice of America, and North Carolina Public TV. In 1995 the group was in residence at radio station WUNC in Chapel Hill and in 1996 at WHQR in Wilmington, North Carolina, as part of Concert Artists Guild's "Artist-in-Radio" project. Outside of the United States, Panamanian TV aired a documentary and live performance, and in the Netherlands, Dutch radio presented a live broadcast from the Concertgebouw in Amsterdam.

(continued)

850 Seventh Avenue/New York, NY 10019 ◆ Tel: 212-333-5200
Fax: 212-977-7149 ◆ E-mail: CAGuild@aol.com ◆ Web: http://www.concertartists.org

Page 2: New Century Saxophone Quartet

New Century's first recording, *Drastic Measures*, was released in 1994 by Channel Classics to critical acclaim from *Fanfare* magazine: "They combine great technique and elegant musicianship with a wonderful sense of chamber music." Their second recording, *Main Street USA*, including NCSQ's arrangements of music by Bernstein, Gershwin and Gould, was released in September 1996.

Moving beyond the traditional repertory for saxophone quartet, New Century performs original compositions and transcriptions ranging from classical works to contemporary pieces with funk and jazz influences. In April 1997 the group premiered *Quartet No. 2*, a work commissioned for them by Lenny Pickett, band leader and lead saxophonist of Saturday Night Live; other works written for the group include compositions by Sherwood Shaffer, Benjamin Boone, and Arthur Frackenpohl.

In the 1997-98 season, the Quartet will perform at the North Carolina School of the Arts as part of an ongoing residency supported by Chamber Music America, and will participate in residencies for Quad City Arts in Illinois and Iowa and at Lafayette College in Pennsylvania. 1996-97 season included a tour of North Carolina with sponsorship by the North Carolina Council on the Arts, and a Washington, D.C. debut at the Strathmore Hall Artist Series.

The New Century is based in Winston-Salem, where its members attended the North Carolina School of the Arts.

September 1997

850 Seventh Avenue/New York, NY 10019 ♦ Tel: 212-333-5200
Fax: 212-977-7149 ♦ E-mail: CAGuild@aol.com ♦ Web: http://www.concertartists.org

Note that each of these three biographies has a similar order: competitions or similar accomplishments in paragraph one, press quotes and performance experience in paragraphs two and three, and education and professional or school affiliations last. If you don't have competitions, or press quotes, use what you do have: your attendance at a fine music school, affiliations with particular composers, specialized repertoire, or regional reputation.

In each of the biographies we have reproduced, however, there are one or two main points about each artist which have been highlighted, both through placement in the narrative and the amount of space devoted to them. In Mia's, it is recordings and radio; in Joe's, it is youth combined with significant and diverse performance experience, given his age; in the New Century's, the unusual nature of the group and the very positive response it elicits from many sources. There is no way of telling everything about an artist or ensemble in a brief biography, but the reader's interest should be piqued enough to want to know — and hear — more.

A reminder, and some advice:

∎ DO:

> Make sure that your name, address and phone number, or the address and phone number of the person or organization doing your business for you, is on your biography. Putting it on letterhead that includes this information will do the job. It should go without saying that the biography should be neatly and attractively formatted.

∎ AVOID:

> **Hyperbole, exaggeration, and praise that can't be substantiated.** The purpose of the biography is to inform in a positive way, not to put something over on anyone. "One of the foremost pianists of our day" is only appropriate for someone who is, undeniably, one of the foremost pianists of our day.
>
> **Too much information.** The biography shouldn't exceed a page or two (or three, if you're really famous), and certainly shouldn't be padded to make your career to date seem more important than it is.

Photographs

We asked a friend of the Guild, who once ran a performing arts series in Wisconsin, which materials were most important to her in making booking decisions. She answered that her board, which had to approve all her recommendations, was not very artistically knowledgeable, but that she could usually sell them a performer on the basis of an attractive or arresting photograph. Not a recording. We heard something similar from the very knowledgeable manager of a regional orchestra; he said that, given some good word of mouth, the right photograph would convince him that he is dealing with a serious, important artist.

A very important sales tool, your photographs should immediately tell the person seeing them something about you. They will be sent to both presenters and the press. Our specific suggestions may be ways of addressing the needs of one or the other of these groups, but can apply to all of your photos. A few general remarks, and then — a picture being worth the proverbial thousand words — some examples.

- **You will want to have several good photographs to use for various purposes, but the most basic one you will need is an 8" X 10" black-and-white glossy head shot.** Head shots aren't really only heads; they are portraits which are not full figure, and can, in fact should, include your instrument. Black and white is still industry standard; color is increasingly being requested, but you certainly can get by with black and white at first.

- **If you have only one photo, it's safest to make it one with a light background,** as it is easiest to reproduce in newspapers.

- **Assuming now that you will have at least two photos, usually you will want one formal and one informal pose.** The informal shot can include more, or all, of you, and may well be an "action" shot, perhaps showing you doing what you do. This is always hardest for singers, since you don't want photographs with your mouth open; one journalist we've spoken with is a fan of the "perusing the score" picture in this case. The formal picture should show you in concert dress, whether that's tux or gown, or turtlenecks and jeans - whatever characteristic clothes you wear for an evening performance. The informal shot should contrast with the formal one.

- **Your photo(s) must be relatively recent, and be recognizable as you, NOW.** There have been far too many dismayed presenters who've waited in airport lobbies to meet artists who've already arrived, but whom they've not recognized because the only photo they've seen is a high school graduation picture. Life is full of embarrassments, but this should never be one of yours.

- **Your photo(s) must include your name, telephone number and address,** either stripped in at the bottom or labeled on the back.

There are two reasons why artists don't regularly update their pictures. First, photo sessions are expensive. If this is your excuse you have our sympathy, but not our approval, as photos simply must be a regular part of your ongoing business expenses. Second, some artists feel that being older will keep them out of a job, and that a picture taken when they were younger will help them get a job. This is not necessarily untrue, but submitting a misleading photo simply adds one handicap to another; when the moment of reckoning arrives, you're not only old, you're unreliable and untruthful. You therefore need to find a photographer who can bring out those qualities in you which will be engaging, in one way or another, in spite of or irrespective of your age.

One last comment about making sure your pictures look like you, aimed specifically at women. One of our journalist friends has frequently complained about photographers who overuse a certain look which makes all their subjects look alike: glamorous, high-cheekboned and doe-eyed. Very few of the women in the photographs actually look like that when seen in person. The reporter's feeling, and ours, is that it's great to look good, but not to look like someone else looking good. Make sure that your overall appearance and style generally correspond to the way you actually present yourself on stage.

On to the examples. The first two sets of pictures are of two pianists, Alan Chow and Stephen Drury, who for a time were simultaneously on the Guild's roster of artists.

We've used these photos at *Career Moves* workshops to demonstrate how a good picture says something very specific about an artist. In asking for first reactions to the photographs of Alan Chow, the words elicited usually have included "friendly," "warm," "direct," "engaging," and "accessible." The words people have used to describe Stephen Drury's photos include "unconventional," "adventurous," "serious," "dangerous," and "challenging." These photographs are good because they demonstrate important truths about these artists and evoke responses which are in line with this truth. Alan is a warm and communicative pianist who particularly loves the works of the romantic and classical periods. Stephen specializes in the music of Charles Ives and John Cage, among others, is a champion of new music, and often constructs highly unusual programs juxtaposing new and older works. Some of the qualities which set these artists apart, as musicians and as performers, can be seen in these pictures: in their poses, clothing, even the quality of their eye contact with the camera.

Having two pianists on a small management roster at one time could be a considerable booking challenge; having photographs this distinctive, which quite effectively demonstrate some of their respective strengths as artists, was exceedingly useful. The pictures helped the presenters to determine which artist would suit them best. Similarly for you, managing your own career, a photograph that clearly reveals something of your performing personality can be an immeasurable asset.

ALAN CHOW, piano

ALAN CHOW, piano

Photo examples 1a and 1b: Alan Chow

STEPHEN DRURY, piano

STEPHEN DRURY, piano

Photo examples 2a and 2b: Stephen Drury

The following photos, of the New Century Saxophone Quartet and of violist Scott Lee, illustrate why you should, if possible, have both an informal and a formal shot. The formal shot is one which can be used in many situations; it is serious, attractive, and shows the instrument. The informal shot, if it's engaging and/or interesting enough, could convince a presenter to hire you and can even help them to sell tickets to the performance. Newspapers, particularly in smaller cities, may print it; the assumption that presenters make is that if the photo is fun, or unusual, the concert will also be fun or unusual. A photo can illuminate one aspect or other of your performance personality or of your programs.

Not every picture can, or should, demonstrate everything about a performer. (If it could, the performer would necessarily be of quite limited ability). But every picture should reveal something, and it should be the truth.

Photo examples 3a and 3b: New Century Saxophone Quartet

Photo examples 3c and 3d: Scott Lee, violist

SCOTT LEE, viola

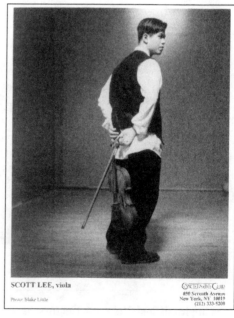

SCOTT LEE, viola

Photo: Blake Little

MIAMI STRING QUARTET
Felicia Moye, violin   Chauncey Patterson, viola
Cathy Meng Robinson, violin   Keith Robinson, cello

CONCERT ARTISTS GUILD
850 Seventh Avenue
New York, NY 10019
(212) 333-5200

Photo example 4:
The Miami String Quartet

This was one of the most attention-getting photographs Concert Artists Guild ever worked with. Everyone loved it, and it's everything you want a photo to be: arresting, unusual, saying something about the artists, instantly identifying both them and their name, fun, you name it. It also breaks a basic rule, i.e., that the instrument(s) should always be in the photo. Every rule has its exception.

Photos we can't show you: What not to do

The best photo examples for a book like this are probably the bad ones, those that all of us have seen which evoke snickers or wisecracks rather than smiles of admiration. Not wishing to be cruel, and being aware that the field is — all the cutthroat competition notwithstanding — a small one, we can't print them. But we can at least describe some of the obvious problems we see with some frequency, with the hope that you'll look at your own materials with a somewhat dispassionate and objective eye.

- **Photographs with terrible backgrounds**: wrinkled backdrops, unrelated scenery, random passersby waving at the camera, etc. They're distracting and look very unprofessional.

- **Odd facial expressions**. A photo of two young women, who would probably have described it as "cheerful," was experienced by everyone in our office as "predatory," given the predominance of teeth. Please have someone other than a loving parent look at the shots.

- **Problems with image**. For example, come-hither may be fine, sexy can be fine, but make sure that the photo does not misrepresent the artist and/or event. Pictures that are overly sexy may be misleading (unless your performances do, in fact, offer something considerably off the beaten path for a classical musician). This principle is obviously true for any other striking, but possibly inappropriate, image.

How-To:

Finding a photographer isn't hard, but finding a good one, and the right one, can be. The local photography studio that does weddings and bar mitzvahs is usually not the right place to go; they have little or no experience with the needs, both professional and technical, of the classical music field. The best way to find the right photographer, as with everything else, is to do some research and look at other musicians' photos. After a while you should begin to see which photographer's work you like, and what kind of pictures might work for you. (Several reliable and creative photographers in New York City and on the West Coast are listed in the Resource Section of this chapter, with their 1997 fees.) Since this is an expensive investment and a very important one, consider the decision carefully.

Budget suggestions:

- If you are still in school, and have access to photography students who are in the process of building up their own portfolios, you may have an ideal opportunity to get some wonderful pictures for very little or no money. You might need to provide the photographer with somewhat more direction and guidance than you would a seasoned professional who has often worked with performers, but the student may well give you more time, effort, and care than her more experienced colleague can.

- Photographers who work regularly with actors or other entertainers rather than with classical musicians may charge less. This may be a very good option, particularly for singers. Again, you may have to provide guidance and be aware that your requirements may be somewhat different from those of the subjects they usually work with, but you also may get a fresh point of view and some very interesting pictures as a result.

- If you live or come from anywhere other than New York, remember that New York City prices are generally higher for professional services, photography included. Even if you are professionally based in New York City, you might explore getting your pictures taken elsewhere, if you can find the right photographer familiar with the needs of musicians.

When you do schedule a photo session, discuss its length and requirements with the photographer in advance, and know what you're getting into. Be prepared to spend at least several hours. Bring several changes of clothing for both formal and informal shots as described above. Make sure that if you play the piano there will be one in the studio, or arrange for a location that will have one. Know what the location offers in the way of background if you're not working in the photographer's studio. Bring your instrument and any other materials that you may require.

The photographer will make a contact sheet of the session, from which you will usually select two photos that you like. Depending on your agreement, the photographer will make "portraits" from each selected shot, which are slightly retouched, good quality 8X10's; these are what you're buying. These portraits will be your visual equivalent of a master tape. **You'll duplicate them, but never send these originals to anyone.** The negatives are the property of the photographer, and you will never own them. The artistic content of the portraits is also the property of the photographer; you must credit him whenever the photo is used. (He needs to get work too, and this is how he gets his name around.)

Since a good photographer is very busy, and since she doesn't want to spend all her time making duplicates of photos for your press purposes (and since it would be far too expensive for you if reproduced on that basis), she will usually give you permission to have the portrait commercially duplicated in quantity. This is the standard arrangement; the arrangement may vary with different photographers, or in the case of color sessions which result in slides, so be very careful to get everything clear before beginning.

Take your portraits to a commercial photo duplication shop that specializes in bulk orders (several, with rates, are listed in the Resource Section) and have them make a copy negative from each one, which you will then use whenever you need prints. The copy negative is an 8X10 negative which the duplication house may be willing to keep on file for you. Order glossy prints to be made from the copy negative in a quantity that will be both useful and economical. (Don't go to a FotoMat type of place, as they will be far too expensive for this kind of work.) Get them to strip in your name and contact information if at all possible (see the photo examples above). This will save having to type or print labels and affix them to the back of each picture, and it doesn't cost much extra. Remember, every photo you send out, like everything else you send out, must have your name and at least a phone number on it. Some variation of Murphy's Law surely says that if something can get lost or separated, it will. The best picture in the world won't help you if no one knows who it is.

A very important rule:

Don't send a picture, or any other expensive piece of material, unless you are reasonably sure that it will get looked at or read, and that the recipient won't immediately throw it away.

Pictures and other materials will almost never be returned, even if you've provided a stamped, self-addressed envelope. It's too expensive for you to send materials, and too annoying for the recipient to get them, when they haven't been requested and aren't needed.

The Press Kit

When involved in more extensive sales, or when more elaborate publicity is required, you will probably want to put together a press kit. The term "press kit" is somewhat misleading, since it is used for sales and management as well as press purposes. The press kit is simply a compilation of your materials, put together in a convenient way and immediately identifiable as yours. Physically it is a folder, which can be an inexpensive pocket folder from the stationary store, which will contain your biography, picture(s) and additional supporting materials. Since the additional materials will be there to support the story set out in the biography, they will be those items which amplify your basic sales points: i.e., feature articles and reviews (which prove that you've played many different places and the critics love you); a flyer (which demonstrates that you are a savvy performer who can help them with their publicity materials); a repertoire list (showing that you have an extensive and interesting repertoire).

Example 1 shows some of the contents of Mia Chung's press kit, including her flyer, the first page of the biography you saw earlier in the chapter, one review, and one feature article. In the actual kit, there are many of each of these last two items. The folder itself has a copy of the flyer pasted to it. We don't include photos, since the flyer is essentially pictures with a little text.

Example 1: Sample Press Kit Contents

Flyer ↑

↓ Feature Article

CONCERT ARTISTS GUILD   *Biography*

MIA CHUNG, piano

First Prize • Concert Artists Guild Competition

Since winning First Prize, the U.S. Trust Award, the Channel Classics Prize, and the ITT Corporation Prize at the Concert Artists Guild Competition in 1993, Mia Chung has quickly ascended to the top ranks of America's young pianists. Most recently, Ms. Chung was recognized with an Avery Fisher Career Grant in April 1997.

Ms. Chung has received the highest praise for her interpretations of Beethoven's Sonatas. Her debut recording, as part of Channel Classics' Winning Artists Series, features Beethoven sonatas and bagatelles. Of her performances of these sonatas at her New York debut, *The New York Times* wrote, "Uncommonly insightful, individualistic and lively. ... She found balances and rhythmic emphases that made the work's drama seem fresh. ... Her playing was dazzling." Upon selecting this recording as a "Best of the Year" for 1995, *Gramophone* magazine noted: "Chung's performance is inspired ... a totally absorbing musical experience." Channel Classics recently released Ms. Chung's second recording, which features the music of Robert Schumann. Her third recording will spotlight Beethoven and will be released in 1997.

Ms. Chung has been actively involved in radio nationally. In June 1995, Ms. Chung served as the first "Young Artist in Residence" for National Public Radio's *Performance Today*. After working with her, National Public Radio nominated Ms. Chung for "Debut Artist of the Year." Also in 1995, her performances and commentary aired throughout metropolitan Boston when she was "Artist-in-Radio" at WCRB-FM. As the station's resident artist, she brought classical music to inner-city children through in-school concerts. Ms. Chung is currently "Artist-in-Radio" with WGMS-FM in Washington, D.C.

February 1997 will mark Ms. Chung's European debut at the Concertgebouw in Amsterdam. As an artist member of Chamber Music Society Two, a new project of the Chamber Music Society of Lincoln Center, Ms. Chung and her colleague artists will perform in its own chamber music series in New York, collaborate with members of the Chamber Music Society in performances at Alice Tully Hall and Merkin Concert Hall, and participate in educational outreach programs throughout the New York area. Solo performances during the 1996-97 season include engagements at the Concert Society of Maryland, University of Massachusetts at Amherst, the Terrace Theater at the John F. Kennedy Center for the Performing Arts, with the Corpus Christi Symphony Orchestra, and in recital in Parma, Italy. Highlights of the 1995-96 season included debuts in Japan at the Yokohama International Piano Festival, Seoul, South Korea, in recital at the Hoam Art Hall, and Boston at Jordan Hall.

(over)

Concert Artists Guild 850 Seventh Avenue, New York, NY 10019 • Tel.: (212) 333-5200
Fax: (212) 977-7149 • E-mail: CAGuild@aol.com • Web: http://www.concertartists.org

Biography ↑

↓ Review

CONCERT ARTISTS GUILD   *Press: Mia Chung*

THE WALL STREET JOURNAL
Tuesday, April 26, 1994

Mia Enters the Piano Wars

by Raymond Sokolov

Mia Chung came onstage in a green gown, small but moving briskly. She is not a household word, except in a few households. But all of them had followed her to Carnegie Hall to hear her play the piano at her recent New York debut.

Her husband, John Yee, was there, up in front on the right of Carnegie's ornate 268-seat Weill Recital Hall, taking a uxorious breather from his duties as a medical resident at Children's Hospital in Boston. Her nephew Andrew Chung, 4½, was in back, in a serious coat and tie. Many of the others were family members or friends who had caught up with her as a piano prodigy (soloist with the Baltimore Symphony at 12) or at Harvard College or Yale graduate school or while she was earning a doctorate at Juilliard or when she won the Concert Artists Guild New York Competition last year. Almost everyone sat on the left side of the auditorium, the better to see the 29-year-old's hands as she tackled a provocatively ambitious program.

Like dozens of other young musicians who hire this hall every year, Ms. Chung was making a major career move. If it worked, she would get a review in the New York Times, possibly even a favorable one, and that would give her a nudge upward into the brutal jostling for attention in the dense jungle of young pianists, all hoping to break into the small elite of players who really are household words.

In this Hobbesian struggle for public notice, there are many possible strategies. Ms. Chung, who earns her living as an artist-in-residence and

music professor at small liberal-arts Gordon College near Boston, did not hesitate to draw on the broad grasp of the repertory that her very superior education had given her.

She began with Schoenberg's "Six Small Piano Pieces" of 1911, fleeting, expressionistic, mercurial, various and, above all, experimental music. When he wrote them, the composer was incubating his 12-tone system. In her program notes, Ms. Chung remarked that these early pieces point forward to Schoenberg's pivotal "Pierrot Lunaire," but "perhaps with less eerieness."

Having polished off this intricate set of cameos, Ms. Chung segued with high wit to a little-known youthful experiment by Aaron Copland, "Piano Variations" (1930). Copland, then 30 years old, and with his more clubbable Americ-is-beautiful phase yet to come, was laboring under the dark star of Schoenberg's full dodecaphonic manner and straining to bend it to his own happier genius.

Ms. Chung completed this turn toward the light with the final selection of the first half of the concert: Beethoven's joyful "Sonata in G Major, Opus 31, No. 1." Although she told us in her notes that she meant this piece as a "bright contrast" to what had come before, and that, for her, its outer movements "like a good joke, invoke cheerful laughter," the Beethoven she played with such vigor and force was not a serene Mozart clone waiting to find the heroic volume of his maturity. In her rendition, he was all there at once: pure classical background, gamesomeness and romantic storm abrewing.

(OVER)

Concert Artists Guild 850 Seventh Avenue, New York, NY 10019 • Tel.: (212) 333-5200
Fax: (212) 977-7149 • E-mail: CAGuild@aol.com • Internet: http://www.concertartists.org

---

CONCERT ARTISTS GUILD   *Press: Mia Chung*

BOSTON GLOBE
TUESDAY, FEBRUARY 27, 1996

Sophisticated statements from Mia Chung

By Michael Manning
GLOBE CORRESPONDENT

MIA CHUNG, piano
At Jordan Hall, Sunday afternoon

Spend the better part of 20 years, as I did, in classical music broadcasting and you'll find a phrase like "Artist-in-Radio" an annoying portent of something less than it claims to be. That it's a title borne by pianist Mia Chung can only improve the industry's credibility. As WCRB's 1995 "Artist-in-Radio," she was kept busy touring schools, performing educational outreach programs for youngsters and baring her name mentioned often and lovingly on 102.5 FM.

> **She plays the hardest music there is with a degree of intelligence, musical and pianistic sophistication that is rare.**

Her concert Sunday afternoon in Jordan Hall, no classical Top 40 event, was exceptional. Look past all the chatty, friendly, station-frequency-repeating nattering that inevitably accompanies one of these "community services" and you'll be mighty impressed by the judgment that selected this particular pianist. Her technical approach to the instrument is secure and unshowy, and she puts every ounce of it, every pound of it to the service of the music. She plays the hardest music there is with a degree of intelligence, musical and pianistic sophistication that is rare.

When it comes to Robert Schumann, there are the

great works that everyone loves—"Carnival," "Papillons" and the other waltzy pieces—and the even greater works that hardly anyone knows—the episodic and radical "Kreisleriana," "Humoreske" and the eight "Novelletten." Chung played the eighth "Novellette" to open her program, showing right away that she can take a segmented, rhapsodic piece like this, give each section its due, each Romantic characteristic its personality, and still hold it together as a coherent statement. This was to mark every performance of the afternoon.

As a concert piece, Beethoven's "Appassionata" has suffered more than its share of interpretations, and it's a pleasure to hear a real by-the-book, as-written performance. It's always harder to play it Beethoven's way, and Chung had the wherewithal to do it, with extremely clean, clear execution and marvelous dramatic pacing.

And there's more, for if middle-period Beethoven doesn't get you, late Beethoven might. The last of the great 32, the Sonata Op. 111, is one of the ultimate tests of a musician. Chung played it beautifully. There were times in the transcendent set of variations which conclude when the music really achieved that suspension of time that any thoughtful performance strives for, but that few attain even for a moment.

The free program will be repeated Friday night in Pickman Hall at the Longy School of Music in Cambridge.

Concert Artists Guild 850 Seventh Avenue, New York, NY 10019 • Tel.: (212) 333-5200
Fax: (212) 977-7149 • E-mail: CAGuild@aol.com • Web: http://www.concertartists.org

Reviews and other inserts

A review can be reproduced in its entirety if it's all positive. Clip the article, the name of the publication (the masthead) and the date out of the paper, and neatly and carefully glue them to a piece of paper which has your name, address and contact information on it. Have the sheet photocopied, and put it in the kit (see Example 2). If the only copy you can get of the review is in very bad shape and won't reproduce cleanly, it is permissible to re-type it, as long as you don't change anything. You can, of course, leave out the last line, or paragraph, if that's where the critic decided to put the negative comments. If there are less than ideal comments throughout the body of the review, or even only one good comment in a largely negative review, it's obviously better to use only excerpts.

If you have a feature article which is not a review — but is flattering — by all means reproduce and use it in your press kit (see Example 1).

Strings Magazine

September/October 1997

Spotlight on New York
Premieres, Debuts and Double Exposures

by Edith Eisler
(EXCERPT)

While the 1996-97 season's orchestral tributes to Brahms and Schubert peaked during the fall and winter, chamber music festivals predominated in the spring, and many recital programs also contributed to the celebrations. Out of four promising debuts, the most impressive was the June Weill Recital Hall concert given by violinist Joseph Lin, the 18-year-old winner of the 1996 Concert Artist Guild competition. Enormously talented, relaxed and dignified, his brilliant technique and big, beautiful tone always at the service of the music, he played with intense emotional concentration and genuine expressiveness, splendidly partnered by pianist Benjamin Loeb. His winning, youthful ardor and exuberance made Beethoven's "Spring" Sonata a bit too romantic but were just right for the Richard Strauss Sonata, Op. 13. Bolcom's Sonata No. 2, a fun piece in many styles, had flair. Ernst's *Variations on an Irish Air*, a wild bravura piece exploiting every violinistic trick and sound effect, was tossed off with a juggler's ease, leaving the capacity audience cheering.

Concert Artists Guild 850 Seventh Avenue, New York, NY 10019 ▪ Tel.: (212) 333-5200
Fax: (212) 977-7149 ▪ E-mail: CAGuild@aol.com ▪ Internet: http://www.concertartists.org

Example 2: Complete review

45

In excerpts, as in all reproduced written materials, make sure that all the quotes are properly ascribed. You can paste a group of review excerpts onto one clearly identified sheet of paper. Alternatively, you can re-type them (see Example 3). Make sure the stationary you use is, as always, identified as yours, and includes information on how to reach you.

Beware of having too many dots, showing where you've left words or phrases out, since your quote will lose credibility (in other words, no "Mr. Jones was very ... good"). Be careful when quoting excerpts from reviews to let common sense guide your choices; you're not trying to put anything over on anyone, but rather letting the world know that something positive has been written about you. As long as you're not misrepresenting the intentions of your critics, and they actually did have something good to say, you're probably excerpting responsibly.

AS THE CELEBRANT OF BERNSTEIN'S *MASS*

"He's got it all: The high's, the lows, the 'look' and the croon."

—**Leonard Bernstein**

"Douglas Webster was everything you could want--a full magnificent voice with a range to match, stage presence and acting skills that dazzle, and that undefinable human magic that radiates across the footlights and speaks directly to the heart and mind..

—**The Register-Guard**
(Eugene, Oregon)

"He commands a high, wide and handsome baritone."

—**The Boston Globe**

IN CONCERT

"A French art-song interpreter of rare quality."

—**Richmond Times-Dispatch**

"The Schubert set was performed with class, Webster moving from the delicate simplicity of 'Heideroslein' to the hyper-romantic hushed awe of 'Nacht und Traume' with the un-failing combination of natural musicality, a fine instrument, good training and good taste." —**The Buffalo News**

Concert Artists Guild 850 Seventh Avenue, New York, NY 10019 ▪ Tel.: (212) 333-5200
Fax: (212) 977-7149 ▪ E-mail: CAGuild@aol.com ▪ Web: http://www.concertartists.org

Example 3: Excerpted reviews

A repertoire sheet will be useful if you're sending the kit to a conductor or orchestra manager.

ⒸⓃⒸⒺⓇⓉⒶⓇⓉⒾⓈⓉⓈ ⒼⓊⒾⓁⒹ

SCOTT LEE, viola
Concerto Repertory

J.C. Bach	Concerto
Béla Bartók	Concerto (1945)
Max Bruch	Romance
Nicoló Paganini	Grand Sonata for Viola & Orchestra
G.P. Telemann	Concerto in G major
William Walton	Concerto

[October 1997]

**Concert Artists Guild / 850 Seventh Avenue / New York NY 10019-5230
tel 212-333-5200 / fax 212-977-7149 / e-mail CAGuild@aol.com**

Example 4: Repertoire list

Flyers

Flyers can be used for a variety of purposes. A flyer can provide much of the information discussed above in a single sheet for general use; it can, if surprinted with specific information about a particular performance, also serve as a concert flyer (if your design allows for some blank space; these days, we print longer flyers with this space at the bottom for this purpose). On the front of our artists' flyers, we include the following, in order of importance:

- Your name and instrument or voice type
- A photograph, usually your formal shot
- A quote from a newspaper review (if you have one), or other short and intriguing verbiage
- Representation information, if any (management, record label, etc).

Example 5a: Flyer front

On the back:

- Another photograph, usually the informal shot;
- More quotes (if you've got them) and credits;
- A brief biography;
- Recording and other credits;
- Booking address, phone number and contact person.

Example 5b: Flyer back

This format is variable, but the flyer should be concise, feature a good picture or pictures, include some interesting short written information, and perhaps have some blank space available where you or a presenter could surprint the specifics about an event.

Costs

Very roughly, the cost of producing a two-color flyer from scratch might run as follows:

Photography	$700
Design	$400
Printing (2500)	$400*
Total:	$1,500

* Including shipping, using an out-of-town printer. In New York City, this could run about $500.

You may already have photographs; you may be able to do your own typesetting on a laser printer; and perhaps you know a designer who will donate his services. In this case, you're left only with the printing cost, which is quite enough. Shop around outside of New York for printing, even if you're based here; often you can get a real bargain and not lose quality. The printing cost listed above is based on using coated (that is, shiny) stock.

Flyers can be as plain or as elaborate as you want or can afford. In general, you can save money by using one color (which may be black) and white; additional colors cost, and full-color is most expensive, though it is widely used these days. Your choice of paper will also affect the cost, as will the number of photos, since reproducing pictures is more expensive than reproducing text.

Aesthetics are important, and a good looking flyer can be very helpful; however, tastes differ, and ours may not be yours. What you need to do is to look around and see what you like. If you can find a designer whose work you very much admire, and who's affordable, by all means hire her. As we mentioned in the "budget" section in regard to photos, if you're in school, and can hook up with a gifted design student who is building up a portfolio, you might get something very striking for little or no money. Similarly, if you are working with a non-profit group, you might be able to get professional design services donated. If you know a good professional designer, ask.

One additional use for a flyer: it can be pasted to the front of the press kit folder to personalize it. This is very commonly done, and can look very good. If you're having flyers printed in large quantities, it might be useful to ask that several hundred be printed only on one side (the front) for this purpose.

Probably, wonderful flyers have gotten people jobs; probably, ordinary flyers haven't lost anyone a job. Terrible flyers could though. As with all your materials, the flyer must reflect something about you, and must never give anyone a reason to believe that you are anything other than completely professional.

Concert Flyers

Concert flyers come in various forms, from very simple postcards to actual flyers to elaborate season brochures. Budget and scale will guide your choice. You can use a general flyer, if you have one, surprinted or stickered with the specific concert information, or you can design a flyer specifically for the event.

For a single concert, make sure that your flyer (or postcard, or whatever you've chosen) contains the standard minimum information of the news story, i.e., who, what, when and where. Why isn't necessary, though a newspaper quote or some other teaser may tell the reader why they might want to attend. In addition you need to include the following:

- Ticket price(s), including applicable discounts if any

- Repertoire information

- Assisting artists

When putting these together, remember that you will be

- ► Sending them direct mail;
- ► Handing them out, or stuffing them into programs of prior events at the same venue;
- ► Posting them in strategic places, to make sure that someone comes.

Your design should accommodate as many of these possible uses as you will need. That is, if you're mailing the flyers, make sure they have space on one side for an address label and a return address. If you're posting them, make sure that everything reads coherently (not upside down) when unfolded.

Budget Flyers:
When you're just getting started, and want to publicize an event

We made a flyer a number of years ago for the debut performance of a wind quintet which had never played together before; they still had no picture, no newspaper quote and no group credentials. They also had almost no money, and had to do the flyer cheaply. The flyer was formatted on someone's laser printer, and printed on one side of the paper in red on white glossy stock. We placed a large circle with the name of the group - "Solar Winds" - in the center of the flyer, listed the players underneath, and put the information about the event at the bottom. The piece looked fine but a bit bare, but yellow magic marker added by hand around the red circle (looking like a sun?) made it that much more cheerful. The brief written material below the artists' names described their individual credentials, since they didn't have ensemble credentials as yet. The same flyer could have been used for other performances as well, or — if desperate — for general booking, with contact rather than performance information at the bottom of the piece. A similar piece could probably be printed for about $150 now, for 1000 copies.

Concert Flyers:
Embarrassing errors checklist

All of the following are errors that we have made at one time or another, and we hope to help you avoid them. **When proofing your flyers, look for:**

■ *Photo credits*   All pictures must be credited, usually in small print climbing up the side of the photo.

■ *Acknowledgments*   Some supporters require that they be listed on all publicity materials as well as programs. (State arts councils, the National Endowment and other public agencies may contractually require this, so find out and include it if necessary.) If someone has actually paid for or donated the printing of this flyer, that probably should be acknowledged on the piece.

■ *Program information*   Check whether premieres are actually premieres; spellings of composers' names; accuracy of all information.

■ *Date*   Make sure that the day, month, year (believe it or not, we've screwed that one up once), and exact hour of the concert are all correct.

■ *Address*   Since Concert Artists Guild, for example, has an address different from that of the hall where our concerts are performed, we have to include both our return address and that of the hall. In addition, make sure that you have included the phone number of the hall box office, again being particularly careful if the number is different from the one you would usually list for contact information.

■ *Spelling*

Of performers' names, including all assisting artists. Do remember to list all the assisting artists; one of our most embarrassing moments was when we failed to list the pianist for a violin recital. The pianist is both marvelous and a great friend of ours, and we — and he — were devastated.

■ *Layout orientation*

When the printer gives you the "blue" — the blueprint proof copy of the piece — to check for smudges or errors, make sure that nothing will come out upside down when the flyer's folded, and that the front/back orientation of the postcard is correct.

Demo Recordings

One of the most effective sales tools a musician can have is a good demo recording, either a tape or a CD — assuming that someone will listen to it. In many situations, some of them crucial to an artist's career development, a recording will be the means by which colleagues get to know you as a musician. Those listening to it will make immediate judgments about what they hear; your recording therefore should be of high quality, say something about you as an artist, emphasize your strengths — and do all this relatively briefly.

On the assumption that you don't yet have a commercial CD, and that what you need as demo recordings are, first, basic cassette tapes, that will be the subject we tackle first. At some point you may want to move on to creating a comparable demo CD. (See the section on Making a CD for some guidance in this area.) Good demo recordings aren't cheap to make. They require decent recording equipment, extensive rehearsal and preparation, expert engineering and high quality reproduction. Some of the costs of all this may be assumed by others, particularly if you are in school, or may be reduced if you invest in your own equipment and do some work yourself.

Uses of demo tapes

The most obvious use for demo tapes is for those situations in which they're specifically required; competitions, auditions or grant applications. You may also have occasion to send them to radio stations for broadcast (if you have a DAT tape or CD). In addition, demo recordings can serve as basic sales tools when dealing with presenters, conductors, managers, composers, other artists or teachers. When to use them is a subject for later chapters in this book; how to make them and how to use them is the present topic.

Repertoire, Length and Order

The purpose of a demo recording is to say something interesting and intriguing about your performing, not to say everything about it. In some cases, such as a competition with specific length, format, repertoire and order of repertoire requirements for tapes, you may not have much choice; but if you can determine the length, content and order of your recording, do so with the understanding that the first selection has to make a good impression, and that twenty minutes of wonderful performing is probably more effective than anything longer. Just as when you go on stage you can't wear all of your performance clothes at once, even though they all may be very striking, you can't include every one of your favorite pieces on your demo; they may not get listened to. Your customers are almost certainly very busy, and you should leave them wanting more, not feeling they've heard everything you have to offer. Put yourself in your listener's shoes, and try and think about how much someone might want to hear under a given set of circumstances.

As for specific repertoire; do what you do well, obviously, with an ear to variety. In most situations, it is perfectly acceptable to offer single movements of sonatas or concertos, but not excerpts from these. The sole exception is that it's okay to delete long orchestral introductions, in which case a fade in just before the solo entrance is the rule. For singers and instrumentalists except pianists it is also generally okay to use piano accompaniment for concertos and arias.

Sources of recorded material

As with your pictures and biographies, not every recording can serve every purpose, and you will probably want to have several. It is best to have enough recorded material available to be able to mix and match, and come up with the perfect tape for any occasion. Sources of material include:

- **Studio session(s):**
  More about these on page 60.

- **Concert performances:**
  Includes everything from school recitals to your last performance with a major orchestra. Remember to edit out, or have the engineer edit out, all but a very little of the applause. The first burst of enthusiasm, and a fade-out after about 2-3 seconds, should let your listener know that your performance was appreciated, without belaboring the point. In using live performance materials you're trading off recording quality for the special feel of the live performance; but be careful that the trade off is worthwhile, i.e., that you still can be effectively heard. If the recording was made by your uncle, holding his Brand X tape machine on his lap next to candy unwrapping and coughing neighbors, the person listening to the recording may not be able to fully appreciate just how terrific the performance was.

- **Radio broadcasts:**
  If you perform on the radio, certainly ask if you can get a copy of the tape, since it will almost always be of very high quality. Radio stations are usually very nice about this, though you may have to pay a small charge for the actual tape.

- **Tapes made with high-quality portable equipment:**
  You can probably use these when you're starting out, if you're careful to use the best equipment possible, control ambient noise, edit out extraneous material, and listen carefully to make sure that the quality of the performance comes through. It goes without

saying that the performances should be especially good, since you won't be able to have the gloss of professional sound nor the excitement of the concert hall.

Labeling

Always assume that anything you give anyone will be misplaced, or at least separated from your letter or other materials. So make sure that your tape is neatly labeled, and includes your name (unless you're specifically told by a competition or audition committee not to do so), the works being performed, other relevant program information, and technical information about the tape, such as whether you've used Dolby B or C or other noise reduction.

▪ AT ALL COSTS, AVOID:

▪ **Major flaws in sound quality.**

Everyone expects high quality sound reproduction these days. A listener will be somewhat understanding of unevenness of quality in a live performance recording, but static or excessive ambient noise in a studio recording is absolutely unacceptable. Also, obviously, if the sound doesn't sound like you, it's a flaw, though your listener may not know it.

▪ **Major performance flaws.**

Again, a few wrong notes will almost certainly be overlooked if they occur in the context of an otherwise wonderful live performance, but only a few; similar technical flaws in a studio recording will be far less acceptable.

▪ **Poor assisting artists or accompanists.**

A bad accompanist or orchestra may well cause your listener to judge your performance by theirs, even if you played far better than they did.

Studio and Other Professional Recordings

At some point you may decide to do a studio session, or have a professional engineer do some on-location recording, for the purpose of getting together some high quality taped material to put together in various combinations later on. You will come out of the session with an industry standard tape, which these days usually means a digital audio tape (DAT); if so, make sure that you get a sub-master of the tape in cassette format, since not everyone will have the equipment to play the digital master. Though this is not an issue on DAT's, when transferring the recording from DAT to cassette format you may want to use some sort of noise reduction — probably Dolby, which is better for classical music than dBX. Many high tessitura instruments don't do well with noise reduction, and sometimes the player will opt not to use it.

The recording studio will also be capable of adding some sort of reverb to the tape, which simulates, to a greater or lesser degree, the sound of a concert hall (more reverb = larger hall).

The advantage of using a studio is that almost all factors are controlled by you. The advantage of the on location recording is that you might be working in a particularly beautiful sounding space, or playing a very fine instrument which is located there. The choice of engineer and studio is one which you should make, like all other professional decisions, after asking around extensively. Get recommendations from friends; ask to listen to samples. Talk to the engineer, and make sure that he or she has extensive experience with classical music, has worked with your instrument or voice type, and can read music well enough to follow what you're doing and do intelligent editing. If you're using a studio, go there to find out what the room is like, whether they have a piano, what kind of equipment they'll be using. When you've narrowed the choices down to just a few, discuss costs, which should include set-up time, the actual recording session, editing time and tape costs. Check out additional costs that might not be included in an estimate, such as tuning the piano, or renting additional instruments.

If you're in New York, a listing of various recording studios, with 1997 costs, appears in the Resource Section. Three hours of recording time should yield about 30 usable minutes of taped material; be prepared for a total cost of about $500 - $600 for this.

The Recording Session

Since time is indeed money in the studio, you should have everything prepared to make the session go smoothly and efficiently. In preparation for the session, you should have done the following:

▶ **Discuss the session with the engineer**, so she knows exactly what you're planning to do, and in what order.

▶ **Arrange to have a "producer" with you.** This may be a friend who is familiar with your playing or singing, and can assist with things like microphone placement, watching the score and marking it for each take for editing purposes, and anything else that arises which might need an informed person on your side. This person should not be the page-turner, if one is needed, since then he couldn't be marking the score; so make sure you've covered this base as well.

▶ **Make sure the piano is tuned** and/or additional instruments are in place.

Bring the following with you:

▶ **A tuner or tuning fork, if you're not a pianist.** If you have to splice, you better make your pitch very consistent.

▶ **A metronome.** The same is true here; if you have to splice, you will need to be consistent enough in your tempi to do so. Remember, though, that you may feel that the overall impression of a live, straight-through performance is the priority; in this case, splicing will be minimal, and you may simply run the music several times and pick the best takes of complete movements or works.

▶ **Additional scores** for the engineer and for the producer, with page turns minimized to avoid unnecessary noise and metronome marks indicated. Don't forget your own music either.

▶ **Music stand(s).**

▶ **Lights.**

▶ **Your instrument.**

Keep in mind:

■ When deciding the order in which to record, keep in mind that you will almost certainly get tired by the end of three hours. Therefore, it's probably wise to begin with the most challenging work, and plan to finish up with something which you could perform well just about asleep.

■ If you've never done a taping session before, try to do a dry run (or several dry runs) with a portable machine at home before setting foot in the studio.

■ During the session, the engineer and producer should be making notes — and writing down your comments — about the quality of a given take. Very little or no playback can fit into a three hour session from which you hope to get 30 minutes of usable music; listening to cassettes recorded simultaneously with the master, which the engineer should give you when you walk out the door, together with the comments on the take sheets, should allow you to choose much of what you will want before going back to the engineer to make the final decisions.

- Don't let the session go longer than the allotted three hours, as you won't get much good material after that anyway.

Listen to the tape as soon after the session as you can be positive yet objective. Check at that point whether the decisions you, the producer and the engineer made about what material to keep are accurate.

WHEN YOU'VE GOT YOUR TAPE, REMEMBER:

> **Save the master! Never, never, send a master tape to anyone.** Each year at the Guild we receive one or two tapes from applicants to our competition which turn out to be someone's master; inevitably, these are the ones which get lost in the mail, aren't returned by the judge to whom they were sent, or are chewed up by someone's dog.

When you duplicate the tape to send out, copy it, or have it copied, at real time. High speed tape reproduction is cheaper than real time reproduction, but you lose significantly in sound quality. Make sure that the tape used is high-bias (CrO_2) 70 us. Normal bias tape and high speed reproduction are not kind to classical music.

You can save yourself significant money in a relatively brief period of time, if you're going to be making tapes in any quantity, by investing in a dubbing deck - a cassette deck which can accommodate two tapes and record from one to the other. As of now, these decks cost about $350-$400 for a machine that can record on both decks, which allows you to make two copies at a time from a CD or DAT; since sending out tapes to a professional company to have dubs made costs up to $10 each (including tape cost of about $2), you've recouped your investment soon after 20.

Very important: make sure the deck records at the correct speed; the tape may play back at the wrong pitch on other people's machines.

NOW, THE MOST IMPORTANT RULE:

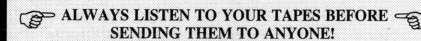

**☞ ALWAYS LISTEN TO YOUR TAPES BEFORE ☜
SENDING THEM TO ANYONE!**

The Guild receives blank tapes every year, which aren't very informative about the performance abilities of those who have sent them. We also receive tapes with multiple takes, expletives, and ambient noise which makes it impossible to hear the performance. Such tapes do not make a positive impression. Don't send them.

Demo CDs

As these have become easier and cheaper to produce, more artists are using them. A Demo CD is like a Demo Tape, but — since it is more expensive, more permanent and less flexible — you have to apply considerable thought to what you would like to represent you for a number of years to the greatest number of listeners.

But if you have good digital taped material, and can imagine lots of possible ways to use the CD (which might include distributing it to VIPs who have some interest in it, selling them at your concerts or giving them to your supporters), you may want to go ahead with the project. Concert Artists Guild produces Demo CDs including all the artists on our management roster, and the presenters love them. We have been working with Channel Classics Recordings, a label based in Holland with which we have collaborated on other projects, through their manufacturer, Mediatrack. Since we start with existing digital tapes, the cost per CD — based on 1000 CDs, which you probably don't need — was about $2.75 each. This included mastering and other engineering, a glass master, manufacture of the CDs, cardboard sleeves to put the CDs in, and design and printing of those sleeves, shipping, and licensing. The cost per disk rises as you order fewer, but you can trade off things like design, printing and packaging; a quartet represented by CAG recently paid $1500 for 1000 CDs in plain black envelopes.) The cost will rise very sharply if you don't already have excellent digital tapes from which to work.

Another interesting option, if you need CDs but only in very small quantities; there are now machines available that can produce CDs, one at a time, from a DAT. The CDs themselves are called recordable CDs. The machines cost about $1200 (and the prices have been dropping rapidly recently, so it may be cheaper by the time you read this). The blank CDs about $6 each. We are told that these machines have a limited life (we don't have one), so it is an investment that you will want to consider carefully. Also: if you have an excellent DAT you would like to make cassette copies from, but don't have a DAT machine, consider having a CD made by your engineer or at an audio reproduction store. The cost is $40 to $50 for one unit, but it can save a lot of trouble and maintain higher sound quality than working from a master cassette.

There is no question that the time has arrived when, at a certain point in one's career, a Demo CD is simply more impressive than a tape, and more presenters have CD players in their cars in order to listen to them. Also, if the CD includes complete works, and especially if it includes enough material to resemble a commercial CD, you can sell it at concerts, or provide it for broadcast purposes. So think about this as an investment. (More options on places to make these, and prices, in the Resource Section.)

A possible reason for having a demo CD, *even when you have one or more good commercial recordings*, believe it or not: how much it costs to get a sense of the scope of your work to presenters and others. The artist's or insider's price for a copy of a commercial CD might be around $10 per unit, buying them from the record company or distributor; if you have more than one CD, each might only represent one facet of your artistic personality. To present a more rounded picture, and to avoid sending several expensive full-length CDs to many people, it might be far more cost effective for you to compile selections from several sources and make a demo CD, specifically for this non-commercial, promotional, purpose.

A word about video

You'll see that in the Resource Section, where we've listed recording studios, we've also listed places where you can get videotapes made. Increasingly, videotape is supplementing (not replacing) audio tapes and CDs as a sales tool, and if it's possible at some stage to get one, it probably won't be wasted. Schools are often able to make videotapes of your performances, and you should take advantage of this service even if you don't use them for professional purposes. Videos can be incredibly useful in refining your on-stage presentation. Some of the halls you will be performing in can also make videotapes of concerts, and, if it's affordable for you, you should have them made.

Since reproducing video tapes is understood to be very expensive, you can request that they be returned, and they probably will be — unlike your audio tapes, which are almost certainly gone forever.

Making a studio video involves more personnel and a more complex set of technical criteria and expertise than does making an audio tape. Since it is such a specialized area, we will only mention here that the rules of brevity, maximum impact and careful advance preparation still apply (perhaps even more so), and that you should seek the further advice of someone knowledgeable in this field.

Making a (Commercial) Compact Disc, With or Without a Record Company

Today's music world seems to demand that a musician have a CD in order to prove that he exists as a professional. It is also true that it is increasingly easy to produce one, one way or another; the proliferation of small recording companies, increased access to excellent equipment, and the ability of almost anyone to hire the right people, place and hardware and make a professional quality CD themselves, means that all of us can -- with sufficient money -- hand out CDs with our business cards.

The best of all possible worlds is to be offered a recording contract with a respected commercial label; needless to say, this is the least likely scenario, but one which deserves some serious discussion here. Whether you should spend the thousands of dollars that a solo recording can cost to produce a CD yourself (that is, a fully produced sellable CD, not simply a demo in CD format) is another question. It is, as always, wise to know exactly what your objectives are.

Everyone I spoke to in the series of interviews of individuals in the recording industry (which took place several years ago) was sure that careers are made on live performances, not on recordings. Of course, presenters and managers will tell you that it's recordings that do it. The likelihood is that career building will depend on there being access to the artist in the concert hall and on the radio, at home, in the car, etc. There are obvious exceptions; however, for the most part, careers are balances of live and recorded music making.

Recordings can have several purposes; generally, producing significant income for the artist is not one of them. Neither is prestige, unless the recording has been made by a recognized company. In the context of an established or rising career, the purpose is often exposure and publicity, and in order to accomplish this the recording must go somewhere. A recognized, major company then is one that has the interest in and ability to effectively distribute the recording after it's produced, and to back up the disc with a publicity campaign.

There is another use for recordings, of course. If a young artist is held back with presenters (and some others) at a certain point by not having a CD, feels she needs one to establish her credibility, and can find the money to produce one, it can't hurt. The recording will have to be made with great care, and with an understanding of the limitations of the recording's uses. More about this later in this section.

First, the word from the top of the industry. For this section, we interviewed a group of people associated with distinguished recording companies. The interviewees and their affiliations (<u>in 1993</u>), who are identified in the text by initials, are:

- ▶ **Alison Ames**, Vice-President for Artists & Repertoire,
  Deutsche Grammophon
- ▶ **Michael Fine**, Vice-President for Artists & Repertoire,
  Koch Classics International
- ▶ **Wolfgang Mohr**, Executive Producer,
  Teldec Classics International
- ▶ **Elizabeth Ostrow**, Former Vice President for Artists & Repertoire,
  Angel Records
  Former Vice President for Artists & Repertoire, New World Records
- ▶ **Tim Page**, Executive Producer,
  Catalyst Recordings (BMG)
- ▶ **Ellen Schantz**, Director, Publicity & Promotion,
  Elektra International Classics

Though many of these individuals have gone on to other positions during the last four years, their words are still applicable and accurate, and have been left basically untouched for this third edition. We have interspersed the interviewees comments with notes of our own, in italics, from time to time. But for the most part, we allowed them speak in their own words, answering some questions that we, at least, always wanted to ask. (Though the text reads as if they were all in the same room at the same time, they weren't; getting these incredibly busy people together for a discussion probably would have been impossible.)

Can you/your company be approached, and how? Cold? With an introduction? How can someone get your attention?

AA: Cold is pretty useless, though I try to be polite about listening to unsolicited tapes and reading/answering mail. Try to get yourself within earshot of people with some influence: presenters, conductors, managers, the American Symphony Orchestra League, to provide an introduction.

If you do get in touch with people such as myself, with or without an introduction, spelling and courtesy count.

MF: Sometimes, just from talking to someone on the phone, you begin to like them, to know that you want to work with them. I try to listen to everything sent to me, even cold; but we get 50-60 submissions a day, so it's impossible. I end up listening to those tapes for which I've gotten a strong personal recommendation from someone in the business. For me, I need a listenable tape, but something overly perfectly engineered might make me suspicious or wary. I'm listening for something musically interesting and "ready," not necessarily for a well produced tape.

Occasionally I will be intrigued by something sent cold, usually because of the repertoire. Repertoire is often the key to getting something going. Standard repertoire for Koch is not of interest; much of our work is 20th Century repertoire. Passion for a particular project or artist is often what will interest me.

Sometimes we do "charity case" recordings, that I know won't sell much but are really musically wonderful.

EO: A recommendation, often through a conductor, will get you some attention. Standard instruments are traditionally more likely to produce interest than unusual ones — though, with recent shifts in the industry towards unusual repertoire, unusual instruments might be of more interest as well. Looks count, in that you should make sure that you're turned out well and dramatically. Luck and timing count. Having some funds available for public relations in support of the project doesn't hurt.

Introduce yourself with a <u>good</u> (broadcast quality) tape, and a <u>typed</u> cover letter. A good performance tape is a calling card. For me, a self-produced CD is unnecessary. Don't send your Beethoven.

[EH: In other words, be wary of sending the most standard repertoire.]

Be careful about the order of your program, and start and proceed from strength.

WM: Artists can approach us — we will consider that, but it's very, very rare. A specific project, interesting repertoire, etc., is of more potential interest than a general approach.

You don't need a CD; a good sounding recording on DAT is fine.

TP: Theoretically, I'm all in favor of unsolicited tapes but, in reality, I almost never get to listen to them. They just sort of pile up on a shelf — every now and then I'll look at them and get depressed but I rarely have much time to play anything these days. And that's terrible because I know I'm missing a lot of stuff.

Describe a situation in which a new artist might come to your attention, and you might start to work with him/her.

AA: Take a violinist, for example. (Instruments like flute are almost always out of the question.) The violinist would be brought to our attention by another musician: a teacher most likely, or a manager, mentor or conductor.

I would get a tape, and listen to it. An artist needs a good, decent sounding tape. It doesn't have to be beautifully packaged, or in CD format or anything; it has to sound like that artist, playing repertoire representative of that artist.

I would try to get to a live performance by the artist; that's difficult, since I have to go to 50-100 concerts a year by Deutsche Grammophon artists, leaving not a lot of time for more events. A chance to hear an artist at a place like Marlboro, for example, is great, as one goes there in any case. Several hearings may be necessary, so we're talking, possibly about a fairly lengthy period.

Assuming we're interested, we would then try and put them together with other, perhaps older musicians. We would try to get the artist opportunities to play for other DG players and conductors and to arrange concert dates for them.

Along the way, recordings would start to come out.

WM: We're always searching for talent. We read the international newspapers, and spot names which come up recurrently with enthusiasm. We ask around in each city where we're represented what the impressions are of our contacts there, and ask them to go to concerts and report back. You generally hear about those you're interested in from colleagues.

Maxim Vengerov's teacher emigrated from Russia with several of his pupils to a small German city. The story itself had some marketing appeal. Soon two names among the students appeared above the others. I went to a school concert and heard him. He won the Carl Flesch competition, and major conductors began to know about him. We signed him at Teldec soon after this. We negotiated for more than a year with his small, local management before the deal was signed.

TP: An artist will most likely attract my attention either through a direct encounter, or through the strong recommendation of somebody whose taste I really trust. I consider my friends and colleagues among my most important talent scouts.

EH: *A couple of important items to note here. One is that unusual instruments —*
sorry, but that means anything other than piano or violin for many — are
out of the question for many A & R people; there simply isn't a sufficient
market for them. And, in relation to marketing, it's important to remember
that marketing is a real issue, not a superficial one, for these companies. A
recent violin and piano recording by a CAG artist on a major label recently
had a budget of $30,000. This is money that most labels hope to recover in
a reasonable amount of time, so going into a project with a very small sales
potential is a major leap. It happens, just not very often.

Back to the interviews:

How many people are involved in the process when deciding to record a
particular artist?

AA: Ultimately, it's a committee sort of decision, never a solo decision. Four to
five executive producers have access to the boss, the head of A & R in
Germany; each of those will fight for particular artists or projects, but it's
the boss who has the final say. But all have to agree that the artist/project
makes sense in terms of quality, that the artist's repertoire fits the company's
current profile as well as that season's overall repertoire releases, and that
the overall budget can handle the project.

MF: We're a small company; I make the A & R decisions after consulting with
my colleagues and quite often directly with our sales managers around the
country. I'm usually stuck with my decision, as I customarily produce,
engineer and edit the recordings.

WM: It's a team decision, with considerable committee discussion. With Max
Vengerov, the team was choosing one artist out of three possibilities. He
was the farthest along in his career at the time. There's no longer any time
to build up legends.

How do emerging artists fit into the overall scheme of things at your company?

AA: Relying on major artists has a downside. If they're older, you can lose them (Bernstein, von Karajan and Horowitz died within a 15 month period; Serkin and Kempff soon after). Also, such artists may be lured to another label. You need to have younger, emerging talent appearing on the label, being cultivated to assume a more major role with the company over time.

Also, younger, less known artists are cheaper, not a negligible factor. The choice becomes expensive and established, or cheaper and younger. We don't go out and look for such artists; usually a conductor or someone in a position to hear many young players will bring him/her to our attention. Gil Shaham was recommended by his German manager; Matt Haimowitz by Itzhak Perlman.

Nonetheless, a group of major, influential artists on a label can monopolize most of the slots, leaving little room for nurturing younger artists; first dibs on projects go to those highest in the pecking order.

WM: Teldec has a long history of developing and building young artists' careers. Starting in the 50s (Telefunken, our predecessor, started in the 20s), some of the artists we've brought along and are very proud of our role in their early career development, are Harnoncourt, the Alban Berg Quartet and Frans Brüggen. We need to have both ends of the spectrum represented: the big name artists, and the building and developing of young artists careers. Much of our time is spent with the younger ones. There is always the chance that they may leave for other companies later on, but that's not important. The period of investment pays off with loyalty and commitment.

More and more extra-musical factors are important in developing careers. Right now it's a "jeans" mentality; we will perhaps have more dignified presentations in a few years. But right now, age is a factor.

There's no point to a 17 year old playing [and recording] a Beethoven violin concerto -- then, you [might as well] take a 10 year old.

EH: *Note that what passes for a "young" or "emerging" artist for many of these large companies is more what you or I commonly think of as "an infant" or "already has a very glamorous career going," respectively. We don't think of working with these artists as risk-taking, but the companies do.*

What is the role of the recording company in an artist's career?

MF: I like to be very active. Artists make their money on live performance, and get exposure and PR with recordings. I like to see the recordings being able to generate the dates, and I make calls to conductors, etc. to make this happen. It means something to have a recording on the Koch label. I spend a lot of time therefore on advocacy on behalf of the artists. What you [the artist] need in the business is someone, well-placed in the field, who believes in you. That could be a manager, but it's someone who can and will make calls on your behalf.

AA: For every recording made, there are 300 concert dates. Success and fame come through live performance, not recordings.

ES: We aggressively pursue PR and other opportunities for our artists, and work quite closely with their managers and representatives on career development. But, there are a finite number of dollars budgeted for promotion and more than just a few artists. As much as we'd like to push 100% for every artist, in terms of available financial and human resources, that just isn't possible.

Is outside funding ever involved in a recording taking place at your company? Would it ever make the difference in a project taking place?

AA: Sometimes outside funding plays a role, major or minor, in a recording. Volvo, a major sponsor for the Gothenburg Symphony, underwrote a recording that that Symphony wanted to do, for example. However, having funding in place would never induce or encourage us to take on a project that we didn't want to do in the first place.

MF: The way Koch works, I make sure that costs are covered before we start, and that often means that I raise the money for a recording. So yes, it is helpful if the money is already there. It depends, though. If it's clearly a vanity project, and doesn't fit within the artistic profile of the organization, I won't do it.

EO: It doesn't hurt to have funding in place. Don't ever spend money of your own on spec, though, with the hope of selling or placing the master. It's much too unlikely.

Do you every work with existing master tapes?

MF: Yes, particularly when they're produced by engineers/producers whose work I know well and like.

EO: Yes; more likely at a small company than at a larger one. At New World, we would have considered using an existing master tape. Try to get DAT format, not just good analog; a small company might pick that up.

TP: Yes, occasionally.

ES: Very unlikely. A small company might.

How about an artist being recorded by a very small label, or self-producing a recording? Is there a down side? What about getting effective distribution?

AA: Getting good distribution is a big problem, so that could be a major stumbling block.

MF: Don't go with a label that asks for full funding for the project, even if you have the money; they have no interest in the record finding a market, since they assume no financial risk. The artist should never pay production expenses.

But this is assuming that the artist is interested in the recording selling. If the only purpose of making the recording is to have a calling card to hand to presenters, and you have the money, go ahead.

WM: A recognized label, ok. The recording could be very helpful. But most companies lack a proper distribution network. Even with a big label, this can be a problem. Remember that for the artist the money isn't in the recording; it's in the concert income that results.

ES: If it's not on a major label, it may not be that useful. A good demo tape may be just as good. The up side is that the sound will probably be good. The down side is that you're not fooling anyone. A known, functioning label is fine, it doesn't have to be a big company. In the psychology of promotion, the first thing in a resume is "placement". Is it a major label or not?

TP: I believe that a self-produced CD can be helpful in building a career. When anybody asks whether to shell out for a New York concert or for a private recording, I always suggest the recording. It'll cost only a little more and it is permanent. It can be played on the radio. It can be given to critics. It can be passed on to grandchildren. And so on. If it's an interesting and valuable recording — with the premiere performance of a new work, say, or an important rediscovery — it might be considered "news" and reviewed in the record magazines.

Cassettes really don't have the same cachet. They're not convenient for radio programmers and DAT [has replaced them for broadcast purposes] anyway. CDs have a certain mystique. Everybody has made their own cassette tape of something at some point but — to the general public and, I think, to most critics and programmers — CDs are still mysterious, like artifacts that fell to earth. But whatever you do, it should look (and sound!) as professional as possible.

One important comment, to help keep the above material in perspective. All of the distinguished people quoted above were sensationally nice, and the conversations I had with them would have led me to believe that the folks in the recording business are the nicest in the industry — had this been my only attempt in that direction. Other experiences (with other companies and individuals) have been singularly unpleasant, and this is the part of the field in which I've had the worst rate of getting phone calls returned, for example. The clear conclusion is that many of the people in the recording business are indeed very nice, but that this is a very, very hard group to get in the door to meet: beware of damaged egos and endless frustration if you try without some kind of effective entree.

Summary and commentary

- The definition of a young, emerging, less established (choose your term) artist taken on by most major or established record companies isn't the one you and I usually use. In general, those they do pick up — with great trepidation and feeling like they're taking an enormous risk — are those that are reasonably established, or well on their way to being so, by our standards.

- A major or established label almost certainly won't be interested in you (assuming you are our definition of a young, emerging, less established performer) unless you have a friend at court, as it were.

- Unless your friend is very, very powerful, you're more likely to be of interest if you can offer something unusual in the way of repertoire, approach, or anything that will attract attention to a project. A smaller but still established label may take a risk with you, in a minuscule number of cases, even if you come without a strong introduction, *if* you have this kind of very interesting project, and perhaps if you're in a position to fund or help to fund it.

- The single factor that was mentioned again and again, in various contexts, was the issue of interesting, innovative repertoire.

- You don't need a CD to approach a company about making you a CD. You do need a very good quality recording, preferably digital.

Self-Produced CDs

If you make an investment in a self-produced CD, it should be with a clear idea of what you hope to achieve with it. If you want to sell it, or at least for it to appear in the record stores and get some airplay, you must find a way to work with an established label, whether big or small. (If you want a Demo CD to add to your professional outfit, to impress presenters or other sponsors, and to have a excellent quality recording for radio and other promotional purposes, it will be sufficient to work with respected people that do good quality work — or to follow the advice on making very limited numbers of CDs, that is, one at a time, on page 65. You can, of course, sell CDs at your concert performances and the like, even with no commercial distribution at all; indeed, for a young artist, more CDs are likely to be sold backstage, or at a table at intermission, than in stores anyway.)

But in the case of a CD conceived as being commercially available, the advantages of working with an existing independent label over starting your own are clear. The independent record label generally has a distribution mechanism in place, can assume the entire manufacturing an administrative headache, absorb financial risk, and probably ultimately move more records, if they have any kind of reputation at all. The negatives are that they may not be that effective, and that you will realize less income — if you believe there is potential for some. There actually are a considerable number of small independents which are willing to look at your project, or your master tape, if you've gotten that far. Since these are, to a greater or lesser degree, seen as vanity labels, and since they don't like to think of themselves this way, we can't give you a list here. Do your research by looking into which small labels do the kinds of recordings which are most similar to what you are interested in doing or have done. Write to the company, again with an introduction if possible, but without one if necessary, and see if you get a bite. If you do, try to talk to other artists who have been recorded by this company, and discuss their experiences with them.

Or you can do everything on your own, soup to nuts, sort of like acting as your own contractor when building a house. This will involve developing the program, finding an engineer and the other personnel to do the recording, and doing all the production, right down to buying the jewel boxes, designing the artwork and the program and having it all printed, etc. You will even have to follow up yourself with sending out press releases to let the world know your CD exists, and getting copies to record reviewers, assuming you have a mechanism in place for selling the CD direct (you cannot expect a reviewer to write about a recording that's not commercially available). It's hard, but you can do it. You can also find a producer who will do much of this for you, and/or one who will try to place the recording with a label once it is mastered. Ideas about costs and a couple of suggested folks to go to about this may be found in the index, as well as more sources of information and professional associations in the recording industry.

A note about contracts

If you decide to work with an independent record company (or a large company, for that matter), you should have a lawyer experienced in such matters look over any contract you sign. Volunteer Lawyers for the Arts (see the General Resources chapter) can direct you to someone knowledgeable, if you don't know anyone yourself.

A contract probably will cover contract duration, royalties arrangements, recouping expenses and advances against these royalties, financial statements, the authority to use your name in promotional activity and other promotional arrangements, and publishing rights. One item to make sure is in their is that the artist should have a buy-out right, in the event that the recording goes out of print, or even out of the company's catalog. This way, the artist may be able to provide the master to another label should they become interested, or at least to have the material for archival purposes.

The Internet

This topic is too much on everyone's mind (and takes up too much of many people's time) to overlook. The question, for purposes of this section, is "Should [I] [my group] have a WebSite? And what will it do for me if I do?"

Most reasonable sized, and even many small, music organizations now do have websites, mostly to disseminate information about themselves and keep in contact with whomever their constituency is. Concert Artists Guild has a website (www.concertartists.org), which at the time of this writing provides visitors with information about our competition and our roster artists. In the near future we plan to have information about our publications (including this book) and Guild membership.

But do *you* need one? and if so, when?

The following interview presents what we've come to know as a typical profile of a musician's website. We spoke with Mike Seltzer, trumpeter with the Manhattan Brass Quintet, a group established in 1991.

"We established our website in November 1994 (Address: http://quicklink.com/~antman/MBQ). I had friends in the computer field, and wanted to set up the website for practice; I hoped it would get us exposure, and work — or get me work setting up websites, in publishing or design. It doesn't cost much to do if you already have an e-mail account. I did it myself; it took a lot of time, particularly to do the graphics. With help, it took a month to get it going. I basically did it in stages. It took as much time as practicing the trumpet does. I used Adobe, and am pretty happy with the program.

"The results have been mostly contacts and networking. Old friends have found us on the net, and gotten in touch; composers have found us and offered to send us scores. We haven't gotten work through the website yet, but it may be starting to lead to that now.* But it's really not a booking site; rather it's for public relations. We add to our mailing list (there have been 600 visits to the site, and about a piece of mail a week). It's cheap, since I did the work, and it can't hurt. It could facilitate touring, probably, and presenters like the website. I like it for the group, but I think for an individual it seems kind of hokey. Our website includes pictures, bios, sound clips, anecdotes, a calendar, mailing list opportunity, and contact information."

* *Note that the Guild's website has begun to produce some booking inquiries by e-mail, and we are now referring presenters to the site for quick access to bios and other artist information.*

The important points to note, then, are as follows:

▶ It can be quite cheap to design and set up a website if you, or a member of your group, can do it, or even if you have a generous friend who wants to gain experience by using you or your group for practice (that's what CAG did). It can also be a bit expensive, if you hire a professional designer; costs can run about $75 per hour. But with a simple page consisting of a bio, photo and quick sample of your playing, the designer should only need to spend an hour or two. For something zippier, the designer may request an additional "creative fee" of perhaps $100.

▶ Maintaining the site costs about $20 per month for a page that takes less than 25 megs of memory (if this means something to you), but these prices can vary drastically; you should check with a local internet service provider for the for the best deal. (Many online service providers offer e-mail customers a small free site, though you have to design it yourself.) In selecting a provider, look for stability and reliability. Ask the provider for some examples of web pages that they host, and look at those pages in the early evening (when traffic is usually high). If it takes a long time for the majority of pages to load, try someplace else. Many online service providers offer their customers a small free site, though you have to design it yourself. Last, make sure your website is registered with popular internet search sites such as Yahoo, Alta Vista, etc. This will make it much easier for people to find you!

▶ It probably won't make you any money, at least at first. But it may make you friends, which can lead to money.

Resource Section

Photographers

The following is a list of several photographers with whom Concert Artists Guild and/or its artists have successfully worked over the years, based in New York City and Los Angeles.

In choosing a photographer, more than price should guide you. It's essential to meet, like and admire the work of the photographer you choose, so make sure all of this is in place before making your decision. Also, note that some photographers will work with you on clothes, make-up or locations, so be sure to ask about these items as well.

In alphabetical order:

Jeffrey Hornstein
137 West 14th Street, #301
New York, NY 10014
212-352-1186

Fees: *$500 per black & white session: includes two prints*
         $20 per additional print

The photographs of Mia Chung and Mariko Anraku (see pp.43, 49 & 50) were done by Mr. Hornstein, who does a great deal of fashion photography as well as fine work for musicians.

Don Hunstein
533 West 57th Street
New York, NY 10019
212-664-0813

As Director of Photography for Columbia Records for over 20 years, Mr. Hunstein photographed many famous artists for album covers and publicity, but enjoys working with emerging artists as well. The "formal" photograph of the New Century Saxophone Quartet is Mr. Hunstein's work.

Fees: *$600 per black and white session; includes two prints*
$200 additional for color, if added to b&w session.
Fee may be negotiable; rates the same for location or studio.

Lisa Kohler
202 West 82nd Street, #4C
New York, NY 10024
212-799-7687

The photographs of Alan Chow and Stephen Drury which appear in the preceding chapter are Lisa Kohler's. Ms. Kohler has worked with many CAG artists, and does excellent, interesting work.

Fees: *$925 per black & white session: includes one print*
$175 per additional print
$125 per roll of color, if added to the b&w session
$125 on location charge

Blake Little
6442 Santa Monica Blvd. #201
Los Angeles, CA 90038
213-466-9453

Mr. Little has photographed for the Kronos Quartet, the Los Angeles Guitar Quartet, Simon Rattle, David Byrne, Delos International, and Elektra Nonesuch. The "informal" photograph of Scott Lee on p.36 is by Mr. Little.

Fees: *Based on usage and individual jobs. Call for information.*

Steve Sherman
161 W. 54th Street, #1403
New York, NY 10019
212-757-5977 (phone)
212-977-2775 (fax)
e-mail: sjsherman@earthlink.net

Fees: *$800 + expenses for a session which can include black and white
and/or color; expenses run about $200 for film, processing and prints.*

Another fine and experienced young photographer; call for more details.

Christian Steiner
300 Central Park West
New York, NY 10024
212-724-1990 (phone)
212-724-7861 (fax)

Fees: *$1,000 per black and white session; includes one print; $200 for
additional prints
Prices per roll of color depend on various costs (film cost,*
production, etc.)*

*Mr. Steiner is highly respected in this field and does very elegant work. Though none
of his photographs are represented in the examples in this book, he is so much in
demand that it's very easy to find samples of his work.*

Photo Duplication

We referred in the text to places where you can get a copy negative made
from your original portrait, and then keep that negative on file for duplicating in
bulk. We can recommend several places which are commonly used in New York
City. Look at their work, and see which you prefer. We've listed prices, for
comparison purposes, for making the copy negative of an 8X10 black and white
original; adding line stripping (a one-time charge), that is your name and other
information printed on the bottom of the photograph; and making glossy 8X10
reproductions of your photos in quantity.

Wace Imaging Network
222 East 44th Street
New York, NY 10017
212-661-5600

Prices: *Copy negative*   *$25.00*
              Line stripping   *(included)*
              Prints, for orders of 52-100   *$1.70 each*
              For 101-150   *.90 each*

              For 150 and over .75 each

Modernage
1150 Avenue of the Americas
New York, NY 10036
212-997-1800
There are two other Modernage offices in New York City.

Prices: *Copy negative*   *$13.00*
              Line stripping (per element)   *$7.50*
              Prints, for orders of 100 and over   *.52 each*

Pro-Lab
111 West 24th Street
New York, NY 10011
212-691-0191

Prices: *Copy negative*   *$12.50*
              Line stripping (per line)   *$6.50*
               Prints, for orders of 100 and over   *.55 each*
              For 150-200   *.47 each*

Ken Taranto Photo Services, Inc.
39 West 14th Street, #504
New York, NY 10011
212-691-6070

Prices: *Copy negative*   *$17.50*
              Line stripping (per line)   *$7.50*
               Prints, for orders of 50-100   *$1.70 each*
              For 100-150   *$1.10 each*

Designers

Finding a designer who can create a flyer for you that expresses what you want, and with whom you are compatible, is very important. If you're working with a manager who regularly uses a particular designer, you may not have much choice. But if you're on your own, here are some suggestions, in New York City. These are designers that Concert Artists Guild has worked with frequently, and of whom we think highly.

When you hire a designer, you want to give them your photographs and text, and get back either film or a computer disk, either of which can go straight to the printer. We've indicated the average price each charges for a flyer design; film may or may not be included in the price, so check on this.

Carol Bobolts *(sample: Anraku flyer, p.49)*
Red Herring Design
449 Washington Street
New York, NY 10013
212-219-0557

Flyer design: $800 (possibly negotiable)

David Hughes & Tanya Ross-Hughes
Hotfoot Studio
237 East 28th Street, #5B
New York, NY 10016
212-684-1957

Flyer design: $400

Elvira G. Moran
39 West 14th Street, #507
New York, NY 10011
212-691-0937

Flyer design: $400

Marino Zullich *(no samples in this book, but he did the Guild's roster, CD cover and competition poster — all excellent)*
44 Willow Place
Brooklyn, NY 11201
718-834-1272

Flyer design: $600 (possibly negotiable)

Printing

There are a <u>lot</u> of printers out there. If you can use a specific recommendation, though, we found a company in North Carolina that has consistently given us very good prices, service and quality. They are:

Morgan Printers
P.O. Box 2126
3001 S. Evans Street
Greenville, NC 27834
919-355-5588, or
800-962-1972 (phone)
919-756-2559 (fax)

Two printers we work with in New York City:

Admiral Photo Offset Company, Inc.
47 West Street, 2nd Floor
New York, NY 10006
212-422-6848

CAMA Graphics, Inc.
480 Canal Street
10th Floor
New York, NY 10013
212-941-4645 (phone)
212-941-4664 (fax)

Demonstration Recordings:
New York City Area Studios & Engineers

STUDIO *	Adrian Carr	Cedar Sound
ADDRESS	630 Ninth Avenue New York, NY 10036	90 West Street New York, NY 10006
TELEPHONE	212-977-5390	212-227-3896
SET-UP COST	none; on-location fee varies	none
RECORDING	$125 per hour (Discounted rates available for artists)	$60/hour
EDITING	$125 per hour (Discounted rates available for artists)	$55/hour
TAPE	Various formats & prices	Call for rates
PIANO	1897 Steinway B	Steinway B
EQUIPMENT	Multi-track and digital mastering available; digital editing. Classical instrumental & vocal recording.	2 track (up to 24 track and digital mastering available)
CONTACT	Adrian	Mark

Christopher Greenleaf	Lobel Productions	MSK Recordings
42 Avondale Rd. Westerly, RI 02891-5004	5810 Bergenline Avenue West NY, NJ 07093	200 W. 15th Street NYC 10011
401-596-3699 (ph) 401-596-7171 (f)	201-869-0744	212-989-1986
none	none	$50/hour
$300/ app.3 hours (Flat fee for most jobs, all inclusive)	$50/hour	$50/hour
Additional digital editing available at studio rates	$50/hour	$35/hour
	none	none
N.A.: ON-LOCATION ONLY; NEW YORK OKAY	Steinway L full array of electronic digital keyboards available at no extra cost	NA: SPECIALIZES IN LIVE CONCERT DOCUMENTATION. **ON LOCATION ONLY**
16 track DAT recording from two or more microphones	2 track 8 track 24 track analog / 24 digital DAT available 64 Track sequencer available	Digital. Typically $200 to record concert. $50 to purchase digital master. Specializes in early music **ON-SITE**
	Mike	Michael

STUDIO	Planet Sounds	Sadler Recording Studios
ADDRESS	251 W. 30th Street NYC 10001	118 E. 28th Street NYC 10016
TELEPHONE	212-594-7554	212-684-0960
SET-UP COST	none	none
RECORDING	$50/hour	$50/hour
EDITING	$50/hour	$50/hour
TAPE	$35 (½");$12 DAT	$10 DAT
PIANO	Yamaha 7½ ft.	Sohmer 6 ft.
EQUIPMENT	up to 24 track and digital mastering available	up to 8 track: Also DAT High speed and real time audio and video duplication
CONTACT	John	John

WK Studios	Intermedia Arts Center (IMAC)	NOTES
611 Broadway Suite 721 NYC 10012 212-473-1203	370 New York Ave. Huntington, NY 11743 516-549-9666	
none	$50/hour (audio rate)	
$60/hour	$125 per camera-hour (video rate): $1,500 day location rate	
$60/hour	$75 per AB roll (video)	
$22.00 (¼")	3/4" video tape S-VHS	
Electronic keyboards / Samplers	Baldwin 9 ft.	
up to 16 track isolation booth	**VIDEO** $15/audio engineer hour. includes lighting, sound, stage technician, video director. Also ON-SITE	
JoAnn	Michael	

Self-help regarding video

The California Arts Council's Performing Arts Touring and Presenting Program produces a guide called *Creating An Effective Promotional Video*, covering topics from "Why A Good Video Is Essential," to "Low Budget Techniques/Shooting It Yourself." It costs $7.50, + $1 for shipping. Send a check or money order made out to **California Arts Council** to:

Performing Arts Touring and Presenting Program
California Arts Council
1300 I St., Suite 930
Sacramento, CA 95814

Making CDs

If you want to make a digital master to be used to produce CDs, you could talk to one of the studios listed above, or you might talk to Tim Martyn at Classic Sound Inc. Tim and his company regularly record artists' recitals at Merkin Hall; they now mostly do recording for various major labels. Their rates are much higher, therefore, than those above. However, they do excellent work, and will talk to you about your possible CD. They can be reached at:

Classic Sound Inc.
211 W. 61st Street
New York, NY 10023
212-262-3300 (phone)
212-262-3380 (fax)

The company that the Guild works with to produce our demo CDs is:

Mediatrack
Jacob van Lennepkade 334F
1053 NJ Amsterdam
The Netherlands
31-20-616-1775 (phone)
31-20-616-0258 (fax)

Our 1997 price was $2,150 for 1000 CDs in cardboard sleeves. This included shipping. It did not include graphic design, for which we provided film. We provided all the master tapes.

Another possibility:

Disc Makers
7905 N. Rte. 130
Pennsauken, NJ 08110
(800) 468-9353 (phone)
discman@discmakers.com (e-mail)
www.discmakers.com

This company offers a very wide range of products. Their prices aren't the lowest, but their customer service is said to be excellent. They also publish a number of free guides which are very useful and are available to anyone who calls and asks for them, including:

- ▶ Guide to Master Tape Preparation
- ▶ Finding Fans and Selling CDs, A Guide to Releasing and Promoting Your Own CD
- ▶ Guide to Independent Music Distributors

For further information:

A source book for information on where to get everything related to making your own CDs is:

The Billboard International Buyers Guide
P.O. Box 2016
Lakewood, NJ 08701
800-344-7119 (phone)

The book costs $125. You can consult this for sources of CD manufacturing, printers, distributors, and anything else related to the recording industry.

If you've made a CD which you actually want to sell on the Internet, you might call:

Circum-Arts
31 W. 21st Street, 3rd Floor
New York, NY 10010
212-675-9650 X17 (phone)
212-675-9657 (fax)
biles@circum.org

Contact Richard Biles for information on this program of Circum-Arts, whereby they act as a broker for artists or arts organizations. The Internet users who visit the "store" can browse the products and purchase the products on-line.

Self-help with your webpage:

There are books which will help you to build your own web site without having to pay for a designer. Three stood out for our staff:

Setting Up an Internet Site for Dummies, 2nd Edition, by Jason and Ted Coombs, published by IDG Books Worldwide. Like the other ...*Dummies* books, it explains everything in plain English, and allows the reader to come up with her own solutions.

Dummies 101: Creating Webpages, by Kim Komando, published by IDG Books Worldwide. Another one, perhaps even more "dumbed down" than *Setting Up...*

These two books seem slightly geared to PC users. If you're a Mac user/fan, try:

Create Your Own Homepage (Mac Users), by Tonya and Adam Engst, published by Hayden Books. Described as a perfect reference book by at least one of our Mac friends.

All three of these books come with a diskette or CD-Rom that contains numerous programs to help you get started.

III. Assembling Credentials

Before anyone will hire you to do something, you have to have done something. In order to make yourself appealing to a presenter, you have to have some negotiable credentials, in the form of performance experience, competition wins, or other evidence of your level of accomplishment. In this chapter we'll deal with competitions and self-produced concerts; for more advice on getting performances, see Chapter VI, part 2, "Self-Management."

Competitions

The great number of music competitions indicates, among other things, that consumers in the field are most comfortable with easily identified testimonials which validate a performer's expertise. Competitions seem to provide this by applying objective, recognized and respected standards to the selection process.

The problem is that music competitions are not like sports competitions. There may be someone who can run the fastest, or someone who can be described as the best tennis player in the world, at least for a brief time, but there simply isn't someone who is THE BEST at playing the Brahms *Second Piano Concerto*. The standards by which music competitions are judged are, thankfully, subject to human sensibility rather than to quantifiable criteria. But this means that they are also subject to inequities and frustrations.[1] Nonetheless, the general public, and even professionals in the field, often behave as if winning a given competition actually means that the winners are THE BEST, and pay them attention accordingly. Which adds to the general disgruntlement.

In spite of which you will probably do some competing at some point, perhaps because in a crowded field, with limited opportunities, you need to get someone's attention. *Competitions are one way — not the only way, but a way which is available to most everyone — to get someone's attention. Perhaps just about everyone's attention, for a minute.*

Certainly competitions can be an important part of a performer's career-building (for some individuals, the most important part). Doing well in a particular competition or audition may sometimes be a necessary in order to reach a particular goal. Some benefits which can come out of competitions are:

- Opportunities for those not well-connected in the field to develop some important connections

- Opportunities to hear other emerging musicians perform; opportunities to be heard, by one's peers as well as by judges; and the chance to broaden your peer group, talk with colleagues about the field, learn about other opportunities, and get comments or input

---

[1] The problems and irritations of competitions are too frequently discussed and complained about to spend many words on, but to let you know that we know about them (and sympathize) we will mention only that they can be restrictive, biased, unimaginative and unpleasant.

- The chance to begin to define what you do best, what you do well, and to learn how you perform under stress

- Performance experience

These are all benefits which can be obtained from competitions win or lose, if you know how to go about getting them. If you win, of course, you can add to these:

- Cash and other valuable prizes, including performances

- Public recognition and attention

- Something to fill out your biographical materials

What no competition ever is, is

- *An instant career.*

We will address some possible benefits individually, and provide some guidance about how best to obtain them; but first, you need to think about how to find out what competitions exist, and how to pick which ones to enter.

■ Where are they? What are they?

We assume that you know about the competitions closest to you, those run by your school while you're still enrolled. As for all the others, performers often find out about them in a hit-or-miss fashion, either through word of mouth from colleagues, teachers and others, or by seeing a notice on a bulletin board somewhere. This method may work reasonably well, but probably isn't the most efficient way to plan your time and allocate the money and effort you'll put into competing. Some more organized research is in order. Concert Artists Guild publishes an annual Guide to Competitions for performers, which is cross referenced by performance category and location; the annual <u>Musical America International Directory</u> has an extensive listing of competitions including many for performers (see the Resource Section for additional information about these sources). Most colleges and universities, and all conservatories, maintain a listing of competitions for their students' (and often their alumni's) use.

In addition, many orchestras have competitions for which the prize is a concerto performance. Often, these kinds of competitions will be aimed at younger or local artists, and you can inquire with the orchestras you think are likely to hold them in your area. Music teachers' organizations often sponsor competitions, as do instrument-specific societies. A bit of detective work can ferret out competitions which will be useful to you. Don't neglect your local papers as a source of this information; for younger artists, competitions which offer scholarships or other similar prizes are often announced through the local paper, and major city newspapers will occasionally print deadline information about the major international competitions.

▪ Which competitions to enter

Participating in competitions, as stated above, can require a significant investment of time, effort, and money. Therefore, your choice of which competitions to enter should be informed by reasonable and specific goals. Looking through lists of past winners of any competition, including the biggest and most prestigious, should convince you that the winners, overall, have by no means been guaranteed a wildly successful future. Conversely, among today's most famous young solo artists, a good number have never won any competitions — or entered any, to our knowledge — but have gotten onto the "major career" track by a completely different route.

Goals should be as specific as possible, and should match what the competition offers as a prize and how the competition is run. For example, if your goal is to gain experience in performing with an orchestra, you might enter one of the orchestra-run concerto competitions which are held all over the country. If your goal is to be heard by some important musicians in your field, a competition that has several rounds, at least some of them live, where many judges will hear you, is the right one for you. Your goal can be solely mercenary (entering because you need the prize money is legitimate), or just wanting to know how colleagues outside your normal sphere of activity like your playing. You can have several goals; the important point is that they be specific (so that you can evaluate whether you've achieved them) and realistic (so that you don't waste valuable resources).

In choosing which competitions to enter, the rule of thumb should be as follows:

You hope to win, and believe that it's realistically possible for you to do so, so you should want and be ready for the prize when you do.

This means that the competition should 1) be appropriate for your level of performance and experience; and 2) match your musical strengths.

The major international competitions, for example, may well include very extensive concert tours — 100 or so dates in a year — as part of the prize package. If you've never performed more than three or four times during a season, and have not done much (or any) touring, you're unlikely to have the stamina that such a schedule requires. Also, some of the 100 concerts will be in major halls, in situations where you will be judged by the same standards as any of the other artists, seasoned professionals, who regularly play there. No matter how gifted, you may find yourself prematurely facing the world's most critical public.

Similarly, if you enter a contemporary music performance competition and you dislike contemporary music, you're certainly unlikely to win, but also — if by some chance you do — you're unlikely to be able to take advantage of the performance and networking opportunities which will arise from it.

Aside from the clearly stated mission of the competition, it is possible to get some insight into the kind of artist that a given competition is looking for by learning something about its recent winners. If you consider all the winners of a given competition over the past five years to be colorless, middle-of-the-road, boring performers, and you think of yourself as outrageous, iconoclastic and absolutely unlike anyone they've chosen, you may in fact be at a disadvantage in this one. Of course, you may be determined to become the X competition's first artist-winner of any interest, and if so, it's worth a try.

Once you have a clear idea of which competitions you might want to enter, start to think about scheduling. Since traveling to competitions outside your immediate location requires money (for transportation, lodging, food, practice time and more, certainly for yourself and sometimes for an accompanist as well), and since preparing repertoire requires great care and effort in all cases, it's wise to carefully budget these resources. Try to do several competitions which allow you to overlap or repeat repertoire within a season, rather than simply doing one a year. (Given the age limits most competitions have, you won't be able to do very many if you do one a year anyway.) If you've traveled, say to Europe, to enter a competition, see if you can build yourself a small competition circuit. Winning a prize in one or some of them may help to pay for the trip, more people will have heard you perform, you'll get more mileage and experience with the repertoire you've learned, and you'll begin to gain smoothness and confidence in your auditioning ability as you go along.

Don't try, however, to do more than you can take on and still do well. It's not useful to do a bad audition, and you're creating perfect conditions for performing poorly by being exhausted or distracted. Artists in our competition have been known to travel back and forth between our semi-final and final rounds and the equivalent rounds of another competition in some far away city; none of these musicians has won ours, nor have they won the others, to our knowledge. There are always exceptions, of course, and you know your own stamina and ability to perform under stress better than we could. (One singer, who won a first prize in our competition several years ago, knocked the socks off the judges in spite of having just walked off an all-night flight from China at the end of an opera tour.) Still, think about this before plunging in.

Build in time during the circuit schedule to allow for sufficient rehearsal with accompanists, if you're not going to be working with the same one for all your auditions.

One last thing to consider when doing your selecting and scheduling is to try to allow time during and after each competition to take advantage of the professional and social opportunities that will almost certainly be a part of winning, and which may well be a part of simply participating in, the competition. The competition administration can give you an idea of what will be happening; whether you can attend auditions by other artists, for example, or receptions with your fellow competitors, judges, patrons of the competition and the press, and — should you win — whether you should be available for any special events. More about this further along in this section.

The following ideas are dispatches from the field, advice based on the collective experience of our friends on the competition circuit, and on our own experience of who does well in our competition, and how.

▪ Choosing repertoire

Some competitions have required repertoire which you will have to prepare; others have some required works or categories of works; still others have no requirements at all, and may consider your ability to create interesting programs part of their evaluation of you as an artist. Whatever you do,

**DON'T BASE YOUR REPERTOIRE DECISIONS ON AN
ATTEMPT TO OUTGUESS THE JUDGES.**

It is far better to impress with what you <u>can</u> do than to dutifully perform something you think you should. To whatever degree you have any flexibility, choose repertoire which emphasizes your strengths and individuality as an artist. If you are given a great deal of freedom, remember that a competition program should almost never be a conservatory graduation program. You may need to demonstrate your versatility and breadth of musicianship, but you don't have to show that you can play particular works in order to do so. Also, don't try to play the way you think the judges will want you to; play your own way, which is the only way you can really be consistently convincing.

Frustratingly, both of the following are true:

> *War horses, certainly the greatest and best known of them,*
> *can be dangerous, and a jury will almost certainly have specific*
> *ideas about exactly how a well-known work should be played. Also,*
> *they may have heard the work twelve times just before your turn*
> *comes up.*

> *On the other hand, a program of completely unusual and*
> *unfamiliar works, unless you're a specialist in a certain area, can*
> *make a jury uneasy about their ability to judge your performance.*

So, there you are: the choice, ultimately, has to be determined by what you do best.

One other consideration. If you are an instrumentalist or singer who will be performing with an accompanist, and if the accompanist will be provided by the competition or is someone with whom you've not worked before, it's obvious but important to remember to take into account the ensemble difficulties of the works you're programming. Don't provide yourself with an additional and unnecessary challenge when there are so many you have to deal with already.

And if you are working with an accompanist that you provide, the pianist should be absolutely excellent. The quality of your musical collaboration, and your musical judgment in picking someone with whom to collaborate, will (or should) be a factor in assessing your performance. And working with a fine musician will require — and inspire — you to do your best.

▪ Program order

This is the same story. Many competitions allow you to start with a selection of your own choosing. Play to strength; start with what you do best, and what makes you comfortable and relaxed. Don't choose a work to start in which there's a danger that you may completely self-destruct, even if it's a sure dazzler when you hit it just right. If it's that impressive, the judges will likely ask for it later, when you're apt to be more caught up in the flow of the performance.

■ On-stage presentation

The stage director and performance coach, Janet Bookspan, who often takes part in the Guild's workshops, sums up how to make the best of the audition situation as follows: "There are no auditions, there are only performances." This is probably the best single piece of advice on the topic I've encountered. Granted, an audition can often be a weird sort of performance, where your audience may be entitled to interrupt you at will, where you don't always know exactly what you will play, and during which you may not be able to see or hear the people to whom you're playing. Nonetheless, if you are able to maintain the integrity of the "performance," thinking of the piece from beginning to end and wanting to share your performance with your listeners, you're much more likely to draw them into your experience and convince them of your musical vision.

In addition to your actual performance of the music, the "no auditions, only performances" idea means that the etiquette of performing remains, modified, of course, according to the specific situation. If there's no actual audience but only a small judging panel (or just one judge), you probably shouldn't bow when you take the stage, but a gracious smile as you enter, and an equally gracious acknowledgment — plus a thank you — when you leave are essential. (Since smiling also actually is a tension reliever, it can help with performance nerves.)

Dress: for the weather, which may mean that you have to be comfortable rather than glamorous, and for the occasion, which means finding out as much as possible about what the occasion is, and what is the suggested level of formality. As always, ask for information.

▪ Memorization

Certainly do memorize your music if you can. Singers and pianists almost always have their music memorized; string players usually do if it's a concerto, and usually don't if it's a sonata; wind players and others often don't, but should. There is widespread feeling that a sonata, played by an instrumentalist with piano, should not be memorized, backed up by either "tradition" or a desire to not make the pianist look less like an equal partner. In our opinion (and we realize that this is a minority view), this is silly. It would be nice if the pianist would also memorize the music, but we're a long way from that; meanwhile, the less there is to come between performer and listener, the better. The performer's eyes fixed on the music, and even the presence of a music stand, can quite effectively create a barrier to communication. If you must use music and a stand, position it so that it can be ignored by the listener, and don't allow yourself to stare at the pages. (This last advice applies equally to <u>actual</u> performances, not just to auditions.)

▪ Attitude

We've often felt that before musicians enter competitions they should judge several of them. Judging is a difficult process, challenging in both musical and emotional ways; some judges find themselves on firm ground with the former, and yet uncomfortable with the latter. Though they may feel that it's inappropriate to express any direct reaction to your performance, the judges almost always want to like you. There is nothing more exciting for a competition judge than to be overwhelmed with wonderful performances, even if that means more difficult challenges in making their decisions. Assume that even if the physical circumstances make a particular audition less than comfortable, the goodwill and sympathy are there. Such an attitude can never hurt, and may well help you to create the most positive impression possible.

▪ If you don't win

Not winning can mean everything from not even getting through a first
round to getting second prize. Assuming you performed at all creditably,

▪ DON'T:

> Slink off, and try and forget the whole thing as quickly
> as possible;

▪ DO:

> Try and squeeze every last possible benefit out of the
> competition before you pack your things and head home.

Among the things you can certainly do:

- If you have been eliminated, try to attend the auditions by your peers.
  You'll learn a lot about who's out there in the field, about repertoire, and
  about the subtle factors in performance technique that influence juries. It
  certainly will be interesting, both musically and otherwise. You may have a
  chance to meet and talk with people involved with the competition;
  administrators, judges, colleagues, patrons, press. Even when the auditions
  are technically closed, the powers-that-be might let you attend with special
  permission. Of course, if you're still an active participant, don't do this; it
  would probably be both inappropriate, and is likely to be disturbing to your
  own concentration to listen to everyone else's performances.

- Attend any social or press events which are scheduled in association with the
  competition, for the networking reasons stated above.

- Try to get as much feedback as you possibly can about whether anyone who heard you liked your work. In addition to the judges, there might have been others — managers, teachers, conductors, composers, presenters, patrons, press — who attended the auditions. If any of them, including the judges, were interested in you, they might be willing to give you advice or other help. We've known performers in our and other competitions who didn't win, including some who didn't even get past the preliminary tape round, who were able to find a teacher, gain scholarship assistance, get performance engagements and financial help with special projects and establish important ongoing friendships, by simply making sure they met and spoke to as many sympathetic people as they could. The competition administration should advise you as to what is appropriate and when to back off gracefully. It's good etiquette to ask the administration's advice in approaching judges and others.

- If you do well, make sure that someone knows about it. Your hometown newspapers will certainly be interested if you place among the top winners, as might such publications as your alumni newsletter. Send out a letter or press release (see page 154).

▪ When you win

The advice for what to do when you win a competition is, surprisingly, much like that offered for when you don't. The difference is that the *possible* opportunities for learning, networking, and publicity outlined above become *certain* opportunities when you've been chosen as a winner. You're now the star. There will almost certainly be social events; go to them. There will certainly be people who were impressed with your performance; meet them, learn about them, and add them to your mailing list. In addition, make sure the people who have been interested in or have even supported your career up to this point learn of the victory, and that you thank them for their part in your success. Learn about the competition's public relations efforts on your behalf, and find out if you can help them by being prepared with photos, bios and the like. If the competition is a very major one, they will almost certainly be doing equally major publicity for you. Nonetheless, get on the phone yourself, and see whether the excitement surrounding the win can turn possibilities into realities. (If you've been doing well overall, and this is a major event in what could now be a major career push, seriously consider hiring a good publicist right away.) If a management firm has been looking at you, or if a concert series has been considering including you in their season, make sure they know about your triumph immediately.

Find out about what resources the competition has that they can use on your behalf, in addition to the specific prizes listed in the brochure. You shouldn't expect to learn all this instantly; rather, expect to find out gradually and gracefully. We've known artists who have won competitions and developed ongoing relationships with the administration and/or sponsors; these friends have sometimes provided assistance far beyond the amount of the original award. Actual examples, small and large, of these items include:

a tuxedo;
funding for a recording;
a London debut;
a collaboration with a well-known television star on a special project;
a generous living stipend for a year.

None of these was included in the prize the artists originally won. They were given later on, as the result of continued interest in the artist by people involved with the competition, combined with the artists keeping up contact and making their career development needs known.

A final word on competitions. Have some perspective, and be prepared for the fact that no one can please everyone, and that, though you may do marvelously at X competition they may not respond equally well at Y competition. Don't call the competition administration and yell at them for their bad taste. It won't help you any, except to relieve your feelings slightly; it probably won't hurt you either, since most competition administrators will not hold an angry phone call against you forever — but it might, and certainly isn't particularly polite.

Debuts ... and alternatives

If one defines "debut" as a New York debut, and if the intention of the reader is to self-produce such an event, the advice is very short:

DON'T DO IT.

Here are some of the reasons.

1. **The New York debut is something of a musical dinosaur, without the importance it may once have had.** Having a New York debut under one's belt almost never makes any difference at all to one's career development. The phone will not ring the next morning with offers of management, engagements and the like. Almost certainly, <u>nothing will happen</u>.

2. There is only one newspaper in New York which has the staff, space and ongoing interest to try and regularly cover debut recitals: *The New York Times*.[2] And even they have limited numbers of critics, and a limited number of inches devoted to classical music reviews. If you're spending the vast amounts of money a debut can cost for the sake of a review, know that anything — a snow storm, illness, too many conflicting musical events, or, forgive us, a lack of interest in your event — can prevent you from getting one. Then, consider the likelihood of getting a <u>good</u> review with reprintable lines. (How often do you agree with the critic's assessment of a concert?) So much for the newspapers.

3. New York debuts can be fiercely expensive to produce. (See the Resource Section for 1997 costs of concert halls regularly used for such events.) In addition to the hall costs, you must add in the extras: everything from the cost of a recital manager should you use one (perhaps $2,000), to advertising, accompanists or guest artists, travel, hotels and food (if you don't live in New York), and more. If you have the $5,000 to $15,000 such an event costs, there are better ways to spend the money, all of which are more likely to have a positive effect on your career.

This isn't just our jaded view. Every year or so, newspapers in New York City write about the demise of the New York debut, often with some relief. In 1993, Alex Ross wrote an article with the headline, "The Debut: Grand Rite of Passage Now Passé" in *The Times*. He said, "The interesting question is ... whether this much respected ritual has become less significant in recent years? In an age of proliferating technology and information, this neat event - a private, solo debut in a New York concert hall - seems somewhat superfluous. Foreign artists more often make an impact on these shores first through the medium of recordings. Young artists can make their way to possible fame through competitions, auditions, radio broadcasts and select debut series." And later, "The very idea of a New York debut clings to memories of a time when the city revolved around the symphony, the opera, the recital. The rituals and institutions of classical music cannot shake nostalgia for a long-lost age of splendor and innocence. Young artists have discovered new, less

---

[2] Note the word "try:" even *The Times* has changed its editorial policy, and doesn't particularly prioritize debut reviews when making assignments.

cumbersome modes of establishing themselves and getting noticed: recordings, venturesome programming, involvement with new music." Right.

Does this mean that one should never make a New York debut? No, since there are circumstances which would make doing so at least slightly more sensible. They include:

1. **When someone else is paying.** The best possible debut is one for which you receive a fee. If someone hires you to perform your New York debut as part of their "Great Artists" series or whatever, take it. If the debut is a competition prize, it has a greater chance of attracting some press interest. If it's the gift of a patron, and you can't convince this person to put the money into something more practical, it may or may not prove useful, but at least you're not risking your own money — which presumably is in short supply.

2. **When your career has reached a stage where, in spite of significant exposure and serious credentials established in many other locations, you have not had and are not expecting an offer to perform in New York.** Combined with the expectation that a particular group of important people will attend — critics who have been following your career outside of New York, managers, conductors, presenters, other influential musicians — and the potential for attracting a respectable audience (not entirely made up of friends and family), a self-produced debut might be worthwhile.

3. **When you specifically need to have done a New York recital to get tenure at a teaching job.** You should still try to get some outside source to pay, but an investment in your employment future is understandable. However, it would be still better to work within the system to move beyond this outdated benchmark of performance achievement; there are many other things a teacher can do to prove her stuff, and even to do some real good for the field in general.

4. **You're not an individual but rather an ensemble, based in New York, and the debut is not really a debut but rather the first concert of an annual series.** Many groups want to have an annual concert or concert

series of their own in their home base, in which they can have artistic control, experiment with repertoire, and develop a home base following. If your home base is New York City, well, there you are. Whether or not it's New York, your group may — following rule number one above, that it's better to have someone else pay, at least in part — choose to follow the not-for-profit route, and may then apply to various funding sources to support these programs. (See the General Resources chapter for more of this information.)

A New York critic we know has pointed out, very sensibly, that the debuts he is most interested in are those which are scarcely debuts at all. These are concerts performed by artists who have been heard regularly, even frequently, in other situations, whether as guest artists on other programs, as part of a chamber ensemble, or as soloists in concerto programs. Also included in this category are artists who have developed a strong following outside of New York, and whose first performance in this city is an occasion of significant interest. These artists come before the public with a certain amount of credibility and reputation; not only do they attract somewhat more interest than would the average untested and unproven debut artist, the expectations may be more positive, and the general attitude toward them may be kinder, less "show me."

New York Debut Alternatives

If you think about what you would hope to get from doing a New York debut, you can probably achieve the same thing cheaper, and with greater potential for success, by other means. If your aim is to gather reviews, you have a much better chance of doing this by developing regional opportunities, either in your home location (more about this below) or in a variety of important locations around the country and abroad. For the same cost as a self-produced New York recital, you can produce recitals in two or three other major cities where there are excellent papers and good halls — Chicago, Washington and Boston, for example. Your chances of getting press coverage are much improved; and, because you will be performing in several locations, your chances of getting exposure, creating a regional following, and doing other significant networking are greater as well.

Many cities, though rich in musical events, are not as absolutely saturated as is New York. If your goals include accumulating credentials, the preceding advice holds true: if your goal is to test yourself in a major musical marketplace, the same again. In other words, think about self-produced performances as a career investment, and always be looking at any investment in a hard-headed way, with an eye on the payoff. Be specific about this; know what you want, and think of how best to get it.

In thinking about what you want, realize that not all successful and fulfilling careers are national or international. Several artists we know have made fine, rewarding careers limited to their own city or region. In these locations they are in great demand, have loyal followings who wouldn't miss one of their concerts, and are both lauded and devotedly followed by the local critics. (We're thinking right now of Boston and Baltimore, by the way, not of tiny rural communities.) They work all the time, and have musically very fulfilling lives. In the section on the press, we've described how you will almost always have an advantage in your home town (as long as it's not New York) in attracting attention, so do remember this when considering where best to invest your financial and creative resources.

Always try and get someone else to produce the recital if you can. There are concert series in important cities around the country which produce debut recitals and pay a fee to the artists; it may not be much, but at least you won't have hall and related costs, there is usually a built in audience of non-relatives, and the fee may cover some of your other expenses. Some of these concerts are broadcast on the radio, and are that much more valuable as a result. Needless to say these opportunities are limited and highly competitive, but are worth trying for if you're ready for them. (See the Resource Section for several such venues.)

One other avenue you may want to explore, if you are self-producing and don't want to come in completely as a new kid on the block. With sufficiently respectable credentials, you can approach the producer or presenter of an appropriate concert series (meaning a series which sometimes includes emerging or debut artists, or might do so, given a good reason), suggest that you have managed to raise the financial backing and would like to be considered for inclusion in the series. The producer / presenter may just possibly bite, since, if you are of any interest to them, you'll be saving them money on their overall season costs. No one but you and the producer need know that the arrangement is any different from that with any of their other featured artists. You will have the advantage of the built-in audience, critics who regularly attend these programs, and a more important showcase than you would be able to manage on your own.

About recital managers: You can hire someone to take care of all the non-musical aspects of a self-produced event for you, for a fee. In New York, a recital manager will cost approximately $2,000 plus the expenses you would assume anyway (for postage, flyers, etc.), a fee which will generally cover the following services: writing and sending out press releases; arranging for the design, printing and mailing of flyers; helping to plan and place your advertising; sending out special invitations; working with the concert hall and arranging your rehearsal schedule there; assisting with your overall planning; and overseeing the event (and coping with last minute problems). They cannot guarantee reviews or feature stories preceding the concert, and if they say they will, they're probably not honest and you shouldn't hire them.

One other item which a recital manager can often take care of for you is hall "papering." Unless you have a massive number of friends and family in addition to the V.I.P.s that you hope will attend, your hall might look a little forlorn with only a few folks in it. The answer for many artists is making tickets available at no charge to deserving groups — senior citizens, students, foreign visitors, and others. Though you can contact the appropriate centers yourself, it certainly is helpful to have your recital manager take care of this for you.

As to whom to hire, there are simply too many to list, so you should ask those who have done recitals at that location for recommendations. Shop around, be very choosy, and make an arrangement which clearly states everyone's responsibilities.

Resource Section

Sources of information about competitions

The Guide to Competitions
Published by Concert Artists Guild

     Concert Artists Guild publishes the only very comprehensive, affordable and cross-indexed directory of competitions open to performers in the U.S.A. and abroad. Published annually, it is available direct from CAG or at music bookstores including, in New York City, Patelson's Music House and The Juilliard School bookstore. The 1998 Guide *costs $17.95, plus shipping and tax (if you live in New York State). For more information, or to order a copy, write or call:*

     Mary Madigan, Publications
     Concert Artists Guild
     850 Seventh Avenue, Suite 1205
     New York, NY 10019
     212-333-5200

Musical America International Directory of the Performing Arts

     See Resource Section, Chapter 1, for information on this directory; it includes listings of competitions worldwide, including more extensive listings for opera, conductors and composers than are included in the Concert Artists Guild Guide.

Rental costs, for debuts and other concerts

The numbers below are high enough to make you think at least twice, hopefully, about booking a hall and producing your own New York debut. Note especially what is not included in the totals listed, which will make the bottom line significantly higher: stage labor, insurance (in three out of the four halls), program printing at Weill, and variable costs like advertising. However, there are often good reasons for some people, ensembles particularly, to produce a single concert or a concert series. In any case, here's the information, accurate as of late 1997, generally applying to the 1997-98 concert season.

New York City Hall Rental Costs

	Weill	Merkin	Tully
Basic Rental	$ 875	$ 1375	$ 4415
Stage Labor	*	+	*
Minimum Staff	410	265	965
Piano Tuning	130	140	174
Programs	x	+	+
Tickets	75	*	187
Box Office	+	*	+
Rehearsal (time varies)	+	+	345
Recording (cassette)	200	355	500
Insurance	x	x	x
Totals	$ 1690	$ 2135	$ 6586
Hall capacity:	268	451	1096

+   indicates the item is included at no extra cost
x   indicates the item cannot be provided (though it may be required).
*   variable: see notes.

Weill Recital Hall at Carnegie Hall
- Contact: Gilda Weissberger, 212-903-9710
- Basic Hall Rental for Saturday or Sunday twilight concerts (5:30 p.m.) is $775. $1530-1580 includes rental, ticket printing, piano tuning, personnel and security.
- No programs can be provided; you must provide your own.
- Box office is for 60 days; tickets can be charged over the phone.
- Recording quality varies.

Merkin Concert Hall
- Contact: Vicki Margulies, 212-362-8060
- $75 includes day-of-performance service (including ticket printing). For $155, service can be provided for the entire season.
- Program consists of biography page and listing of works to be performed. Additional material can be included at extra cost.
- 2½ hours of rehearsal are included.
- Recording quality excellent.

Alice Tully Hall
- Contact: Trudy Dawson, 212-875-5000
- Rental cost quoted is for Friday, Saturday and Sunday evenings; Weekday matinees, $3120; Monday through Friday mornings, $2605. Rehearsal charge is $345 for 3 hours, including ½ hour setup time, and does not include stage labor.
- Stage labor costs are quoted on receipt of technical requirements; the cost may vary significantly depending upon performance needs.
- 90 days box office. Additional cost for subscription service, $263 per performance.
- Program is printed by Stage Bill, and can include program notes (which you must provide) at no additional cost.
- You must provide your own insurance.
- Recording quality variable.

Alternative halls

New York has many small (and large) halls, churches and other presenting facilities which can be rented for presenting your concert. Rental costs are all over the place, but some are very reasonably priced, and may offer just the right ambiance, acoustics, hall capacity and other features for your event. Our experience is that for fairly standard classical music concerts, though, *The New York Times'* record of covering recitals in alternative locations is even spottier than their record for covering them in the three halls noted above. (This isn't the party line, by the way; *The Times*

ays that they are equally open to attending concerts in any public location, and
perhaps they are.)

Nonetheless, since there are reasons besides reviews for putting on concerts
n New York, you should look into sites which suit you. Certainly concerts taking
place around the city are listed in *The Times*, and in many other publications; attend
these events, and see which ones appeal to you.

New York Debut Alternatives

The following concert series present artists who are not yet well-known, are
regularly reviewed, and pay the performers a fee. They require only the submission
of very basic materials, usually a tape and biography, for consideration.

The Phillips Collections
Sunday Afternoon Concert Series
1600 21st Street, N.W.
Washington, D.A.. 20009
202-387-2151
Mark Carrington, Manager

*This series provides the artist with a broadcast on WGTS-FM and a high-
quality cassette tape of the recital in addition to the fee. Send biographical
information, along with a 20-minute cassette of recital repertory of various styles and
periods (live performances preferred). Materials must be received by December 1 for
consideration for the following concert season.*

Dame Mire Hess Memorial Concerts
500 N. Dearborn Street, Suite 1130
Chicago, IL 60610
312-670-6888
Contact: Al Booth

*Fees are $450 for a local soloist, $500 for an out-of-town soloist; $175 more
is paid if there is a piano accompanist. One night's hotel accommodation is also
provided. The 45-minute recitals are broadcast live by WFMT-FM and its 300
affiliated cable stations across the country.*

Getting your New York Recital reviewed, if you have decided to go this route

Getting *The New York Times* to review a given concert, particularly one by a relatively unknown artist, is uphill work, and — not due to any ill will on their part, but often because of the ratio of music activity to staff to inches available in the paper — unlikely to happen. The other papers are even less likely to devote personnel and space to a small scale classical music event.

A publication the mission of which is to answer the resulting criticism vacuum has emerged, called the *New York Concert Review*. Though you pay for the reviewer to attend, you can't ensure that the review will be positive. Nonetheless, at least you will have someone, who is a known critic, and not one of your friends or relatives, validating that your event took place, and perhaps providing you with a quotable line for your press materials. To contact them about getting a concert (or recording, by the way) covered, and to find out current rates, call:

Howard Aibel, Editor and Publisher
New York Concert Review, Inc.
1649 260th Street
Janesville, Iowa 50647
319-273-2449 (phone / fax)

IV. Networking

"Few people are successful unless a lot of other people want them to be."
- Author unknown

First, forget the idea that the music field is controlled by relatively few people, that those who have the work get the work, that success comes about through connections, power, and money, and that the entire structure exists (at least in part) to keep you out. Forget it not because it's not true, but because — except for the last part — it is. And not all the reasons for this are reprehensible.

In the first chapter of this book, we discussed how musicians are trying to find regular work and success in a buyer's market, and how the buyers generally like to work with those they know. You wouldn't pick a doctor out of the yellow pages (or after receiving a flyer in the mail), knowing that your health is at stake; neither does a presenter, or manager, or orchestra administrator want to hire performers without knowing a lot about them, when the health of their business is at stake. Realistically, even with the best will in the world and marvelously discriminating ears, these people can't listen to everyone.

Imagine, then, that the field is like a big room, and in it are all those who have the work, and wanting to get in are all those who don't — yet. Your job is to learn where all the doors into the room are, and what it takes to open them. Though staying in is often as difficult as getting in in the first place, the approach to both is basically the same. One essential key is networking.

Networking is a term which describes making and understanding those relationships which nurture and sustain a career. No career, in any field, can exist without supportive networks.

If you graduate from Harvard Business School, you have more than a diploma and a well-respected credential with which to negotiate a good job. You have developed a group of potentially supportive peers and mentors, who may well turn into customers, providers of recommendations, sources of information — in other words, a "network" of invaluable contacts. All musicians need the same kind of network, and without it they can't effectively do business.

In this section of the book, we've identified several groups of individuals, from the constituency referred to in Chapter 1, with whom forming ongoing relationships is both particularly important and yet not often discussed. There are other groups, equally important, which will be discussed in other sections of this book (managers and presenters, for example). Also, some groups should be obvious, and a brief look at one of them — your colleagues — should serve to introduce principles which will recur throughout each chapter.

If you have attended a conservatory or other music school, and/or have worked for a while in the field, you have almost certainly developed a network of colleagues who like you and your music making. They include your peers in and out of school, your teachers, and your mentors and advisors. They will often be the source - for many musicians, the primary or only source, throughout their lives - of most of the contacts with which you will build your career, as you will be for them. It is our assumption that the importance of making mutually supportive friendships is obvious.

This is perhaps the place to introduce your most important business tool, next to your instrument:

Your address book.

The reason for introducing it here is that, though we would not presume to teach you how to make friends, we can advise you on how to deal with your friends as professional colleagues. Even your friends appreciate thank you's, written or by phone, for introductions or referrals made on your behalf. They also appreciate your making similar contacts on their behalf. They like being remembered on special occasions, or when they've had a musical success; they like being kept abreast of your activities. So, keep your address book correct and current, and write and call.

The person who is recommended for a job — or anything else — is often the person who has most recently been brought to memory. By remaining current with your colleagues you can be that person.

Your immediate colleagues are the most basic and obvious of your networking groups. Some groups that are not so obvious, whose role in the network is more complex than might be supposed, or that are just plain harder to get to know, follow.

Patrons

The ideas in this section are based largely on talks given at the <u>Career Moves</u> workshops by former CAG board president (and a former Managing Director at Salomon Brothers) Leslie Christian. Leslie is an extraordinary individual, a generous patron to both arts groups and individuals, and amazingly honest about her own motivations for giving. Additional important ideas have been provided by another former CAG board president, Edith Greenwood.

Despairing, the musicians sit in the darkened theater, knowing that for lack of funds the concert will not go on. All looks bleak, when Mrs. Musiclover, world-famous patron of the arts, appears in the wings. "The show must go on. Here's my checkbook; name the figure," she announces. "The concert season is saved!" exclaim the musicians. General rejoicing.

If you share most musicians' ideas on the subject, you assume that a patron of the arts is an extraordinarily wealthy individual who doles out lavish sums to a well-connected few, all of whom are less talented and less deserving than you would be. A community of especially well-heeled philanthropists does indeed exist; we all know the names of the most celebrated of the music patrons, as their last names are usually thought to be Hall, or Pavilion, or Space. They are regularly and tenaciously approached for assistance by all and sundry, since their interest in the field is at least known, and since — like most of the world — musicians are not very imaginative about investigating new possibilities, and have a particularly difficult time imagining why anyone, perhaps excepting these mysterious few people, would give their money away at all.

However, patrons aren't simply **PATRONS**; they are also patrons, individuals who are able and willing to lend various kinds of support to another person or project for a variety of reasons. You already have patrons within your existing network: friends and family who wouldn't miss one of your concerts, for example. They could, after all, make some excuse, and stay home and watch television - but they choose instead to attend and applaud, and sometimes bring their friends and even pay for their tickets. In other words, patronage involves a pattern of supportive assistance which can range from small commitments of time to large financial donations. It can include any or all of the following:

- **Physical presence;**

- **Getting the word out and networking on your behalf;**

- **Contributions other than money;**

- **And, yes, money.**

Unless this range of patronage possibilities is understood, you will close off potential sources of support, pay too little attention to smaller patrons who may be just as valuable as larger ones (and who may turn into the latter at some point), and approach the development of this constituency in the wrong way. Don't just focus on the very rich. It's important to realize that those who can't give $5,000 to a project of yours but who could give $100 may be actually better suited to you. Donors of large sums may require famous recipients, whereas a younger or beginning philanthropist might identify more closely with you at your career stage.

Though you're almost certainly reading this chapter to learn about the people who can help you finance big projects, and not to learn how to remind people to come to your concerts, the former really can and does develop out of the latter. Developing a group of fans who can be counted on for various kinds of help means developing mutually satisfying and mutually beneficial relationships — and that takes years of careful cultivation.

If this notion of cultivating helpful people is upsetting or daunting, we remind you again to think in terms of building your business, not your art. You would be less wary about remembering and identifying people who might invest in your business than those who might invest in your career; however, there probably is little reason for your ambivalence and hesitation. There is great potential for *mutual benefit* to be gained from the investment, as will be discussed later in this chapter.

Know your customer

The first comment we almost always get at our workshops in discussing patronage is, "But I don't know any patrons." Wrong, on two counts. First, given the expanded definition of patronage, you probably know a great many people who can be counted on to assist in your career building efforts. And second, you often don't realize whom you actually know. It's important to identify individuals who do or may support you, and then to understand their motives for doing so.

Patrons are people who have enough time and/or money to be able to spend some of it on you. They may be found among

- Your family;
- Organizations - religious, fraternal or civic;
- Alumni associations;
- Your students/ Parents of students;
- People at your outside jobs.

All of these include people *who have some reason to be interested in you already*. This is vital, for reasons which will be explained later. To these can be added:

- People you meet through your performing activities.

The people who will ultimately support you and your work are people who a) are able to do so, and b) like and/or admire you. Look for potential friends in potential sponsors. Find something in common. And then, keep these people in your address book, with correct spellings and current phone numbers and addresses. Add to the list regularly.

Knowing your potential individual patrons involves understanding what their philanthropic motives might be. They might include the following, in no particular order:

- Many of today's potential patrons came of age during the '60s. The values they embraced then may have been submerged during the scuffle to make a significant place for themselves in the business or professional world, but will often surface again when they've achieved some success and perhaps had a family. At this point, they may seek ways to reintroduce more spiritual values into their lives.

- They may want to feel important. Being a patron of the arts usually brings with it a special status which can enhance other areas of the patron's life.

- They may be frustrated musicians, individuals who took piano lessons as children and dreamed of performing on the world's great stages, but took the safer route and went into the family business. Assisting someone who is taking the risk and making music her life may be a way of maintaining their direct involvement with something once very close to them.

- They may, surprisingly, be assuaging a certain amount of guilt about their success. Many individuals who have "made it" are aware that a field like music, requiring complete dedication and endless effort, doesn't offer the same financial rewards that their own fields do, and are interested in righting the balance in some way.

- They may simply love music. Helping to make fine music, your music, possible, will be all these individuals want or expect. These are rare people, and to be treasured.

Remember that we're discussing individual philanthropy, and not institutional giving, where money has been set aside specifically for giving away, and the reasons for support are often clearly stated in published guidelines.

Also, needing a tax break has not been included on the list of motives. For one thing, gifts to private individuals are rarely tax deductible, and you therefore would need a non-profit organization to receive tax-deductible contributions for you (see General Resources section). For another, the tax laws do change about what and how much is actually deductible. Nonetheless, this does remain an attractive reason for a contribution for some people.

If people do provide support of any kind, what do they want in return? **Simply, they want to be acknowledged, in order to share in the glory and experience the pride which comes from having made something significant happen.** When they come backstage after the concert, when you're accepting the congratulations of all, they want to hear some version of "I couldn't have done it without you" from you. The moment of reflected or shared glory is unbelievably exciting, particularly to those whose own lives rarely offer direct applause, but even to those of us who sometimes do perform ourselves. *The degree to which it is exciting, and therefore to which the patrons are motivated to work towards making it happen again, is directly proportional to how well they know, like, and identify with the artist.*

In other words, you need to give away a little, to share the spotlight, in order to get more back. **Whatever you do say, it should be the truth, and should express a sincere awareness that somebody else helped you.** Since no performance is really possible without some kind of support, from the audience or from those behind the scenes, when you say thank you, you should mean it.

Before going into specific advice, it is important to remember that no matter how good the cause for which you're seeking support, how capable the potential patron is of giving it, and how faultlessly a request is presented, you will probably get "no" for an answer. Be prepared for a considerable amount of rejection, and don't take it personally if possible, as there may be endless reasons — none of which may relate directly to you and your project — why someone responds negatively rather than positively. There will be more about dealing with rejected requests later.

How do you start? Specifics

You are probably reasonably comfortable asking people to attend your concerts, at least by mail, particularly if you're willing to provide free tickets. However, asking for anything more can seem an insurmountable problem.

Asking people for support is a kind of sales, which, believe it or not, can be fun, or at least interesting; it can be a challenge to try to convince people to do what you want them to do. If you believe that in fact you're giving them something of value in return for this support — and hopefully the remarks of the previous paragraphs will have demonstrated that philanthropy involves an exchange — you should feel that a successful deal will benefit both parties.

Here are some possible requests, in ascending order of commitments of money or time, and some approaches to getting a positive response.

Request_____Strategy

To come to your concerts:_____

- Don't just send a flyer; write a note on the flyer, asking them to come.
- Keep on writing these notes for every event.
- If at all possible, call or write a note later thanking them for showing up.

To hold a special performance
at the patron's home or business_____

- Perhaps you (or your group) want to do a fund-raiser for a project you have in mind, or need to increase the attendance at your concerts and beef up your mailing list. Perhaps you need to perform in a particularly nice setting for someone important, such as a manager.

▪ **Ask advice**. Sit down with Joe, who by now has been coming to your performances regularly, and with whom you've struck up a rapport over the years, or sooner if you are particularly kindred spirits (you're both from Texas; you're interested in the relationship of computers and new music technology, and he's a computer specialist; you share a special interest in French music; you share an interest in French food). Tell him your goal (as described above) and your problem (that you need the perfect spot and an audience for a special performance). Let him help you come up with the answer, which might be,

> "Why don't we hold the recital at my apartment? I could serve wine and cheese, invite a group of music lovers, and ask for contributions to [the new recording]."

Or,

> "I don't have room to host a party myself, but I'm a member of a club which holds a concert series; let me make a call or two for you, and we can take it from there."

You might get a completely different response, suggesting an alternative approach to solving your problem:

> "If you want to increase attendance at your performances, perhaps instead of holding a special performance I could offer a block of free tickets to people at the office. I could even take several of them out to dinner first, to make sure they get there; I would get everyone's names and addresses for your mailing list in exchange for the seats."

You might have to help Joe to advise you, but chances are that given the opportunity he'll be delighted to try to help you come up with what you need. Be persistent, but also be sensitive to when it's time to back off and ask elsewhere. Also know that the responsibility for making an event like this come off is yours. Without being a pain, you will have to keep track of deadlines, remind Joe of what needs to be done, offer much assistance, and **Write the appropriate thank you note(s).**

To provide in-kind contributions

These can be as good as money, and might include such items as free printing of flyers; the donation of a piano from a local company so that you don't have to rent one for a concert; the loan of a tux or gown, or getting someone to buy such an item for you; donated labor, ranging from help with mailings to legal work.

The procedure is the same as above. **Ask advice.** Be sure that the person you're asking is someone with whom you have a friendly relationship, usually developed over a period of time, someone you have reason to know is interested in you. Make sure that your request is phrased in a way that lets the requestee a) give you exactly the response you want, b) propose alternatives, or c) say no, gracefully. Make sure, however, that the request is taken seriously. **Write a thank you note, and keep in touch.**

All of these examples are descriptions of actual contributions made by real patrons for real musicians we know. None of the musician-recipients are rich or well-connected or famous. And these aren't isolated examples, but typical of exchanges between patron and artist.

Money_____

This is what most people feel they want from patrons. Think carefully if money is what you really need most, and for exactly what you need it. Generally, requesting the rent and food money (though this may well be your greatest need) isn't going to get you a contribution; rather, a potential patron will probably be more interested in contributing to the costs of a project. Examples of projects which might attract financial sponsorship include:

- Doing the competition circuit, and putting together the funding for travel, accompanist fees and the like.

- Producing a particular concert or making a recording.

- Commissioning a composer.

- Buying a new instrument.

When asking for money, you can ask in person, which means again following the basic "**ask advice**" format above, and developing a strategy together with your advisor. You may prefer to write, however. A personal letter, requesting assistance with funding for travel, for example, might read like this:

```
Dear Veronica,

        Thanks so much for attending my
recital last June.  It was wonderful to
see you there and to visit at the
reception afterwards.
        As you've been following my career
efforts during the past few years,
you'll perhaps agree with my teacher and
me that the time has come to test my
skills against those of my peers around
the world, and compete in several
European and American competitions.  To
do so, however, requires funding, for
travel costs, accompanists and the like,
and there are no scholarships available
for this purpose.  I've saved $1,500 of
the $3,000 I will need to do the Lisbon,
Bucharest, and U.S. Interesting Artist
of the Year Competitions, and need to
find the additional $1,500.
        Any contribution you might be able
to make would be very much appreciated,
as would any suggestions you have about
other possible sources of assistance.
Please let me know as soon as possible
if you have ideas or can help directly,
as I must complete entry forms by the
end of next month.
        Thank you so much for your help
and support, both with this project and
over the years.  Do give my regards to
Reggie and the children, and I look
forward to hearing from you soon and
seeing you at the next recital!


Love,
      Archie
```

Regarding this letter, particularly note the following:

- Archie knows Veronica well, and refers to the fact that she has been
  following his career over the years. Knowing someone over time is
  especially important in solicitations for money; you need to have built up
  credibility and familiarity with you as a person and as an artist. The only

exception to this is when a recommendation that you write this letter has been made by another individual that the potential patron knows very well - so it comes to the same thing, they may not know you, but they know your sponsor.

■ Archie hasn't indicated a specific figure, since in this case he doesn't want to limit the amount the patron is willing to give, nor to indicate that a given amount is too little. In some instances, you might want to indicate particular figures (a low-high range, for example, or a specific amount being requested from each patron), always keeping the person from whom you're requesting the money in mind.

The amount you request should never come as a shock because it's out of line with the patron's means, the depth of the relationship or the project cost. A board member of Concert Artists Guild, whom we will call Ann Jones, describes having introduced a chamber group of young artists she was sponsoring with in-kind help to a group of friends from her club. It seemed to the artists and to Ann that the club members could be approached for financial assistance; although the artists had just met them, and had performed at the club only once, an interesting project had just come up. After Ann checked with the club members to prepare them and make sure it would be all right, she gave the artists permission to write a letter.

A figure had never been mentioned, and Ann's assumption was that they were seeking a small sum, based on the limited time any of them had known each other. The artists didn't show Ann the letter before it went out. To the club members' astonishment, and to some degree annoyance, the amount the group wanted was $5,000. This was too much to ask, on the basis of a very slight acquaintance. To the patrons' credit, and thanks in no small part to Ann's careful smoothing of ruffled feathers, little permanent harm was done to the developing relationships, though the group didn't get any money.

On the other hand, another CAG board member talks of having received a solicitation for the production of a series of concerts by a young pianist in whom she had developed an ongoing interest over a number of years. The letter limited the suggested donation amount to $100, when she would have been happy to give $1,000.

Though she did give several hundred dollars, she felt uncomfortable about giving more, as it might have seemed that she was throwing her weight around. Both the pianist and the donor lost out.

Back to the letter:

- Archie asks for advice as well as for money, thus giving Veronica a graceful way to help without making a direct contribution.

- The letter is hand signed, and further personalized through the reference to husband and children. This reminder of the personal relationship is very important.

If the amount you're seeking is great enough, if the project is grander, or if you're simply much too uncomfortable about fund-raising for yourself, you might want to get someone to write a letter on your behalf. Individuals could write letters to their friends or to a mailing list provided by you. Using the letter above as an example, Veronica could write to her and/or Archie's friends, stating exactly the same information:

Dear Betty,

It was good to see you at Archie's recital last June, and to visit at the reception afterwards. Clearly, we're both devoted fans of his music!

His teacher feels that the time has come for Archie to test his skills and talent against those of his peers around the world, and compete in several important European and American competitions. To do so, however, requires funding, for travel costs, accompanists and the like, and there seem to be no scholarships available for this purpose. I happen to know that he's saved $1,500 of the $3,000 he'll need to do the Lisbon, Bucharest, and U.S. Interesting Artist of the Year Competitions, but he needs to find the additional $1,500.

I'll be donating several hundred dollars to the "Archie Travel Fund." Any contribution you might be able to make would be very much appreciated, as would any suggestions you have about other possible sources of assistance. Please let me know as soon as possible if you have ideas or can help directly, as Archie must complete entry forms by the end of next month.

Do give my regards to Jughead and the children, and I look forward to getting the families together soon! Thanks again in advance for your help with this project!

Love, Veronica

If a non-profit organization can legitimately act for you — see the Resource Index and General Resources Section for information on non-profits — the donors might well be able to take the contribution as a tax deduction, an added benefit. A chamber group or other musical organization with which you're associated might be incorporated not-for-profit (alternative term, same thing). Other non-profits which might ask for funds on your behalf might include a school, church group, civic organization, or foundation which regularly acts on behalf of individual artists. The following is a letter Concert Artists Guild wrote to potential donors of funds toward the purchase of a new violin for a young artist on our roster. Note that she provided most of the names to which we wrote, though we also sent letters to our own board of directors and membership.

Dear Friend,

From time to time, Concert Artists Guild tries to assist artists on its management roster — winners of the annual international competition — with special projects. This letter is about one such venture.

Violinist Maria Bachmann made her Town Hall debut during the 1986-87 season, as a First Prize Winner of the 1986 Competition. Her extraordinary artistry was lauded by The New York Times in their review, which began, "Maria Bachmann is a violinist of soul and patrician refinement; her beautiful debut recital at Town Hall was one of the most rewarding of the season." Her career is moving ahead with impressive speed, and her recent and near future activities include a tour of China, performances at the Bowdoin Summer Music Festival, appearances with orchestras and in recital around the country, and a New York concerto debut at Alice Tully Hall in the fall.

Ms. Bachmann badly needs a new violin. She has found one that she loves; it costs $12,000, a reasonable price, but well beyond the means of a young artist. Concert Artists Guild is working with Maria to find funds to purchase the instrument; we felt that some of you would be interested in helping her to do so. Any donation you could give, however small, would be welcome, and would be tax-deductible.

We hope that you do contribute, and extend our thanks for your consideration of this project!

Ellen Highstein
Executive Director

The following guidelines, then, can apply to requests for any kind of support:

1. **Ask advice.**
   It's flattering, and doesn't put you or the patron in an awkward spot.

2. **Ask for the specific help that you need.**
   If you're asking for money, don't limit a dollar amount simply through shyness; try for lots, if appropriate, and be informed enough to know when it's not. Be ready with carefully prepared and accurate budgets to back up your request.

3. **Expect more rejections than acceptances.**

4. **Don't phrase requests in a way that will make it uncomfortable to ask the next time.**

5. **Personalize all requests.**

6. **Develop patronage relationships gradually!**
   Start small.

7. **Don't ask for too much too soon.**
   Assume that in general a patron has to get to know you, and you them, before a request (particularly a large one) is appropriate.

8. **Get someone else to write letters on your behalf, if necessary and if you think it will help.**
   Realize that what you may gain, i.e., not feeling awkward, may not be worth what you lose, namely the personal contact which may be vital to the patron.

9. **Be careful regarding the details.**
   Nobody will give you anything if you consistently spell her name wrong.

10. **Ask for support for specific projects, so that the patron can see the result of his support and be properly acknowledged.**

11. **Say thank you and keep in touch!**
    Let those you've asked know what happens with the project, even if they haven't contributed, since this may build credibility for the next time.

Conductors

Many of the ideas for this section are drawn from the caring and informative (and very entertaining) talks given at the <u>Career Moves</u> workshops by conductor Murry Sidlin; other speakers on this topic who provided important ideas are conductors JoAnn Falletta, Ransom Wilson and David Gilbert.

It is important to audition for, work with and get to know conductors for many reasons, not just because it would be nice to have the concerto work. Conductors talk to lots of other people in the business: managers, presenters, administrators, and performers. They may talk about, and recommend, you. They also travel a lot, and can get your name around. They are considered important people in the field, and their opinions are taken seriously, so that simply being well thought of by conductors can be very valuable in your career building efforts.

There are about 1500 orchestras in this country, designated as community, urban, metropolitan, regional, and major, by the American Symphony Orchestra League, depending on budget size. Almost all of them feature soloists at some time or other. About 20 of them are for all intents and purposes inaccessible to you, the emerging artist; these are the most famous orchestras, with the world famous conductors and, generally speaking, the name-brand soloists. Though occasionally unknown artists perform with these orchestras or audition for these conductors, the channels for doing so are carefully and protectively set up: that is, through regular youth competitions, auditions arranged by powerful managers or teachers, and the like. The other 1480 or so, however, are worth a try.

Further, within this large group are those conductors who are your peers, who are of particular interest to you; younger, emerging artists at a career stage similar to your own. The fact that you may already know them as colleagues is a help, and they're probably relatively accessible; not as many performers are vying for their attention, and their schedules aren't yet booked up. If they are gifted and ambitious they will appear in important venues in the future, and will remember you.

In order to get a conductor — or anyone — to pay attention to you, you first have to establish some common ground, an understanding of why knowing each other is in your mutual best interests. Therefore, as with all your other networking, you have to do some in-depth preliminary research (about your customer, the marketplace and what you have to offer) to determine whom to approach and how. Your "customer" at a given time may be the conductor, or may include the particular orchestra where you're contacting her.

Taking conductors first as individuals apart from particular orchestras, you have to know what their musical interests are. What kind of repertoire is he interested in or does he actively champion? Does she seem to enjoy working with young or emerging artists in any of their conducting situations? What kind of musician is he, temperamentally and stylistically? Then, where does she conduct, and what kind of conducting schedule does she maintain?

All the various orchestras they conduct also have artistic profiles and budgetary, seasonal, and structural limitations which are important for you to know. What kinds of concerts does the orchestra produce? Does the orchestra's season include run-out concerts, in-school or "kiddie" concerts, special events and non-subscription concerts in addition to their regular subscription season? (These may offer more likely opportunities for unknown artists than the main subscription programs.) Does the orchestra ever hire lesser known solo artists, for any of their programs, under any circumstances?

There are other general limitations which will be useful to know before contacting the orchestra, including whether they have ever programmed soloists other than pianists and violinists, the lead time on planning their seasons, or how much input boards of directors, orchestra committees, or others have over the choice of programs and soloists. (This last is very difficult to find out, and you can't ask directly, but if you happen to come by the information one way or another it is very useful.)

The next thing to clarify in your own mind is what basis you have for contacting the conductor to request an audition. The very best one is that you already know each other, and the conductor knows and likes your music-making; you might have gone to school together, played together in an orchestra or chamber group (performers do move on to conducting, more and more), or you might have played under this conductor at a music festival or as the winner of a competition. Next best (though sometimes even better) is a recommendation from someone known to and respected by the conductor, particularly if this person is willing to make the call on your behalf, and not simply to let you use his or her name. In either of these cases, it would be much more difficult for the conductor to leave your request completely unread and unanswered (though this will certainly happen some of the time).

If you're approaching someone cold, you have to find something which will interest the conductor, to keep your letter out of the circular file. The reason can be either musical or extra-musical; either can work (or fail).

Examples of the latter, extra-musical reasons:

- You come from the town or region in which the orchestra is based. Many orchestras consider it part of their mission to provide opportunities for local musicians.

- You have some past regional or personal association which gives you something in common with the conductor (a relative, your elementary school, having worked at the same non-music job: you get the idea).

Examples of the former:

- You share a repertoire interest (the music of a particular composer or period).

- You can offer a premiere of a work commissioned by and/or for you which would interest the conductor.

- You do special programs (for children, for example) which would be useful for the orchestra's season.
- You've received glowing notices and packed houses in the area for previous solo performances, and are something of a regional favorite.

If you can offer several reasons to read further in your letter, so much the better.

There are actually factors which make an emerging artist at least potentially attractive to an orchestra. These factors include:

Price: You're cheaper than the famous soloists they may hire for many of their main subscription events.

Diversity of musical services: You may be willing to play unusual works, or to learn something quickly when someone is ill, for example.

Special projects: As mentioned above, you might be able to offer the conductor or orchestra something of particular interest — a premiere, or a series of thematically related programs.

Your letter to the conductor must do the following:

- Open with something which will make it likely that it won't be tossed out;

- Follow up with reasons why it would be interesting to hear you;

- Indicate that you're available virtually anytime and anywhere to audition (recognizing how incredibly busy the conductor is) and that, though you are particularly gifted in the musical areas you've highlighted, you're also wonderfully flexible;

- End up by thanking the conductor for his or her time and attention, and attaching well-produced support materials (see Chapter II).

Example (not to be taken too literally, and only in conjunction with the notes):

Dear Maestro[1] Smith,

I'm writing you at the suggestion of my friend [pianist][2] Ivan Bigwig, who recently performed with the Argumentative Chamber Symphony under your direction, and who perhaps has already spoken to you about me[3]. As I've recently had the opportunity to hear you conduct here in AnyCity, and was very excited by the wonderful performance (the tempo of the 3rd movement of the Brahms made it make sense to me for the first time), I decided to write immediately[4].

As you will see from the enclosed materials, I am a pianist who has studied and performed extensively, both regionally (I come from and am based in AnyCity[5]) and around the country, and have won several important competitions both here and abroad[6]. My repertoire is broad based[7], and includes some unusual works in which I believe we share a special interest. I play a new concerto by the distinguished composer Jane Doe, for example, a work commissioned for me. Knowing of your commitment to the works of American women composers, I particularly wanted to bring it to your attention[8].

I would very much appreciate the opportunity to audition for you at your convenience. I could be available for an audition either here in AnyCity when you are conducting here or at your home base in Chicago[9]. I did notice that you will be conducting in Escapeville next April; as I will be performing in the area then, perhaps it would be most convenient for you if I were to arrange for an audition room in the hall in which you'll be rehearsing at an available time[10].

Thanks so much for your time and attention, and I look forward to hearing from you.

Notes to the above:

[1] It rarely hurts to call a conductor Maestro. They usually like it.

[2] "Pianist" is in brackets because if you and/or the conductor know Ivan well enough, or if Ivan's famous enough, you don't have to say it directly. You wouldn't have to say "violinist Isaac Stern." This goes for other modifiers,

such as "your friend," or "my mother." If you both already know the contact person, better not to state the obvious.

3 You're indicating immediately that you're a friend of a friend, or at least a colleague. Chances are that the conductor may not be the first to read the letter, or may not ever get to read it himself, but knowing that there's a personal connection makes it difficult to completely ignore.

4 Stating up front that you actually are familiar with this conductor's work, and admire it, is a good idea if it's true. (If it's not true, it makes it somewhat dubious to be asking her for help anyway.) Conductors are people too, not unswayed by praise or criticism. Be as specific in your remarks as you can.

5 Bring up the local connection early, as in a small city or a less artistically glutted region this may help your chances of being of interest.

6 Similarly, being a competition winner helps establish your bona fides as an artist to be taken seriously and with some experience. Be specific and name the competitions, if they're recognizable.

7 In addition to letting the conductor know about your musical specialties, you're indicating that you can do the standard repertoire.

8 Ideally this is true, and you do share an area of special musical interest. Equally important, you've distinguished yourself from the crowd by showing that you're willing to discover, learn and perform non-standard repertoire.

9 You're making it clear that you're extremely flexible about when and where you audition, which is just about essential if it is ever to come to pass.

10 Here you've really done your homework; but knowing and making an audition proposal based on the conductor's touring schedule is either flattering or intrusive, unfortunately depending on the particular individual and not subject to any rules. Generally it would be better to leave a very specific suggestion like this for a subsequent letter.

Follow-up:

It is perfectly reasonable to call the conductor's office (where you sent the letter) to ask if it was received. It is also appropriate to talk a bit to the secretary or other staff who might be screening the letters, and learn about whether the maestro holds regular auditions and where, or whether, auditions are arranged on a more ad hoc basis. Perhaps this conductor never does audition, but prefers to hear artists when they're actually performing somewhere. Knowing this will certainly inform your future calls and correspondence. Take this opportunity to ask if there are additional supporting materials which would be helpful for you to send, to be added to your file. (Most orchestras and/or conductors actually do maintain such files.)

Now comes a long period of waiting, during which you have to be both patient and persistent. Write again after three to six months to see if anything has happened. Use this letter to a) update your activities and b) offer a demo tape, particularly if it's one which you know the conductor will want to hear (the world premiere of the Doe Concerto?). Then, periodically write and update your materials. The updating should never be done with a form letter of the "Dear Friends" variety, but should be personal; it can be short, though. A call to the office (never call at home, unless the conductor has specifically requested that you do so) could be appropriate every once in a while, to determine if auditioning procedures are still the same. During this time of courtship, keep yourself informed about the conductor's and the orchestra's doings; who are they hiring, for what performance situations, doing what repertoire.

At some point, give up on this person, if absolutely nothing is happening and if in keeping informed about the orchestra's and the conductor's progress you sense that you are not the ideal person for them anyway. This is probably unnecessary advice, since it is unlikely that you'll have enough time to beat dead horses, and will have little enough time to pursue live ones. This counsel will only be needed by the most irritatingly persistent people, who should tone down a bit.

If you get the audition — and yes, it does happen, from time to time — be careful to present a balanced selection of repertoire, unless the maestro has requested something specific. Definitely include some of the materials you used as bait to interest this conductor in the first place. It isn't necessary to play only concerto material or sing only oratorio arias. Assume that you will need to provide an accompanist. Every once in a while a conductor will want to play for you, but it's very unlikely. Be aware that there may be time constraints, as in any audition situation, and try to maintain an attitude that one Concert Artists Guild friend calls "humble, yet confident."

After the audition, make sure that you write your thank you note, quickly. And then, keep in touch. It is very possible that the conductor or the orchestra can't use you now; by keeping both informed of your activities and repertoire you're remaining well-positioned to be available should an opportunity arise, as well as keeping your name current in their respective memories.

There's another long shot chance here, which is that if the powers-that-be are familiar enough with you and your work, have heard your tape, or are otherwise confident in your ability, they may simply hire you — audition or no audition. Be prepared.

The theme of this section has really been getting to know the conductors, rather than specifically getting them to engage you as a soloist with the orchestra, even though approaching them with the latter in mind has been the illustration chosen. As stated before, whatever the outcome of an audition, conductors can be immensely valuable musical friends and allies. However, when you are specifically looking for concerto (and other solo) work, keep in mind that the advice offered above can be adapted to others in positions of power in a given orchestra. These include managers, music administrators, even members of the boards of directors in some cases. If you know or have some connection to these individuals, certainly consider making them a part of your constituency.

Composers ... from the performer's perspective

The ideas for this section have appeared in talks given at the <u>Career Moves</u> workshops by Frances Richard, Director of the Symphonic and Concert Department at ASCAP and former associate director of Meet the Composer.

This chapter shouldn't really be necessary. In a well-ordered world, contributing to the accumulated body of musical wisdom and participating in its creation through performance would be every performer's goal. In that world, the career-building effect of working on an ongoing basis with living composers and championing their works would be the natural by-product of the performer's regular artistic life. Given that we don't live in a well-ordered or particularly thoughtful world, the practical desirability of doing so has to be stated, in so many words.

The career-building value of working with composers is infrequently discussed. The attitude prevalent in many conservatories and among many private teachers is that learning a couple of contemporary works is a burden to be borne as part of a graduation requirement. For many, musical education is the passing on of received knowledge. Some teachers include the contemporary music of <u>their</u> time — Rachmaninoff and Debussy — as part of that knowledge, but most ignore the music of <u>our</u> time as being outside that mandate. This leaves the business of seeking out and learning contemporary works to the students, who approach doing so with some suspicion, fearing that it's all going to be very unappealing and unrewarding. Contemporary music also becomes difficult to fit into an already overcrowded practice day filled with learning the "standard" repertoire. But the result of this is to leave the majority of young musicians at a career disadvantage.

We've already discussed why it is necessary to stand out from the crowd of aspiring musicians in some way, and carve out a special niche for yourself in the musical community. Since, sadly, becoming fluent in new music is something relatively rare, you have an automatic advantage if you are. The skills you need in order to learn and perform new music well — good sight-reading and learning quickly, the ability to count, accuracy of intonation and sometimes the ability to transpose, and more — are valued and appreciated throughout the field.

Yes, it's true that if you're a violinist most presenters want you to play the Mendelssohn concerto, and not the Elliott Carter concerto. However, remember that the competition for the Mendelssohn jobs is incredibly fierce, while those who can play the Carter, when there is a call for it, are scarcer than hen's teeth. Interestingly, there is considerable call for performances of new music, since — remember how you have to know where the money comes from, and how it's allocated? — funding sources, both government and private, feel a strong obligation to support the creative work of our time and the groups or individuals that champion it. For example: an orchestra may support its pops concerts on ticket income, and squeak by in its war-horse programs on a combination of ticket income and donated funds, but can get money over and above subsistence for presenting the works of living, preferably American, composers. And someone — you? — is needed to play them. Add to this the number of festivals that feature new music which take place around the country, as well as the new music groups which regularly present concerts, and you're looking at a fair amount of work.

So, playing new music can get you some work: it can also get you significant attention from the press. This is also discussed in the chapter on the press; here we'll say only that by featuring new works on your concert programs you'll intrigue and interest critics, who may come as a result. You may get the interest and attention of your colleagues and mentors as well. A program performed in New York by a former Concert Artists Guild pianist, Stephen Drury, featured a John Cage premiere and two works (one not performed since the 30s) by Charles Ives — Drury specializes in the music of these composers — along with Mozart and Liszt (see the press release sent out about this, cited in Chapter V). A very famous pianist was in the audience, and, when asked, said that she had attended because of the interest and variety in the program, and because she wanted to hear the new and rarely performed pieces.

Your effectiveness as a performer of new music can be maximized by seeking out particular composers whose music you very much admire, and becoming a champion of their work. The networking value of working with selected composers and becoming identified with these performances is greatly enhanced, and the chances are greater that you'll get at least some of the calls when their music is programmed and a soloist or chamber musician is needed. (Think particularly of younger, emerging and less well-known composers, whose career stage again is comparable to your own, and not just the new music superstars.) In addition, you and the composer can perform together, with the composer appearing with you at performances of his or her music; adding this feature to the performance can make a special program that much more attractive. (There is funding available specifically for composer appearances; see the Resource Section for information on <u>Meet the Composer</u>.)

The effect of performing new music on the way you perform more standard repertoire can be considerable and profound. The musicians who play both are often the ones who are the most interesting. Dealing with wet ink, understanding that each note written represents a decision to go one musical direction and not another, and that such decisions may not be carved in stone (particularly if a work is written for you, and you have some input during the process), can forever change the way you approach even the most well-known works.

Considering all the reasons <u>for</u> performing new music, you might rather wonder why the question isn't "why not?" rather than "why?" We can only think of two reasons, and both involve money. Commissioning can be expensive (though it's not necessarily so), and performing new works, particularly with a group, can involve extensive and costly rehearsal time. Remember, however, that there may be money available from both public and private sources to underwrite the commissioning and performance of new music even when there's no money for anything else, so these obstacles shouldn't be impossible to overcome.

(There is one other possible reason which is sometimes expressed for not playing new music, but it has not been included in our list because it's nonsense. To the thankfully dwindling group of musicians that still can be heard to say, "I don't like new music:" please remember that there is no one specific "new music." We live in a time of extraordinarily broad-based musical eclecticism, with something to everyone's taste. It's simply a matter of being musically curious and listening actively to find music you at least like, which everyone should do anyway.)

If you decide to commission, which confers the greatest prestige and may offer the opportunity to work with the composer on the creation of the music, the how-to's of commissioning, including suggested fees, contracts and more are laid out in a booklet (<u>Commissioning Music</u>) available from Meet the Composer (see the Resource Section for the address and phone number).

When you perform new works, remember — or learn, if you never knew — that most composers belong to one of two licensing organizations, ASCAP and BMI, which act for them somewhat as a union does for performers. That is, these organizations protect the composer's interests. A composer is entitled to a fee for the performance of her work under most circumstances, and the fee is paid to the licensing group which sends checks to the composer. The fee is generally modest, and is based on the hall's ticket price structure or other factors. These fees form an important part of a composer's income. It is unfair, and also illegal, to deny a fee to the creator when the work is performed. Make it your business, therefore, to know whether a fee is required, who is assuming the fee (often the hall or radio station will take care of this), and whether you should assume this expense as part of the concert budget. For further information on performance licensing, call ASCAP or BMI directly (phone numbers in the Resource Section).

Resource Section

Patronage: Other Sources of Support

The "patrons" section of the chapter deals with support which can be provided by private individuals. In addition, there are some sources of assistance and help for individual musicians, financial and otherwise, in the public sector, including government agencies and private foundations, and many for chamber groups with non-profit status. Some of these agencies and foundations are listed in "General Resources," the last chapter in this book. Also to be found there is an explanation of the term "non-profit," a brief word on whether you need or want to obtain such status, and some advice on who will help you get it if you want it.

More Information about Working with Composers

The American Music Center
30 W. 26th Street
Suite 1001
New York, NY 10010-2011
212-366-5260 (phone)
212-366-5265 (fax)

This organization maintains a large circulating library of scores which are available to performers and performing groups, very useful for getting acquainted with the work of various composers or finding works appropriate for your ensemble. The Center's staff will prepare lists of works for special instrumentation.

AMC makes grants to composers to help pay copying costs; since commissioning fees may have these costs built in, reducing them significantly helps performers as well.

Meet the Composer

2112 Broadway, Suite 505
New York, NY 10023
212-787-3601 (phone)
212-787-3745 (fax)

This group funds composer appearances at performances, workshops, etc. in which the composer's work is included, as well as longer composer residencies in schools. The organization also publishes a very useful little pamphlet, "Commissioning Music: A Basic Guide, " which explains the commissioning process in detail and is very helpful for performers.

MTC also organizes and administers several major composer residency and commissioning programs. The organization has affiliates in many cities around the country.

Performing Rights Organizations:

The Federal Copyright Law specifies that copyrighted musical works cannot be performed publicly without obtaining the permission of the copyright owner (the composer or the publisher). Performing rights (licensing) organizations collect fees paid in return for such permission (royalties), and distribute them to their composer members. The hall at which you're performing, or the series in which your concert is included, may already have an agreement with ASCAP and BMI, and the responsibility for paying the licensing fee may not be yours. But it is someone's, so check.

ASCAP
One Lincoln Plaza
New York, NY 10023

Robert Leibholz
212-6407

ASCAP is the oldest performing rights licensing organization in the U.S.A., and the only one which is owned and run by its members. To find out if the work you intend to perform is by an ASCAP member composer, call Robert at the number above.

BMI (Broadcast Music, Inc.)
320 W. 57th St.
New York, NY 10019

Barbara Petersen, Assistant Vice President
Emily Good, Associate Director
Concert Music Administration
212-586-2000 (phone)
212-262-2824 (fax)

BMI is the world's largest performing rights organization. Most composers who are not with ASCAP are with BMI, and the organization maintains informational brochures about their composers, available on request. To find out if the work you wish to perform is under BMI license, call Concert Administration at the above number.

V. The Press

The ideas expressed in this section were largely drawn from very candid and enlightening talks given by Allen Hughes, former music and dance critic and editor of The New York Times. *Additional helpful information was contributed by Anthony Tommasini, of* The Boston Globe *at the time of his participation in our workshops.*

The press is an essential element in an artist's career building, though not necessarily, or even principally, through reviews. To most musicians, "press" means "critic," and, since an artist's view of musical criticism generally includes both unrealistic hopes and negative expectations, the best of what is to be gained from the press is lost before it's found.

The press is not actually in the business of providing good reviews with which you can fill out your press kit, or even positive, quotable lines for you to reproduce in your public relations materials. Obviously, reviews aren't useless; nice ones are encouraging (and reproducible), and a body of reviews can give you and your supporters some idea of how you are being perceived by your audiences. But it is important to recognize that any particular review won't give you much beyond one person's opinion about your concert. A good review won't create a career, and a bad one won't stop one.

But since your goals include getting people beyond friends and family to come to your concerts and getting hired for additional performances, you must make yourself known to the public. As one member of the press has often said at our workshops, "First the public knows your name; then the public knows your face; then the public comes to hear you play." **To accomplish your goals it is necessary to get the word out, and the press is often the means by which the word is gotten out.**

The press, of course, includes more than the newspapers, comprising the electronic media as well as the vast array of print publications that, in one way or another, serve the field. However, the daily interaction between the arts community and the local newspapers is perhaps the best place to start. As always, it is important to understand their point of view before considering how to convince them of yours.

Newspapers

■ **Newspapers exist, basically, to report the news. They also determine what for them is news — i.e. what are undeniably items of universal importance, and additionally what are the particular interests and priorities of its staff and readership — and therefore what gets reported.** For very many newspapers, the way they determine what is news is by counting heads: how many people will be interested in a given item. By this measure, classical music, except in very special circumstances, isn't news, so the very fact that it is regularly reported on at all — whether by reviewing concerts, announcing coming events, or including feature articles of more general interest — is a matter of conscience, a bow to "culture." In almost all cases, someone famous is news, and therefore coverable, in a way that you are not. This is not an insurmountable obstacle to being featured or reviewed, but important to keep in mind.

■ **Much of classical music coverage does indeed consist of reviews, and in many cases reviews are a specialized kind of news.** When an opera production or an orchestral concert which is part of a longer run is reviewed, readers can follow up by attending a subsequent performance (as they could in the case of a movie or a play). Performances by individuals or chamber groups are generally one-time only events; even if a concert is part of a series, the specific repertoire won't be repeated. The reader can't respond to a good review by saying "That sounds great!" and rushing out and buying a ticket. In the short term, what the readers get is an opinion as to whether they missed a good concert or were saved from a dreadful one. What the newspaper tries to provide beyond this by printing reviews of single concerts is a sense of who's doing what, where, and — in the newspaper's view — how well.

For each newspaper in each location, therefore, what's news? what's reviewable? what gets covered? is determined by the relationship between the priorities of those in charge and the perceived interests of the paper's constituency. You will need to read your local newspapers to learn who the music writers and editors are, what are their interests and priorities, and what gets printed.

In New York City only one newspaper — *The New York Times* — somewhat regularly reviews concerts by small groups, or lesser-known artists, or debut recitals. *The Times* seems to assume that their readership includes enough people who are interested in classical music to keep more critics on staff and to cast their critical and reportorial net more widely, and with greater regularity and predictability, than other papers in town. Though a review of a young artist might appear in another paper, it's far less likely. (It's not all that likely even for *The Times*, given the many variables involved; see Chapter 3.) This situation may be slightly — or even greatly — less egregious in cities and towns outside New York.

For *The Times*, the inclusion of new or unusual repertoire in a concert program, perhaps a premiere, will be of significant interest and may increase the chances of a program getting reviewed, for three reasons. First, it seems to be the policy of the paper to pay attention to creative work and composers as well as to performers; second, a review which describes a premiere, say, serves both the composer and the performer and brings more information (news) per inch to the general readership; and third, the reviewers are more interested in attending this program, since they won't have heard that same piece twenty times previously in the same season.

For a newspaper in a small community which doesn't have the saturation of musical events that New York City does, a program featuring quite standard repertoire might be of great interest — depending on who the artist is, the artist's relationship to the community, or the group presenting the concert. Even in a larger city, a featured artist who is from the area might be attractive enough in a more "human interest" way to rate a feature article before the concert as well as a review. When this chapter was originally written, we had just read a review of a performance in Miami by a young pianist represented by CAG; the Guild had presented concerts in that same city on this same series for two years, but this was the first time a Miami paper was willing to review one of them. The concert did take place in the summer, when almost nothing else of musical interest was happening, which helped; but even more important, the pianist was born and raised in Miami. This seems to be true in Boston as well; for the *Globe* the priority, in addition to covering the most high profile events, is Boston based artists.

Your information on the interests and concerns of the press in New York or other major metropolitan areas will probably come from familiarity with the publications as a reader, plus some good detective work. In smaller communities though, the people of the press may be considerably more accessible to you, and you can learn a great deal in a much more direct way. It is possible, when planning a concert appearance in such a city or town (and with the approval of those presenting your event), to research the papers that may write about the event, find out who the music or arts editors are, and call them up. You can tell them that you are excited about coming to the community and would like to know more about its musical life, and you might want to ask advice about some aspect of this or a future performance. You certainly want to indicate that you will provide any information about the event that they might require, and that you would happily be available for an interview if that would be helpful. What you're establishing is a friendly relationship, indicating respect for the press' need for information and role in your career development, and laying the groundwork for mutual interest.

Your successful dealings with the press, then, will be based on **mutuality** — on everyone's getting what they need. In spite of the fact that you may feel that you're fighting for space in a newspaper that's basically uninterested in you, this is only partially true. As long as there's interest in music in the community, and the newspapers have to fill the allotted space with something, it is essential to a paper to have information about the field. **You are helping the journalist and critic by giving them something of interest to cover and keeping them abreast of your activities in the field; they are responding by putting your name before the public.**

If any of the advice below on reaching and working with the press results in your being interviewed by a newspaper reporter, consult the section below on <u>Radio: Being Interviewed</u> for guidance.

One additional important word, on the relationship of paid advertising to critical coverage. The mutuality referred to above does not include a quid pro quo of "buy an ad and get reviewed." This is certainly not the way most publications do business; it is against stated policy for music staff to communicate with advertising sales staff before deciding on who gets covered. Should you decide to pay for an ad, do it for its own publicity value, since that's all what will get you.

The Press Release

Your most basic form of communication with the press will be through the press release, a general, non-personalized communication sent to those on your mailing list who might want your information. The release is generally short, ranging from half a page to three or so pages; for most releases, one to two pages will do the trick. You will send a press release (or one will be sent on your behalf) when you are giving a concert, when you or your group has accomplished something special, or when something worthy of public notice has occurred or will occur. Press releases, sent in plenty of time to be useful (see calendar below) are always

- **Typed**

- **Double-spaced** (our examples aren't, exactly, but that's to save space)
- **With wide margins**, so that a reporter or editor can make notes.

They always include

- **The name and phone number of a press contact** (who may be you) at the top, who can be called if the release is considered of interest and if further information is wanted. The release is typed on letterhead or will have the name, address and phone number of the group typed on it, so that it can be easily identified. There is a standardized format for these things, so that press people — who are, after all, barraged with such material — can quickly and easily read them.

In addition, format conventions include

- **A release date at the top.** Usually your release will be headed "For Immediate Release," meaning that the paper can print the information upon receiving it. We imagine that there are some special cases where a later release date is specified, perhaps to give the press time to prepare for some kind of news bombshell, but we've never seen one.

- **The word "more" at the bottom of the page,** if the release goes on to a second, third, or — heaven forbid — fourth page.

- **Pages numbered at the top** with five repetitions of the page number, i.e., "22222," or "33333." Yes, it's peculiar, but that's the form.

- **"# # #" marks, or the word "End" at the end of the release.**

The release is written in journalistic style, with the traditional who, what, when and where in the first paragraph, and in the inverted pyramid format of the news story — with the most important information up front and the more general, less important, or background information following. The headline which introduces the release should briefly emphasize the most important fact, or facts, about the event being described.

You may want to have several press releases: one short release to give the specifics of a concert for inclusion in an events calendar; one slightly longer release, including some background information, to send to critics who you hope will review the concert; and one lengthier release with detailed background information for those journalists who might be interested in writing a feature, or who need to be lured into the concert hall with stronger ammunition. Examples of each of these follow. Note the dates on which they were sent, relative to the date of the concert.

Example 1: A release intended for calendar listings in magazines (note the long lead-in time), with just the most basic information. An events calendar release for a newspaper would only need to be sent a month or so in advance.

Concert Artists Guild

                              FOR IMMEDIATE RELEASE
                              September 15, 1988

                              Press Contact:
                              Robert Besen: 212-333-5200

CONCERT ARTISTS GUILD PRESENTS
PIANIST STEPHEN DRURY

On Tuesday, January 24 at 8 p.m., pianist Stephen Drury, 1983 First Prize winner in Concert Artists Guild's international New York Competition, performs at Merkin Concert Hall, 129 West 67 Street. Tickets are $10; students and senior citizens $6; TDF also accepted. For further ticket information, please call the Merkin Hall Box Office at (212) 362-8719.

Program

Fantasy in C Minor, K.475	W.A. Mozart
Selections from Transcendental Etudes	Franz Liszt
Celestial Railroad	Charles Ives
One (1983)	John Cage
Three Page Sonata	Charles Ives

                    #   #   #

              850 7th Avenue, New York, NY 10019

Example 2: A more complete release, and the kind you would want to use if you have only one. This can be sent to your entire press list.

Concert Artists Guild

FOR IMMEDIATE RELEASE
December 20,1988

Press Contact:
Robert Besen: 212-333-5200

**STEPHEN DRURY, PIANO, IN MERKIN HALL
CONCERT JANUARY 24**

Distinguished CAG Alumnus Returns in Program
Featuring Works from Mozart to Cage

Pianist Stephen Drury, 1983 First Prize Winner of Concert Artists Guild's international New York Competition, will return after five years for his second New York solo recital, to be given at Merkin Concert Hall on Tuesday, January 24th at 8.00 p.m.

Mr. Drury, a specialist in contemporary music, will include two rarely performed works by Charles Ives and a recent work by John Cage, along with works by Mozart and Liszt, on his program.

Drury, a member of the faculty of the New England Conservatory, has drawn great praise for his performances of both traditional and contemporary music, in particular the works of Ives and Cage. He has been soloist with the San Diego, Spokane, Springfield, and Portland (Me.) Symphonies, and with the Boston Pops. Mr. Drury was chosen as an Artistic Ambassador of the U.S. Government in 1986, which has since sponsored his tours of Asia and Europe. He has performed at contemporary music festivals in Boston and New York, and 1987 brought "Best of the Year" honors from the Boston and Albany press for performances of the complete Ives Piano Sonatas.

(more)

850 7th Avenue, New York, NY 10019

158

Concert Artists Guild
22222

Mr. Drury's recital will begin at 8:00 PM at Merkin Concert Hall, 129 West 67 Street. Tickets are $10, $6 for students and senior citizens. For further ticket information, please call the Merkin Hall Box Office at (212) 362-8719.

Program - January 24, 1989

Fantasy in C Minor, K.475	W.A. Mozart
Selections from Transcendental Etudes	Franz Liszt
Celestial Railroad	Charles Ives
One (1983)	John Cage
Three Page Sonata	Charles Ives

#　#　#

850 7th Avenue, New York, NY 10019

Example 3: More detailed release, to stimulate special interest. Note emphasis on unusual repertoire, with commentary by the artist. This release would be sent only to carefully selected individuals on your press list (see later in this chapter about press lists).

Concert Artists Guild

FOR IMMEDIATE RELEASE
January 12, 1989

Press Contact:
Robert Besen: 212-333-5200

RARELY PERFORMED WORK BY IVES TO BE FEATURED IN PIANO RECITAL BY STEPHEN DRURY

Concert Artists Guild to Present Recital at Merkin Concert Hall on January 24

When pianist Stephen Drury performs at Merkin Concert Hall on January 24, the concert will mark not only the return to New York of the 1983 Concert Artists Guild International Competition winner, but also a very rare performance of one of Charles Ives' most important and least known works for the piano.

Called "The Celestial Railroad," the piece was sketched out by Ives in 1925, but never published. Working with manuscripts he found at Yale University and the Lincoln Center Library, Drury arrived at his version of the work by combining elements from both drafts and devising his own notations. Drury's performance of this seldom heard work will be one of the highlights of a program that will also feature works by Cage, Liszt and Mozart.

Drury notes that the major theme of "The Celestial Railroad," which was inspired by the Nathaniel Hawthorne story, reflects Ives' awareness of the temptations many artists face in the modern world.

"The piece describes an epic journey that contrasts the glitzy, entertaining qualities of the temporal world with the slow, quiet pace of a pilgrim's progress toward the Celestial City," he explains. "It's actually rather terrifying in its force and subject matter, and it has all the wildness and inventiveness that characterize a major work by Ives. It's a work that should be performed."

(more)

850 7th Avenue, New York, NY 10019

Example 3, continued

Drury, who usually plays at least one work by a twentieth century composer in his recitals, finds the music of Ives particularly rewarding because he shares the composer's interest in adventure, both spiritual and musical.

"People tend to think of Ives purely in terms of Americana," he observes. "But it's clear to me that personal adventure is what's at the core of his work--which is why it's no surprise that he was able to conjure out of the piano sounds that no one had even heard before.

"What fascinated him was the question of what happens when you try something new--and that's what fascinates me as well."

Drury's interest in composers whose sound images defied received notions about the piano is evinced by the inclusion in his Merkin Hall program of works by Liszt, Mozart and Cage, as well as Ives.

While acknowledging that such juxtapositions are unusual, Drury maintains that the composers have much in common beyond the virtuosity that their music demands of the pianist. All four, he says, were also intent on describing spiritual journeys of one kind or another, and all wrote music which has redefined the possibilities of the instrument.

Presented by Concert Artists Guild, Drury's January 24 recital will begin at 8:00 p.m. in Merkin Concert Hall, 129 W. 67th Street. Tickets are $10, $6 for students and senior citizens. For additional information, please call the Merkin Hall box office at (212) 362-8719.

Program - January 24, 1989

Fantasy in C Minor, K.475	W.A. Mozart
Selections from Transcendental Etudes	Franz Liszt
Celestial Railroad	Charles Ives
One (1983)	John Cage
Three Page Sonata	Charles Ives

#　#　#

850 7th Avenue, New York, NY 10019

In all the above releases, note that the information about hall and tickets ends the body of the release, and that the program is restated last of all. This should be done even if you have enclosed the concert flyer along with your press release (which you should do), as, of course, everything will get separated and something will get lost.

The Pitch Letter

In some cases you may want to send a pitch letter to a selected critic or reporter, suggesting possible areas of interest and reasons why an event or artist is worth covering. This personalized letter might be attached to a release, sent as a follow-up to a release or sent on its own, as long as all the relevant facts are reiterated in it. An example of a pitch letter:

CONCERT ARTISTS GUILD
850 7th Avenue
New York, NY 10019

December 7, 1988

Ms. Sympathetic Reporter
111 Main Street
Anycity, Anystate

Dear Sympathetic:

As you know from having covered us during the past few years, the artists under Concert Artists Guild's management often present programs including works which are rarely performed or otherwise of unusual interest. Knowing of your particular interest in the works of Charles Ives, I'm writing to invite you to attend the January 24 recital of pianist Stephen Drury, which will feature a rare New York performance of "The Celestial Railroad," as well as the wonderful "Three Page Sonata."

Mr. Drury, whom you interviewed when he won our competition in 1983, believes that this is the first New York performance of "Celestial Railroad" since the 1920's, and is very excited about the coming performance. In addition to the Ives pieces, the program will feature John Cage's "One," written in 1983, as well as works by Mozart and Liszt — an unusual and fascinating juxtaposition.

The concert will take place in Merkin Concert Hall at 8 p.m. We would be delighted if you would attend, and will hold tickets for you at the press table. I hope you will agree that the concert will be an especially rewarding one, for you and your readers.

Sincerely,

Robert Besen
Associate Director

In this pitch letter the writer is reminding the recipient of two important facts: one, that the program includes at least one work which should interest her; and two, that she already has some interest in or relationship with the performer. There has to be some kind of hook in a pitch letter which is introduced quickly and which grabs the recipient's interest enough to make sure she reads it to the end, whether she acts on it or not. **Don't forget to double check the spelling of the reporter's name and address.**

Note: It may be worth a try to do your follow-up to a press release on the telephone if you have a particularly ingratiating phone manner. If you don't have a good phone manner, forget it. Even if you do, keep in mind that getting people to return phone calls can be a challenging (and possibly futile) undertaking.

Sending Your Materials:

What to send

When you send a press release, you will want to accompany it with a minimum amount of support material, if appropriate. If you have a concert flyer, for example, certainly include that (it probably won't be ready for the three-month-in-advance calendar listing release). Don't, however, send a complete press kit, as most of the material in it — reviews from other papers or repertoire lists, for example — won't be of any interest to the receiver, and it will immediately get pitched. Send a photograph only if you have good reason to believe that it might be printed. It won't be returned, and most large city papers will request one or send their own photographer if they really want one. (That's why you have a press contact and phone number listed, among other reasons.) If you have a general flyer or an interesting background sheet (perhaps your brief biography), these might be all right to attach.

> Don't send all three releases plus a pitch letter to everyone. Understand and target your customers, who should <u>each</u> get no more than two of these items.

When to send materials

For music or arts calendar listings, call the paper, magazine or radio station (see below) and find out what their timing requirements are. Some magazines need as much as three months to place you in this section. For general and review purposes, three to six weeks lead time is usually enough notice. Much more than that and you may get lost in the shuffle; less, and you stand little chance of being put on the reviewer's schedule. For more extensive releases and pitch letters, two to three weeks before an event may remind the recipient of the concert, and give her an additional reason to attend.

Tickets

Find out (by calling) the paper's policy on tickets: whether they prefer to have them mailed with the press release, or held at the box office or press table on the night of the program in the name of the publication. In any event, tickets must always be

- Complimentary;
- A pair, not a single seat;
- On the aisle (or some designated favorite seats, if you or the hall — ask them — know which are the preferred seats of that reviewer or paper).

Don't call the paper to find out if the tickets will be used if your purpose is getting them returned; they won't be. Assume that the dozen or so best seats that you set aside for press use are part of the cost of doing business.

When a critic does show up, please remember the following two additional etiquette items:

- Start your concert reasonably on time. Critics are driven crazy by having a long wait for the first note.

- Don't plant a friend or relative near the critic to
  a) try and read over his shoulder what his comments are, or
  b) listen in on his conversation with a companion, or
  c) engage him in conversation to try and find out if he likes what he's hearing.

That this would be very rude and irritating should go without saying, but, astonishingly, people do it. You won't, of course.

The Print Press: Beyond Your Own Daily Papers

In addition to your community's daily and weekly newspapers, large and small, there are many other outlets by which your information can be brought before the public. Other print media, the way they relate to your activities, and their geographic coverage, include:

- **Weekly or monthly newspapers which are community-based,** and which list future events even though they do not review concerts. Local.

- **Home-town newspapers,** even if you no longer live or perform in your home town. They will be interested in you anyway.

- **Alumni magazines, publications issued by organizations or companies with whom you (or someone close to you) have a relationship, and the like.** Special constituency, local to national.

- **Weekly or monthly magazines which include concert listings** of future events, and may include reviews of past events, like *The New Yorker* or *New York Magazine*. Regional/ National.

- **Special interest magazines,** such as *American Record Guide*, which both review concerts and recordings and include feature articles. National.

- **Special interest magazines, journals, and newsletters, which are primarily "to-the-trade,"** such as *Keyboard Classics, The Strad, The Tubaists Quarterly*, and which publish articles of interest to their own constituency. National (and sometimes International).

- **The large national weekly magazines** (*Time* and *Newsweek*) are unlikely to be writing about you, but if there's a specific interest angle it may be worth a shot to keep them informed. Similarly, other magazines, monthly and weekly, which do not usually include articles about classical music, might be sold on a particular story if you can find an angle which interests them (*People*? *Elle*? *Fortune*?).

The Electronic Media:

Radio

An awful lot of people listen to the radio. In almost every community there exists a mix of stations: commercial, public and college or university based. These may include classical music in their programming, or may feature classical music only. Since the people that would come to your concerts may well be listening to these stations, getting exposure on the air can be enormously worthwhile, and even more useful than print coverage. Often these opportunities will be related to promoting specific concert performances, whether in your home base or while on the road; sometimes, though, they will simply be occasions for the public to get to know you better.

To get the information to a station, about a particular event and about your own availability, you first have to find out what stations are out there, what programs would be interested in you, and who are the producers of the relevant programs. The producer is generally the person who makes programming decisions, and usually is not the on-air person. Sometimes the producer is the on-air person, and sometimes an on-air person does have a say in the programming. To find out who the behind-the-scenes people are, and who is involved in programming, you have to call the station.

Send these folks your press release, and follow up with a phone call to emphasize that you would be delighted to come down to the station to perform, if they have facilities for that, or could come down to be interviewed in connection with your coming concert/record release/national tour/whatever. Ask if they would like a copy of your broadcast quality tape (in advance), so that they could play some of it for their audience.

Being Interviewed

The ideas in the following section were, for the most part, generously provided by Thomas Bartunek, Vice President, Programming & Operations, at WQXR-FM, the nation's largest classical music radio station.

If any of the above advice is successful, and you are asked to appear on the radio to publicize your concert (or just to fill an interesting hour or so), you will probably be asked to play something, or provide a playable tape — and to talk. It's not that hard and it can even be fun, but there is a knack to giving a good interview. Unless you are very experienced at this, practice, keeping a few guidelines in mind:

- **Think about what makes your event terrific, and be prepared to say what that is.** Write it down, and think about it. You can't say everything during the course of a short-ish radio interview, but you can say something which may draw a potential audience member into the hall. Think about what might intrigue you, were you the listener. There might be two, or three things on your list, but no more than that, Too much information will result in a loss of focus, confusing the listener, and making it harder for you to get your point(s) across. Your interview should sound extemporaneous, but it should actually be very well prepared.

- **During the interview, give answers that contain the above information, no matter what the questions are.** Have you ever noticed how politicians handle the press? They keep coming back to the points that they want the public to hear, whether or not they manage to also answer the questions posed. Listen, note the technique, get disgusted with the state of the world, and then adapt the method for your own use. It can be annoying (or infuriating) in a political interview, but it is actually useful and important in an interview with a performer. In this case, the interviewer is not trying to put you on the spot, but rather is looking for that nugget of excitement that you've prepared to give him. He doesn't know what it is until you tell him.

- **Be prepared with an anecdote or two that will create a personal note and create a connection with your listeners.** A story about how you choose your repertoire, or what it means to you, is usually more engaging than the history of the works and the dates of the composers. Something that reveals your humanity - how the string broke during the last performance and what you did to deal with the emergency, for example - creates more sympathy and engages the listeners more than a list of your credits. Try to also show that you care that the audiences enjoy what you will present. Listeners need to know why they should attend your event, and for that they need to know *why you?* and not *why Brahms?* and, above all, *why me — why should I go?*

- **Don't be thrown by an interviewer who is less-than-perfect, in one way or another.** Some radio interviewers are overly enthusiastic, and may never get to interesting content (what our friend from WQXR calls the "Golly! Gee!" school of interviewing); some are hostile; some are friendly and willing, but not knowledgeable; some are quite knowledgeable, but determined to use your interview as a chance to demonstrate this, and make some points for themselves. If you've prepared properly for the interview, just keep coming back - in the most charming way, of course - to the focal point.

- **Personalize the interview, in or out of town.** Always use the interviewers name at some point during the interview: it keeps the interview personal, and shows that you're interested in them as well. If the interview takes place when you're out of town (perhaps as part of a tour), try to include some reference to something local: the sports event which happened the night before, an election result, a concert which took place recently. Find out this information by leafing through the local paper, or by listening to the local talk radio show for a few minutes. It can be very engaging to listeners to feel that you, the visiting artist, are interested in them.

All of the above advice about being interviewed on the radio can be used equally well for an interview with the print press. In that case, you may have more time to consider what you say as it's happening; on the other hand, you have to be extra careful, since what you say won't pass by quickly, but rather will be in print to be read and re-read. Stick to the basic idea of knowing what your message is, keeping it simple by keeping it to one or two important points, including a personal angle, and being interested in and informed about those that are interviewing you, if possible and appropriate.

Getting Other Radio Publicity, Free: Public Service Announcements

Even radio stations which otherwise have no interest in reporting on or playing classical music may help you to publicize an event. Most stations have mandated time devoted to public service announcements (PSAs), and you can try to get your concert included in their public service calendars by always mailing the station the same calendar type release that you send the print press. Find out who at the station receives such notices, or whether they prefer to receive them addressed to "Calendar Listings Editor," or some such title.

It is remotely possible that some station, sometime, somewhere, will be interested in playing your own produced 10, 20, 30 or 60 second spot (taped, ready for broadcast material) on this basis. If you would find it fun and not a huge effort to produce one, either musical or descriptive, go to it and let them know that it's available. More likely the station will be delighted to sell you airtime to play the above; if you have the budget, this can be excellent advertising. (When written PSAs are submitted, your chances of having them read are also increased if you provide 10, 20 and 30 second versions.) Note that you may not be able to include ticket price information in a PSA, so check on this before getting down to the typewriter. Needless to say, paid advertisements certainly can include this information.

Television

As we all know, most people watch television, and most people's view of what's important in the world is formed by what they see on it. Chances are that network television will not be much interested in you. If <u>Tonight</u> or <u>60 Minutes</u> does call, it will probably be at a stage in your career when you have a public relations representative, and you can oversee his efforts on your behalf instead of implementing the work on your own.

However, with the advent of cable television, the increase in regionally based public television and the enormous expansion in the number of community access and campus stations, opportunities for making yourself better known in a community or publicizing a particular event through this medium are indeed available. Once you've determined what stations feature community programs or special programs which might be interested in what you do, call and find out who the producers are and add them to your press list. You can then use your calendar listing releases, your general press releases and particularly pitch letters to interest them in featuring you on a program, inviting you on a talk show, or simply including your concert in a community bulletin board listing. Follow all the above procedures about radio as well as the general guidelines for press releases when sending them information. If you have a promotional video of the required length, it also won't hurt to let producers know that you could effectively fill some airtime for them.

Warning!

(How about using a Press Agent?)

Everything written above (and below) refers to <u>you</u>, working on your own behalf. With rare exceptions, artists at the early, or even middle, stages of their careers don't need the services of a professional press representative or public relations person or agency. There simply isn't enough there for them to sell. Without the goods to sell, it's ridiculous to hire an expensive salesperson. You can open most of the doors that you need to open at this level yourself; at the point that someone with more savvy, ability and clout is needed, you'll almost certainly know it. Obviously, when you need help with a project, or some additional expertise in a specific area, get it.

Press lists:
Who's on them, and how you assemble them.

Before you re-invent the wheel, find out who already has a good press list that you can use to get started, or, preferably, several lists that you can combine. If you can't get access to a press list, you can go to the library (head for *Bacon's Magazine and Newspaper Directory* for this information — see the Resource Section) and the local newsstand, and buy and read an assortment of publications. Spend some time listening to the radio and watching television. (You should do all of this anyway, because you should — to belabor the point yet again — know your customer.) But it's never sensible to spend lots of research time when someone has done it for you. Your school or other organization may be a good source for getting a press list, or an orchestra or other ensemble that you're associated with. Mailing lists are often fiercely protected, but press lists less so than, for example, subscription lists which represent cash to their compilers. Ask around, and, if worse comes to worst, do the legwork yourself.

Questions to ask when starting a list or updating one.

Some of this has been referred to above, but it's handy to have a list of questions to ask when confronted with an actual person from an actual publication on the other end of the line. Information, obvious and not-so-obvious, that you should have, includes:

- Who is in charge of music reporting and reviews? This may be a complicated question. You may have to address your releases to the Cultural Affairs Editor, the Community Affairs Editor, the Community or Events Bulletin Board, the Music Editor or Music Desk, the Features Editor, or any of dozens of other departments and individuals who may have gotten the job of dealing with classical music. (Remember: You should be sending information to editors as well as to the writers whose by-lines you see in the paper, as the editors make assignments. Again, ask how things should be done.) Be open-minded and creative in getting the operator or department secretaries to give you the names and titles of everyone interested in the field. An important word: Be especially nice to the secretaries or other middle people, as they frequently are the only people you will actually speak to, and who therefore hold your press life in their hands. (This presumes that you're lucky enough to speak to a human; voice mail is tougher, though you can try not-responding to the requests to hit various buttons, and wait for an operator to direct you to a person.)

When you've identified the correct people, get

- the correct spelling of their names and their exact titles;

- the address to which you should direct your communications;

- their policy about sending or holding comp tickets at the gate for events;

- their preferred lead time for receiving information for various purposes.

Even starting with a ready-made list, count on an initial investment of several hours on the phone to check all the information. What will make your list better than those you've been given is that it will be up-to-date, will use everyone's correct and most recent title, and will be correctly spelled. Please don't underestimate the importance of this It takes an extraordinarily broad-minded and understanding reporter to write an article about you when you've chronically spelled her name wrong, or addressed her as "Mr."

Astonishingly few people or organizations update their mailing lists with any regularity. Though correct information will probably not win you points, incorrect information will evoke such negative responses that you should try, at all costs, to avoid it. The easiest way is to have your mailing lists, all of them, on a computer. If you have your own computer, or have access to one through work, a relative or friend, or school, so much the better; if not, many public libraries rent computer time these days, and you need only bring your disk. Some copying/faxing type stores (such as Kinko's) are offering computer time for sale, and these are worth investigating. You can, of course, keep up your lists by hand, but it really is much easier to simply format the computerized list for labels or envelopes, note changes as they reach you, and make a series of calls every six months or on an annual basis to check for overall accuracy.

The Public Relations Campaign

All of the techniques we've described for communicating with the press, and all of the care you've put into creating interesting and impressive materials, are part of an overall public relations campaign. It might astonish you to know that if you do any of the above, you've embarked on a public relations campaign on your own, or your group's, behalf. This may horrify you, but breathe deeply and consider.

One public relations consultant who has frequently spoken at our workshops says that though business people distrust public relations, and certainly are unable to say what it is, they're sure that they need it; whereas musicians, equally hostile and mystified, are sure that they don't. In the largest sense public relations is simply making sure that those in the public eye, or those with extensive public contact (you?), make the most positive use of all opportunities so that they'll be able to stay in the public eye or have more public contact. Everything that you do in regard to getting yourself and your events known should be informed by this understanding. And, given that you understand this, consciously taking charge of your public relations efforts should become somewhat less off-putting.

The public relations campaign consists of all the activities you do and the materials you create in order to promote your artistic ventures, and to make you better and positively known to all your customers. Principles which guide most effective campaigns are logical and simple (though the techniques involved can be very complex, which is why there are specialists in the field). The five which follow are particularly important for you to remember:

▶ Your message about yourself should be truthful, clear, and limited to a few important points at a time. Though at an actual concert the audience may be receiving a message of great complexity and depth, when they get the flyer, or press release, or telephone call announcing it they should get a powerful message of great simplicity and clarity.

▶ As much as possible, the same important points should be featured in all of your messages and materials, so that your customers are reminded of your strengths with consistency. In other words, it is helpful to coordinate the various aspects of your campaign.

► Remember that effective public relations requires persistence. Though you may go through long periods of feeling ignored, keep plugging away — politely and pleasantly, and with an understanding of when frequent is too frequent. Positive impressions and recognition are being created, even when no immediate results seem to be forthcoming.

► Effective public relations also requires creativity. If your audiences are too small, and seem not to include the people you're sure would like to hear you, find out what vehicles you could possibly use to get your information to them, and think about what aspect of what you do could be emphasized to bring them in. If the traditional music press is simply not going to give you much coverage, perhaps some aspect of your work would attract the interest of non-traditional branches of the press.

► Remember non-traditional, non-press vehicles as well: If you're a computer whiz, what about E-Mail? If you are involved with your church, what about church bulletins? The possibilities are endless.

► Last: If you're really not at all good at one aspect or other of the public relations tasks described in this chapter or in Chapter II — writing, phone, coming up with unconventional and new ideas, producing or assessing the quality of your designed materials — get someone else who's more gifted in these areas to help, or to do them for you.

Resource Section

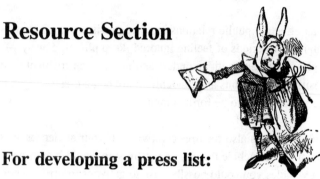

For developing a press list:

Bacon's Magazine and Newspaper Directory
Bacon's Information, Inc.
332 S. Michigan Ave.
Chicago, IL 60604

312-922-2400
Ruth McFarlend, Editor

Available in most libraries. This directory includes staff listings for newspapers and magazines. It is issued annually in October, and there are mid-year supplements. There are other such directories, but this one is the best known.

For other suggestions about developing mailing lists, both for the press and for audiences, see Chapter IX, General Resources.

VI. Management
& Self-Management

All management is really self-management. No matter how far you advance in your career, the responsibility for making sure that you keep working, in the way you want to, remains with you. No manager can magically create a career for someone, though it may seem so sometimes.

We've divided this chapter's information into two parts; first we'll deal with the technical details of how professional management works on your behalf, and then with how to manage these aspects of your career on your own.

Management

Many of the thoughts about management, and much of the technical detail about how major managements operate, have been provided by two regular speakers at the Career Moves workshops: Thomas F. Parker, now President of Parker Artists and previously vice-president with Shaw Concerts; and Charlotte Schroeder, vice-president of Colbert Artists Management. Information was provided also by Robert Besen, the Guild's own artist manager, who performs all the services of a major commercial manager, without the 20%.

In the classical music field, managers perform a variety of services for their clients. They act as booking agents, finding and negotiating engagements. They "service" the contracts they negotiate, which involves making travel and other arrangements and working out production details with the sponsor. They represent their clients in the marketplace — at trade shows for example — keeping their clients' names and activities current with the customers. They may act in a sort of secretarial capacity, keeping track of their clients' various commitments. They will almost certainly arrange for the design and production of the artists' public relations materials, and will, to a limited degree, do public relations work for them. A good management will assume the responsibility for overseeing an artist's entire career development, making sure that engagements are paced appropriately, that the right level of work is being sought and accepted, and that the artist isn't doing things that will damage him artistically in the long run.

But it is for the first of these — getting work and negotiating the fees — that most performers not yet under management desperately want to be. They feel that with a manager they would have as much work as they could handle, and could forget about all the "business" and concentrate on practicing; performers not under management are convinced that if only they were, their career problems would be over.

There is a small amount of truth in this view of management, though not so much in the area of getting a reprieve from non-musical career efforts. The manager's assuming responsibility for dealing with the physical details of a concert engagement does relieve the artist of a certain amount of work, but you'll still have to write your thank you notes, work the room at the reception to make sure that you get re-engaged, etc. More important, though, a good manager can sometimes do two very important things you can't do for yourself:

1. There are doors that will be closed to you, acting on your own behalf, that a very well-connected management may be able to open for you;

2. Having a manager enables you to say "Please speak to my manager," at times when that may be absolutely essential to a negotiation. There are some customers out there who simply don't understand that an artist can be absolutely first class and not have a manager. Not as many as you would think, but some.

To begin our discussion, we'll deal with the kind of major international management that, in the United States, tends to be located in New York City around 57th Street (obviously there are lots of geographical exceptions). Many of their clients are more-or-less famous. These firms are probably the ones you think of first, and theirs are the rosters that many of you hope to join. These are useful to use as models, not only because they present the most daunting challenge to those artists aspiring to sign with them, but also because the way they do business holds true for many smaller firms as well.

What are managers looking for?

Commercial artist managements are in business for two reasons: first, because whoever started the business thinks that it's more interesting and rewarding to work with performers than to make widgets; and second, to make some money (the money coming from commissions on artists' fees). In order for the second of these to proceed from the first, the management needs to have artists on their rosters who 1) interest them artistically, and 2) have the potential to earn significant fees. A handful of artists can make money for pretty much anyone who represents them, since the world comes to them. Everyone else — and you would probably be in this category — needs a significant sales effort in order to get to that point.

How do I know that I'm ready for management?

The usual answer to the question of when are you ready for management is, "when you have something to manage." Though somewhat flippant, that's not a bad answer. You need to have at least the beginnings of a career: to have developed some connections with conductors, presenters or other influential types; won some competition(s); or otherwise gotten into the spotlight in order to make it likely that you'll get some engagements fairly soon (thereby financially justifying your place on the roster). In addition, both you and the manager have to know how you fit into the existing roster: how you complement the current list or who your in-house competition will be.

Are there exceptions to this rule, and does anyone ever get onto a major management's roster without this kind of package? Obviously yes, since managers are people, with interests and enthusiasms (and obligations and relatives) like anyone else. If you're a complete unknown, have never made more than $100 per engagement, but have somehow gotten yourself onto such a roster, your job becomes staying on it.

How do I get a manager?

Most performers will not, in fact, get a place on the roster of a major management (those with the great connections, that can open the important doors). That's simply a fact, resulting from the laws of supply and demand. There are a great many of you, and, relatively speaking, not very many opportunities for work, and therefore not a lot of room on the rosters of the middlemen and women (the managers) who make their livings from putting you and the opportunities together.

But some of you will. Even the most prestigious and powerful managements do take on new clients, and some of the largest do so all the time. Their decision to take someone on is based on a number of specific factors (referred to in general above), and may include any or all of the following:

- A very strong recommendation from someone — or more likely many people — whom they trust; that could be another artist on their roster. For example, the recommendation of one pianist by another on a given roster is taken very seriously, since it means that he's willing — if it comes to that — to share a limited amount of work. Conductors' recommendations, whether they're on that particular roster or another, also carry a great deal of weight, as conductors opinions are respected, and their position in the field means possible engagements for a soloist in the future. Recommendations from other very well known musicians, or important individuals in the business, can be equally important. Another manager might even recommend a gifted artist, whom they are unable to take for one reason or another, to a colleague.

- An important career achievement, such as the winning of a major competition, can result in management offers. A manager may feel that even if she is interested in a particular artist, there must be some initial push to help launch a major career, and she may look for the moment when you've gotten everyone's attention as the right one to start further promotion and career building efforts.

- A good fit between the management and the artist. Each management has a style, emerging from the kinds of artists they select to work with, the personalities of those in charge, and the way in which they do business. The management will usually look for artists with whom they expect to work most effectively.

- Who is on their roster at a given time, and who (and what) they think they can sell. A management may have excellent connections in the opera world, for example, but might be hesitant to take on a clarinetist, even one they admire and like, if they have few or no contacts among recital presenters and are not comfortable or familiar

with the clarinet repertoire. However if the management has lots of
singers already, and doesn't specialize in voice, they may be more
interested in working with a clarinetist than in trying to find work
for yet another soprano.

- Their own opinions and preferences. Managers do hear artists
perform all the time. They are often trained musicians themselves,
and even those who aren't quickly develop very strong feelings
about artists they want to represent and those they don't. As they
should: no one, no matter how gifted, should have to sell something
he doesn't believe in.

**To sum up, you will probably need to have three things to bring to a
manager, after you've gotten their interest through some strong personal
recommendations:**
- The probability that you can get work;
- An artist-manager compatibility that makes sales possible;
- Enough of a name or reputation, or the potential to develop one quickly, to
command a minimum fee of which 20% would be a respectable sum. On a
gross fee of $2,500 a manager would generally make $500; the minimum
asking fee would probably have to be around that, with the potential to
command much more.

Which management is right for me?

Most major management firms are looking for artists who have both the
potential for and the interest in an extensive international career. Believe it or not,
not everyone — and you may be one of these — wants what this entails. It means
being on the road much of each year, having little or no traditional family or home
life, having only a very limited amount of private time, constant pressure, and more.
Some people thrive on this, others hate it. The management will decide whether they
think you have the artistic potential; you have to decide whether you have the all-
consuming desire to have the career which makes the sacrifices worthwhile. If not,

there are good management firms which work with artists regionally, and these might be ideal for you. You can get an idea of which firms do what from looking at rosters in the Musical America Annual Directory, and knowing or learning something about the career activities of the artists on specific rosters.

Such research is also helpful in figuring out which company [needs] [wants] [might be interested] in you. Above, we've briefly discussed this from the manager's point of view: now, once again from yours. Since some managements clearly work only with singers, don't bother to approach them if you play the cello. In looking over a roster, you may notice that a given management has a very diverse roster but doesn't list a cellist; that could be because the management doesn't want one, but it's just as likely that it's because they're between cellists, and might look at you more seriously as a result.

Each management has its own personality and way of doing business. Some of the major management firms have enormous rosters, and the amount of direct contact you have with the person representing you may be limited. Some of them are smaller, however, and there may be more personal attention. There may or may not be a direct relationship between the amount of personal contact and the amount of work you get, by the way, so to some extent your decision about which kind of management you prefer has to do only with where you're most comfortable.

Once you've made a short list of which managements might be of interest to you, and might be interested in you, it's time to figure out who you know that might recommend you to them, as described above. Don't bother to write cold (without an introduction) to a management, even if you have reason to believe that you'd be perfect for them. It's a waste of time, materials and postage. At lunch one day a highly respected manager from a very major firm said to us, "If [in the letter] they address me as Mr. Smith, and not as Joe, I don't bother to read any further." In other words, if he was being approached by an artist who didn't already know him on a first name basis, he simply wasn't interested. This is an extreme, but the principle — that the manager already knows about you and has indicated some interest even before you approach him — is valid.

Should a letter approach be indicated (if, for example, your conductor friend has said that a particular manager is expecting a letter from you on the basis of a recent conversation), write a simple, friendly letter which refers to the recommendation right up front, and include some relevant press materials. Don't put in too many things; less is more, as always. Include a bio, a picture (if you have a flyer, that's better than a photo) and reviews. Most important, invite the manager to a concert if you are performing in the area in the near future. Managers will travel reasonable distances to hear someone they're interested in, so send a list of coming engagements; if it's long enough, it makes a good impression about your level of activity too. If you have no performances that the manager would be able to get to, offer to send a tape or arrange an audition at the manager's convenience.

If you don't hear anything after a few weeks, you certainly can make a follow-up call, particularly if given permission to do so by your mutual friend. Follow up with this manager periodically, always with the same friendly tone (it doesn't pay to get resentful, even if you feel that your best years are passing by), letting him know about your current activities. When this level of interaction is reached (what Robert Besen calls a holding pattern), very infrequent calls when something special comes up, mixed with more regular cards, notes, concert flyers and reviews, is a good approach. It may take years to get him to notice you, so don't give up, but don't be intrusive or irritating.

If all the factors listed which would cause managers to be interested in you are in place, they may approach you. You'll almost certainly be approached by someone if you've done something particularly splashy, like winning a first prize in one of the major international competitions, or rescuing a child from a well while not missing a note of the Symphonie espanole. If you do find yourself with the possibility of management, let's consider whether you can afford it.

How much does management cost?

Generally, managers take 20% of the gross fee negotiated for an engagement as their commission fee[3]. This means: if a manager has gotten you a fee of $2,500 for a recital performance in Toledo, they will take $500 off the top. Out of the remaining $2,000 you will have to pay your air fare to Toledo, your lodging (unless someone there is putting you up), your meals (same exception), your accompanist's fee and her expenses, an airline seat for your cello if necessary, not to mention having the gown or tuxedo pressed and hiring the cat sitter. (Typically, this will leave you with $500-$1000 as your net fee.[4])

This may suddenly make what seemed like an awfully good fee seem far less wonderful. However, you and the manager will (or should) have worked out a level of fee which builds in the commission and expenses and still leaves you with the net fee you've decided you can accept after all is paid. Also: tax laws change, but as of now all expenses — including commissions — are tax deductible.

The 57th Street managements and their peers elsewhere will limit their fees to commissions and not take a retainer (more on retainers later). They're able to do this since the more established artists on their rosters bring in enough commission money to pay the rent and everyone's salaries, thereby floating the cost of getting you established (a period estimated by at least one of our expert consultants as 5-10 years) for at least a while. Until your commissions start rolling in, the firm will cover the costs of staff time and overhead.

---

[3] The standard commission fee for conductors is 15%; for singers in the case of opera engagements, 10%.

[4] Using a net average fee of $600 per engagement as an example, if you play 50 concerts a year you'll net, that is get to keep, $30,000 annually (on a gross of perhaps $60-75,000); hardly a princely salary, but a living wage by most musicians' standards. At this level of activity and fee, you'll be the envy of many of your colleagues, and you'll be considered very lucky to be able to maintain it. We know that you've not chosen to go into this field for the money anyway, but a few numbers to confirm this are sometimes helpful.

What they can't cover are the direct costs related to the handling of your account. Your management will probably do the following, all of which you will pay for:

- Have flyers designed and printed; possibly require new photos, and certainly have photos printed

- Do mailings on your behalf (photocopying, labor and postage)

- Place advertisements (your part of an overall ad for the management, say in the *Musical America International Directory of the Performing Arts*, will be pro-rated)

- Produce, make copies of and distribute demo tapes, videos and other such materials

Other items which, depending on the management firm, you will often have to pay for:

- Phone calls made on your behalf. You'll be billed either for all telephone charges made while servicing your contract, or these plus a pro-rated amount of the general phone bill, or according to some other formula.

- Travel and expenses related to attending sales conventions. Some firms may not charge you for this, but others will pro-rate an amount which will appear in your billing statement.

All of these costs will be charged to you as monthly (or other periodic) bills, or will sometimes be deducted from fees before they reach you. In any case, an itemized statement will accompany your bill, or should.

Some real numbers: Here are some average start-up costs for a young artist newly on the roster of a major management.

Photographs_____**$1,000**

    (Many young artists newly on a big management roster (a competition winner, for example) will either not have good photographs, or will need more up-to-date ones. Probably would need to include color, as would the flyer cost listed below.

Flyers_____**$2,500-5,000**

    This is for a run of about 15,000; presenters at this level usually expect to be provided with 3,000 flyers at no cost to them, so the management wants to be prepared for at least five such engagements.

Mailings_____**$700**

    Though the management may well absorb many of these costs if part of their general mailings, this item reflects a typical one-time piece — say, to announce the artist's new management affiliation. We're assuming one such mailing in the year.

Ads_____**$300**

    This represents a pro-rated amount of major ads in the Musical America annual and the Symphony Magazine annual, divided among 50 artists.

Demo tape duplication_____**$200**

    Since many managers feel that high speed duplication is adequate for their purposes, we've assumed that the cost per tape would run about $1.50 - $2.00.

    Since these items may vary we've not totaled them up. However, it's clear that an initial outlay of almost $10,000, often without much income coming in that year to offset it, wouldn't be very unusual.

What am I responsible for, and what is the management responsible for?

Remember what was said above about what you will be bringing to a management in the first place? You will have already developed a list of possible jobs on your own, which, depending on the stage things have gotten to, need to be seriously pursued or only to have the arrangements completed by your manager. In the course of your work, you'll develop more such contacts, and refer them to your manager to pursue, negotiate or complete. In these cases you'll have made the original contact. And in these cases, the manager will almost always take the standard 20% commission. Leading to the main complaint we all hear about managers:

"I get the work, and all she does is take her 20%!"

Let's lay that one to rest immediately. For the first couple of years on anyone's roster, the manager usually will rely on you to provide work opportunities, since it takes her that long to make contacts for you, build up some credibility, and book you several seasons down the line (most engagements are contracted six to eighteen months in advance). The artists who complain the loudest about this problem are often the ones who change managers every two years, thereby almost insuring that their complaints will continue to be justified forever. Next, the 20% is only partially a "finder's fee"; it also goes toward the servicing of the contract, which is a lot of work. From the manager's point of view, the commissions she gets on artist-referred engagements, which are relatively easy money, help amortize the expenses incurred trying to produce engagements that don't come through.

In addition, many good managers in this area of the business (that is, classical music) do not see themselves primarily as booking agents. Though your manager should in the long run be getting you work, and increasingly good work at that, at the start (and much of the time thereafter) she will use your contacts as a starting place for negotiating higher fees than you could get on your own and providing follow-up by servicing the contracts in a highly professional manner. You have to have a talk with the manager to find out what her contacts are like, in addition to how much she expects from you, and how much and what level of work you can

189

reasonably expect after a few years. In other words, in the area of getting the jobs, you have to assume much of the responsibility, and with some managers — even very fine ones — you may have to assume almost all of it. (Further information about where these jobs come from in the first place is in the self-management section.)

It is the manager's responsibility to find out everything about a concert that will help you to make it a success, and to let you know this information as clearly as he can. The management will be making travel arrangements, finding out whether there are opportunities for publicity through radio broadcasts or press interviews (and checking your availability for these), investigating whether a performance could be paired with a master class to make you a little more money (if you want to do these), and whether there will be a reception at which everyone will be offended if you don't attend. You may have to prod a little to make sure all these bases are covered. Sometimes he will provide even more information and assistance, like finding out whether there's anyplace to eat at midnight, or how you can get back to the airport if the sponsor's ride falls through.

Though your manager will arrange for you to have sufficient promotional materials, and will probably want to make them consistent with the materials of other artists on the roster, these materials do represent you to the world; you should know what's being used and whether you think there's room for improvement. In addition, you are responsible for keeping an ongoing dialogue going with your manager. She should certainly call you when she's trying to set up an engagement; but you may call her when you want a press release sent out on your behalf (that you will pay for) — say, when you're doing the premiere of a commissioned work that you know will evoke some interest. You'll want to call her to discuss programming, both overall and for particular performances; you'll probably be calling each other if you win a competition. So, the responsibility for the public relations and internal communications aspects of your career is a joint one, though primarily yours.

What alternatives are there to major management?

Medium Size and Smaller management firms: Personal Representatives

A brief glance at *Musical America* will convince you that the world doesn't lack managers. There are hoards of them. Though many of them are in the mid-size range, we will pass right on to discussing small managements; for the medium size companies, you should average out the remarks about major managements and those about small firms. That is, not quite as much power as CAMI (Columbia Artists Management) or ICM (International Concert Management), but more than a small firm just starting out, and so on.

Needless to say, few of the small firms out there have the clout which enables them to pick up the phone and get, say, an audition with a famous conductor for a young artist. When you join the roster of a smaller firm without these major contacts, however, you may be trading off clout for hard work on your behalf, since you might represent a more significant part of their action.

If you are offered a place on such a roster, certainly check the firm out before signing on the dotted line. They should have <u>some</u> contacts. Even a young manager just starting out should have developed a few relationships, through previous jobs or other circumstances, which could yield performance opportunities for you. Speak with others on the roster, with presenters who might have worked with them or their artists, or with anyone else who might be acquainted with the firm's operations and reputation. Organizations like ISPAA (International Society of Performing Arts Administrators), APAP (Association of Performing Arts Presenters) and NAPAMA (National Association of Performing Arts Managers and Agents) act to some degree like Better Business Bureaus for managements. That is, they define a code of ethical business practices for their members, though they don't check up on them as far as we know. Membership in these may indicate a certain level of substance and of participation in the musical community. However, it is still particularly important for you to be assured, through personal recommendations and experience, that the people with whom you are entrusting much of your professional life are going to treat it with honesty, care and ability.

Generally, even a small management firm will operate according to the general financial arrangement outlined above. However, since they may not have the built-in bankroll that established artists represent, some may ask for a monthly retainer to keep them in business while they, as well as you, are getting established. We used to advise artists to stay away from retainers, and still vociferously advise against them in the case of large, major firms; however, the realities of the field have changed enough to justify such retainers in the case of smaller firms and those just starting up. You'll have to be absolutely convinced that the manager will be working hard on your behalf, and will take on even more responsibility for keeping in touch and up to date than usual, in order to justify this arrangement. Investigate the firm thoroughly before accepting such an arrangement, and try to move to a commission basis as soon as possible. In addition to retainers and commissions, you will still be paying all expenses, so this can amount to a lot of money. (Retainers are often in the $200 a month range.)

An artist's representative may be your manager at a small management firm with a staff of one, or he may be an unaffiliated person you specifically hire to perform any or all of the services listed in the beginning of this section. The person you select may therefore be your secretary or assistant, in effect, helping you develop press materials and sending out press kits on your behalf, keeping your calendar, making sure your mailing list is up to date, dubbing tapes, etc. This person would be paid for such secretarial work by the hour or as a weekly or monthly salary. If he has an interest in and talent for sales and booking, by all means train him to assume these responsibilities too — assuming that he's better at sales than you would be. When he starts to work on getting you performance jobs, he can be paid both by the hour and by commission; if he's doing well at booking, you can move to paying on a strictly commission basis. For more about this, see the end of the next section, "Self-Management."

Artist-run group managements

A group of musicians can get together and hire a personal representative (on a commission basis, preferably, but possibly on retainer) to act on behalf of all of them, thereby starting up a small management themselves. Another alternative to commercial management is an arrangement whereby like-minded performers get together and assume administrative and financial responsibility for management activities for members of the group. Both these possibilities can have several advantages over individual self-management: they can enable group members to pool information and contacts, to spread the work and cost of self-management among the members or allocate it to a salaried person, allow the member musicians to control the kinds of musicians on the roster and allow the members to say, "Call my manager," with honesty and confidence.

A group management can be set up according to the preferences and abilities of the members. If there is one individual who is particularly good on the phone, that person can do much of the telephone booking work; if someone is good at graphic arts, he can assume responsibility for designing the graphics. Someone with a good business sense should take care of the bookkeeping and financial management, and those with no particular skills (other than playing) can certainly pitch in to do mailings and other time consuming tasks. Almost certainly one energetic individual will actually end up doing most of the work; but there should be an agreed upon structure in place, formally, so that this poor person can complain when necessary. The group can decide what everyone's performance fees should be, and how much of a percentage should be charged over and above that to run the management. Be sure to work all this out before starting, to avoid conflict later. You'll be starting a business, and this is always expensive; therefore, do it intelligently, and with as much advance planning and good advice from those who have tried as possible.

It is always possible, in the best of all possible worlds, that the person inevitably saddled with most of the work will a) like it, and b) realize how much money in commissions is going into the general pot which could be providing her with a living. At that point, she will turn into the manager, and the self-managed group will have turned into a group of artists with a commercial manager. In the one case we know in which an artist started a management on behalf of his own and a few other groups, general expenses were shared among the member groups and almost all of the clerical work was contracted out. The artist-turned-manager himself worked only on commission, which was 10% rather than the standard commercial 20%. He enjoyed the excitement of the work and the contacts he made, and was willing to work for no retainer — in other words for almost nothing at first — until the firm started moving. He was very successful, by the way, and the firm — now in business for about eight years — is now operating on a standard commercial basis.

For any of the above models, check with local officials to determine what you have to do to start a management business, if you plan to use the management to actually do anything for you beyond picking up the phone. You will need to legally be a business in order to receive and write checks and the like; acquiring a federal employer's identification number and filing a self-proprietorship is not actually that hard to do, and won't take much of your time.

Self-Management

Many of the ideas and methods set forth in this part of the chapter, and some of the actual words, were conceived by William Matthews, a gifted classical guitarist with more than usual skill (and success) in self-management. Another rare musician who shared ideas, information and insight with us was Laura Spitzer, a remarkable pianist who has toured throughout the U.S., often towing her own piano with her to underserved, rural venues. Laura's remarks will be specifically cited below. The "20 second introduction" exercise is the brainchild of Jedediah Wheeler of International Production Associates, one of the more creative and innovative people in the business.

At the beginning of this chapter, we stated that all management is really self-management. For most musicians, having a manager doesn't solve the problem of getting work, and you will still be handling much of this responsibility yourself. All the rest — producing materials, determining travel and other schedules, and all the endless detail of making a performance happen — simply means an investment of time of which most artists could and would like to make other use.

Also, for many musicians with management but not with the large and prestigious firms, the economics of the situation seem to make no sense. It's quite possible, after paying the costs of printing a new flyer, the monthly charges for mail and phone, and possibly a retainer fee, that there's little or no profit left for you out of the fees on the few dates you'll get. If this situation is still true after a number of years, with your career stabilized at a limited number of engagements each season, self-management seems a logical and possibly better alternative.

But there are two immediate problems in grappling with the concept of being self-managed. The first has to do with self-image; usually, artists can't help but feel — albeit deep down — as the general public does, that if they were really all that good they would have a manager. The second problem: It is exceedingly difficult, emotionally more than technically, to gracefully blow one's own horn, verbally rather than musically.

In dealing with the first of these, it may help to remember that the field is not fair. Demographics are against you, as stated before; there simply aren't enough openings on management rosters, or enough well-paying engagements, for everyone deserving of representation to get it. And miscarriages of justice do occur. You simply may not be the artistic flavor-of-the-month, or all the choice management opportunities in your field may be taken up for a number of years by others, perhaps, in your view, not as worthy as yourself — it happens all the time. This is not sufficient reason to deprive yourself of the chance for a fulfilling life in music, nor to deprive others of what you have musically to offer.

The second is a thornier problem. It may be most helpful to detour around the emotional question at first, and remember that there are learnable skills involved. Self-management is sales, and salesmanship is a learnable skill, which we will try to demonstrate in this chapter.

It's true that being a sufficiently good sales person to sell yourself requires enormous confidence, both to try it in the first place and to withstand the amount of rejection that you certainly will face. (A manager will experience as much rejection, by the way, but he can always feel that he's not being rejected — his client is.) A shift in your point of view may help you here; remember that some of the skills you have as a musician are applicable to management efforts. Effective performance is effective communication, and it is possible that you can communicate as effectively off stage as on. You can use what you already have as a performer, and try to generalize these skills to a broader arena.

Some self-management principles:

- Keep in mind a clear idea of what you have to offer to each potential sponsor.

- Be interested in others, listen to them carefully, and ask advice when you can.

- Assume a limited success rate, which, after all, is the norm in any business.

Realize that there are actually some advantages to self-managing over outside management. For one, you will actually be more attractive to some presenters because you'll be cheaper (no built-in commission to raise the fee). Some presenters, particularly the smaller ones, enjoy the personal contact with the artist. Also, you know what you have to offer, and may be better at describing it than someone else would be. And overall, you will be actively involved in your own career development, rather than feeling passive or powerless.

Now: how do you get started?

Booking a date in four not-very-easy steps

In Bill Matthews' research, he found that most presenters at the level we're discussing expected to be called before being approached by mail. They explained that they receive so much unsolicited promotional material that unless they're expecting it, they'll pay little attention to a flyer or resume received in the mail. When you reach the person in charge of a performance series, they'll listen to you — it's actually their job.

Making phone calls is harder at first for most people than writing, though following the steps outlined below should help. If you're simply far too shy to make the initial approach by phone, or if you're dealing with presenters on a higher level who can't be reached by phone, a letter can be substituted; the same general format will do. At some point, though, you will need to use the phone for follow-up. (See step 3.)

Before you start, get together all the publicity materials you will need to send to the presenters when they request them, as they almost certainly will. It takes longer to get these together than you think, and you need to be prepared.

1. Whom do I call? Making a list of possibilities.

Make a list of possible places where you might perform. In making the list, you will take into consideration:

1) Where you have some kind of contact or connection,

2) Who presents artists like yourself, or can be convinced to do so, and

3) Where you would really like very much to play.

Almost everyone can come up with at least a short list based on one or some combination of the above. Unambitiously, you might know that your alumni association has functions which might include live music; that the church you attended growing up, or the library in your home town, has a concert series; that your Aunt Sadie is on the board of directors of the local chamber music society. You might find a place where you performed as a kid on a special young person's concert, where they also hire professional artists. Any connection will get you at least a foot in the door, and will provide something concrete with which to start your dialogue.

A little research in the newspapers and other listings, such as the lists of presenters of concert series in the *Musical America Directory*, as well as conversations with colleagues, can also tell you about performance opportunities for which you might qualify. Lists of concert presenters are often obtainable for a fee from many state arts councils. Even a strong desire to perform on a particular series can provide you with an opening for discussion with the presenter. Cold lists, however, should always be followed up with some research before you do your calling or writing; such listings can be misleading, and you will waste time and money. The Guild, for example, is listed as a presenter of a concert series in *Musical America*, and we do produce some; the concerts only include our competition winners and alumni, however, so the many letters we get every day from hopeful artists are simply thrown out, since there are too many of them to answer with a letter of clarification.

Laura Spitzer, who is cited in the chapter credits and who runs a unique class in self-management at the University of Southern California, has assembled a "don't overlook" list of possible contacts. The sources from which she suggests creating a list of family, friends, friends of friends and acquaintances, some of which are mentioned above, include:

- Chamber of Commerce
- Parks and Recreation
- School District Offices, Principals, Teachers, Music Teachers, Parents and PTA Members
- Community Music Schools; School "Gifted and Talented" Programs
- Associations of Music Teachers
- Community, Junior, and Four Year Colleges and Universities
- Rotary, Kiwanis, Elks, Women's Clubs, other similar organizations
- Museums
- Churches
- Senior Citizen's Groups
- Institutions: Hospitals, Prisons, etc.
- Veteran's Groups
- Alumni Associations
- Music Stores
- Local and State Arts Councils

or even

- A business or corporation which might want to host an event, for employees, customers, etc.

Once you've got a list assembled, prepare to make a series of calls. Don't plan to make only one call, as the emotional investment should be amortized a bit by making several of them. And don't make your most important call — the engagement you want the most, or the one where you have the best chance of getting the job — first. After a few calls, you'll develop a certain fluency in your presentation, as well as a more devil-may-care attitude to either rejection or interest.

2. What should I say?

To get the person you want on the phone, use any introduction you can, preferably a real recommendation from a real person. If it is your Aunt Sadie, say so; if a fellow artist or another presenter whom the presenter knows suggested this venue, bring this up immediately. If you have no name to drop, bring up the connection which you've thought of, whether it is some geographical or historical association (as mentioned above) or simply a desire to perform at this hall.

Your first sentence (as above) will be said directly to the person you will want to talk to, or should get you in to talk to that person. Once you've got him on the phone, this sentence will become part of

The 20-Second Introduction.

For the most part, you will reliably have someone's attention on the phone for about 20 seconds, at which point they will either want to hear more, or lose interest. <u>During that 20 seconds, you must say something which will buy you more time, and interest them in hiring you.</u>

This may sound dreadful, if you assume that you must sum up yourself and what you do in barely enough time to take a deep breath. But you don't. You simply have to establish that you have something worth hearing a bit more about. By starting the conversation with your connection, you're earning some extra seconds; without one, you have to have an even better opening. During the 20 seconds, you'll have to bring up either your most impressive credential to date, or the credential which will mean the most to this presenter.

When Bill Matthews is talking to a new presenter on the phone, for example, he says that he often begins by saying something like, "I'm a classical guitarist who has performed in over 65 countries around the world; most recently, I've returned from a tour of [China and other countries in the Far East.]" Bill has performed extensively as a Cultural Ambassador for the United States Information Agency, and feels that presenters are most impressed by the worldwide nature of his performance experience.

Other examples, made up by us. The format: first, a sentence or two to establish a connection; then, the crucial 20 seconds.

Example 1

Establishing the connection:

"Hello, my name is __. [My Aunt Sadie, who is on your board of directors] [my friend Jill Hill, the pianist who performed on your series last year] [other reference] suggested that I call you about performing at [fill in name of sponsor]."

The 20 second introduction:

"I'm from Eastshore, and performed on the Eastshore Community Church young people's series years ago[1]. Since then, I've gone on to become a professional musician, and perform dozens of concerts each year around the country; recently, for example, I performed a highly regarded concert at the Impressiveville Museum of Art[2]. I would very much like to perform in my own region, and would love to come back to Eastshore as a performer on your regular series."

Note: [1] The reference to the local connection.
  [2] The specific, most impressive credential.

Example 2

Establishing a reason for calling this venue (no personal connection, but a geographic one):

> "Hello, I'm ___. I'm a violinist, concertizing regularly in the Northeast, and I've spent summers here in Eastshore for several years."

The 20 second introduction:

> "I've been a fan of your concert hall for years and attend your summer programs; since next season I'm doing other concerts in the area and I'll be here next summer as usual, I would like to perform on your series. I have a special program for families that I think would work well for your audience."

Example 3

Establishing a reason for calling (no personal connection, no non-personal connection), **and going right on to the 20-second pitch**.

> "Hello, my name is ___. I'm a singer, and I've just won the Interesting Artist of the Year Competition. I'm now seeking opportunities to bring the program with which I won that competition to a wider audience. I know that you produce a young artists' series, and I would be very interested in participating in it."

Example 4

Also combined, reason for calling and 20-second introduction:

> "Hello, my name is ___. I'm a clarinetist, and two years ago I graduated with some distinction from [Well Known Conservatory], and I've been performing extensively in [my area] since then. I would like to get some important

exposure in other areas, and would very much like the opportunity to perform on your series."

This last is perhaps weakest, in that there is no specific credential or connection to interest the presenter; however, it can be a subtle way, if carefully worded, of saying in effect, "I can save you money; the exposure is worth more to me now than the fee."

Example 5

The very best approach is one not listed yet, since it goes,

"Hi Fred, it's Ellen. I've got some free dates next year and a great new program I'd like to try out; any chance of working a concert into your season?"

In other words, the first name, we-already-know-each-other approach.

Note that we assume, in all of these cases, that you are not at all famous, and that your programs are not startlingly unusual. If either of these are true, so much the better — and the easier.

If you've captured enough of the presenter's attention to say a bit more, work in something about why your abilities and their needs would match well. This will show that you've done your homework, and also that you are interested in a successful concert, not just a gig. Concern for the presenter's success is much appreciated by them.

If the conversation runs long enough, and seems to be taking a positive course, mention some educational connection, if you do indeed have ability and experience in doing in-school performances or other events. Funding for concert series may be built around such school events, particularly in out-of-the-way communities.

Note: This last bit of advice is given in the assumption that it isn't a school concert that you have been booking. But it's important to remember that much of your work, often by necessity in the earlier stages of your career and perhaps later on by choice and interest, will involve in-school performances, and many of your calls will be to book such events. Having expertise in this area is no longer simply an extra, enhancing one's performing possibilities, but a required and essential part of them. Make sure that you have at least two programs prepared, for K-5 and for 6-12th grade. And actively look for opportunities to try them out: not only will they form a source of income for you, but effective school programs will help make sure that there is an audience for your concerts in future years.

Back to booking the date:

At some point you may be requested to have your manager get in touch with the presenter, or simply asked directly why you are calling yourself. Have an answer ready. There are perfectly acceptable answers; you're just launching your career, and have not yet looked into the question of management; you're between managers; though several managers are interested in you, you've not yet decided which to go with, and don't want to halt your career while deciding; you might even have a manager, but prefer to work directly with the sponsors.

The fact is that with some presenters your credibility will depend on your having a manager, and with them this prejudice can't be completely overcome. But this won't always be true. Don't apologize, and don't feel — about this issue or any other — that you are at a disadvantage. It is this presenter's job to put together a concert series each year, and you do feel that you have a program which will be a positive addition to the series. The presenter will expect a confidence on your part that reflects your belief in your own abilities; you should be able to indicate this confidence while still being grateful for someone's interest and consideration.

During the course of this phone call, a relationship will begin to form; you will like each other, or not, and will find that you have things to talk about, or not. A degree of liking, apart from artistic considerations, is enormously important on both sides; if you have a good phone manner, it will clearly help, and if one person in your chamber ensemble is making these kinds of calls, please make sure that it is the most charming of you — or the one who enjoys talking to other people the most, which may be the same thing.

Also — keeping in mind principle two stated at the beginning of this chapter, that you should listen carefully — be on the alert for any mention by the presenter of some special feature regarding the series which you might work into your discussion. Laura Spitzer reminds her students to listen for the following and make notes during the course of the conversation: the presenter's profession, hobbies, name of spouse or children (I would add pets to that); anything about the profile of the organization, audience size, venue; certainly, their level of enthusiasm. You can use all this information in later calls.

The fee

If there's real interest, and you've gotten to the point of discussing brass tacks, the question of your fee will come up. The question may arise now, during the first call, or in the follow-up call, but, as it can be an uncomfortable issue to deal with, it's best to be prepared. Amounts mentioned will often turn out to be the final ones, even if discussed as "ball-park" figures.

It is fairly common for a presenter to make the first fee offer when dealing directly with an artist, but equally common for them to ask you what your fee is. This makes things difficult, of course, since your preferred answer to this question is probably, "As much as I can get." If you've done some homework beforehand, you might have gotten an idea of the fees paid by this presenter to other artists through asking around. If the series is funded by a local arts council or other public agency, you probably can get an idea of their fee range by calling that agency. (This information is usually public, though it may be complicated to get. An officer in the program which handles their grant application might be willing, informally, to give you some idea of the range, though they won't name specific fees to specific artists.)

You should also have some idea of how much you really need, weighing travel and other expenses against your need for exposure, experience and credentials, thus establishing a bottom line below which you can't afford to go. Don't be too afraid that you won't be taken seriously if you don't stick to a high fee; you can always state some reason why you'd make an exception, just for them and just this once. You're trying out a program, you want a foot in the door in this community, you will almost certainly have engagements in the area right around that time; all are good reasons which the presenter will accept.

Finally, you can always say, "My usual fee is $ (some figure)..." followed by a pause or a full stop. The stop puts the ball in their court, and it's left to them to explain why theirs is not a "usual" case. If it feels wrong to leave it at that, consider adding, after your pause, "... but this is negotiable, since I realize that you might find it difficult to go that high." Or something to that effect.

To give you some ball-park figures: Fees of $1,000 to $3,000 for a young solo artist are considered reasonable for most serious touring engagements, depending on the artist's credentials and the series' budget. Libraries and similar community venues will not pay fees even close to this level, but they do offer opportunities for warm-ups, trying out programs and gaining experience that may make up for the small fees.

3. Following the initial call

Now, one of two things will probably happen. The most likely is that the presenter is either mildly interested, or not interested but not unfeeling (or honest) enough to simply say so; almost certainly what she will say is, "Please send me some materials that I can look over." **You must, at this point, be ready to immediately — that is, at the most within a couple of days, before she forgets who you are — send out very good publicity materials, including a flyer if you have one, or a** picture and biography if you don't, reviews, feature articles if you have them, plus a short cover letter referring to your conversation and reiterating the important points. Hand write this if your handwriting is good. Otherwise, make sure it's not a form letter, hand sign it, and make sure the presenter's name and title are spelled right. It is exceedingly important that your materials be very slick and professional looking, and that you send them out quickly; one reason that presenters are afraid to deal with artists without managers is that they're afraid the artists aren't very good, and that they'll be difficult to deal with in one way or another. Good looking materials say that you're a first class artist; prompt correspondence says that you take care of business. Don't send a tape at this point, unless specifically asked for one (reason below).

In the event that there is no interest and the presenter actually says so, don't miss the opportunity to ask if she can recommend anyone else whom you might call. Principle number two, asking advice when you can, comes into its own here. Give the presenter the opportunity to be generous; she will often open up, particularly if she's just turned you down, and feels a bit bad about it. If she does refer you to a colleague, you will have accomplished several things: first, you'll have a personal connection, a name to drop, in your next call; second, you will be moving closer to your target, a venue that is actually right for you, where you have a shot at getting a performance.

There is a third, and very unlikely, possibility: that the presenter will be so impressed with your presentation, or your reputation will have preceded you and they know you so well already, that you get a positive response immediately. If this happens, skip to the end of the next section.

4. The follow-up call and beyond

Let's now suppose that you've been asked for materials and have sent them, and two weeks have gone by. You're now entitled to make a follow-up call. The real purpose of the call is to ask whether the sponsor now wants to hire you, but you can't ask that directly, and probably things aren't that simple anyway. You therefore must be prepared with something to say (not just "have the materials have arrived safely"), or something specific to offer. If you are performing in the general area, you might invite him; if you have accomplished something in the interim, such as a competition win or a successful concert, you should tell the presenter about it. Otherwise, now's the time to offer a tape (this is one reason why you didn't send one before; the other is that tapes are too expensive to send to those who aren't really interested in listening to them).

Another item which you probably should bring up in this phone call, or possibly in the previous one, is, "When do you start scheduling your concerts for the coming season, and when should I be in touch again?" This will often set up your follow-up schedule for the next call, and help you to be most effective with this presenter in the future.

A second follow-up call is all right, but more than that is silly. If no deal has been cut by this time, or if no time schedule has been set up for further negotiation ("We've already got next season's schedule set, but call me in the fall about the season after that and let's talk again"), drop the phone calls for a while, but remember to keep the presenter posted on your current activities through periodic (perhaps no more than yearly) notes with reviews, invitations to your other concerts and the like.

What to do if you've got the date

When a deal is made, you should send out a letter confirming it. You could send out a more formal contract, if you wish (a sample contract is in the Resource Section), or the presenter may have a standard form that they use. Whether you use a contract or a letter, it should clearly state the financial terms of the deal, the times involved and the division of responsibilities. With a contract, send two copies for their signature, sign one to return to them for their files and keep one yourself.

When the time comes for the concert to take place, taking the following advice will make it more likely that you'll be re-engaged someday, apart from how well the actual performance goes:

- Make sure that flyers or other materials have gotten to the presenter in plenty of time (ask them what plenty of time means, and make sure you stick to the timetable), and that they're of excellent quality. Similarly, give them program information as promptly as possible; if you can't decide on a program, send your best guess. If there must be later changes, so be it. (Be careful, though; some presenters in some regions are <u>seriously</u> offended by changes, whereas others think that the informality of last minute changes is perfectly fine. If an artist happens to have a tour in Japan, for example, such last minute changes are regarded as discourteous and disorganized, and are a major gaffe.)

- Call a few days before the concert, to make sure that all is well.

- Come early. Never give a presenter a heart attack by walking in a few minutes before the downbeat.

- Help the presenter by making yourself available for newspaper interviews, radio broadcasts or other public relations opportunities, and to the community for before-concert events.

- Attend the post-concert reception, and check with the presenter to see if there's anyone that you should be particularly careful to thank.

- Be easy to work with, and flexible about your times and working conditions (within reason).

- Talk to the audience if you're good at it, and if the concert situation is informal enough to make it appropriate.

- Be sensitive overall to the presenter's concerns. Each event for her is like being the host of a party, with all of the anxieties associated with important social, as well as business, events. She wants it to be a success, and you can help.

If at this point you still can't figure out how to get started at all, the lists of presenters in the Resource Section of this chapter are places to start trying to book dates, if you're located in New York City or Boston. All these presenters are used to dealing with young artists; very few of them expect you to have a flyer, and most will consider an inquiry even if you have only a biography and, perhaps, a picture. You will have to inquire with each to learn how much in the way of follow-up calling is acceptable. Some pay a fee, some don't, but none will expect you to pay to perform. Bill Matthews originally compiled the list for New York by asking friends, from his own experience and knowledge, and from some research, including reading concert listings in newspapers and magazines; kind friends at the New England Conservatory originally compiled the one for Boston. Based on these lists, it should not be too difficult for you to compile similar lists for your own communities.

Some general guidelines, from Laura

The following ideas — not in any priority order — are drawn from Laura's notes for her classes and from talks she's given on self-management.

- Don't ever expect anyone to call you back, and never take lack of response personally.

- Her advice regarding fees: If a presenter cannot meet your asking fee, offer to throw in another school program or service for free, pointing out the revenue this can generate to make up the difference; reduce your fee only as a last resort.

- Never back a presenter into a corner; give them lots of room [and time] to talk and think things over and make relaxed decisions.

- Repeat dates and times over the phone, and again on paper when you write; send contracts as soon as possible, to avoid any misunderstandings.

- Use a booking address that will not change, at least for a few years. In some cases, a P.O. box is the best way to do this.

- Reorder materials before you run out.

- Keep an audience mailing list, by putting a sign-up sheet out at every concert; send them notices about recordings or a performances, or copies of articles that appear about you.

- Overestimate travel time.

- Always assume that your audience is highly intelligent, and don't be fooled by clothes or manner that you think indicates the contrary. The more sensitive you believe your audience to be, the more they will respond to you and rise to your expectations.

Please read this: a final, very important note.

Since forewarned is at least a step towards being forearmed, here are some important thoughts to inform your longer-term perspective. First, none of the performers that we have ever spoken with really likes being his own manager. All said that they would prefer having a *good* manager to being self-managed. But the crucial word is *good*; many artists are dissatisfied with their managers, and some, making a virtue of necessity, find self-management to be preferable. At least one effectively self-managed artist contacted said that, though he would rather have a big, powerful management than be running his own operation, he got no better results when he was with one of the smaller, less powerful ones than he now gets on his own. This is not to say that small managements are ineffective, but rather that the difference in success, for him at least, comes not from management as opposed to self-management, but from effective self-management as opposed to not-as-effective outside management.

Laura notes that it probably gets about 10 years to get a career rolling, and that starting out knowing this will help sustain you through the tough times. She adds that the motivation which fuels this effort is a talent separate from musical gifts, but perhaps as important in predicting how successful your efforts will be. In her own words,

"Talent being equal, how would you answer these questions: Out of ten apathetic, passive, inarticulate, depressive musicians, how many will make it? or, Out of ten enthusiastic, tenacious, driven, verbal, optimistic musicians, how many will make it?"

Laura is a highly unusual person, who is the second kind of musician much of the time. The rest of us are the first kind of musician some days, the second kind other days, and somewhere in between in general. If you tend toward type two though, your chances of being able to sustain your self-management efforts, particularly during difficult times, are improved.

In this regard, it is wise to keep in mind that a self-managed free-lance career as a musician usually has a maximum life span: perhaps the 10 or so years mentioned above. At this point, most people need to have built up sufficient momentum to change the balance from them doing most of the calling to mostly being called: or they start to change the way they live, to look for different and more steady work in the field, or to consider doing something else entirely. And they may make such changes even if their careers are going pretty well.

There are several reasons for this. First, self-managed free-lance careers are really, really hard. Though there are remarkable individuals who are exceptions to the rule, most people can't keep up the level of positive energy and unremitting effort required to maintain and consistently build a career, without much help, for longer than this, and sometimes not for this long — even though expecting a career to take off in a shorter period may be unrealistic.

Second, the self-managed free-lance career is very rarely lucrative, even when the musician is booking an enviable number of dates for himself; the expenses of touring can be high, the level of fee hardly princely, and the amount of unpaid time and effort spent on one's own behalf enormous. Usually, the ratio of gross income to net income, that is, how much of the fees you get you actually have as income, is about 3 to 1, or even 2 to 1, for the typical touring performer. That means that if you gross $30,000 in fees — which many artists would think is excellent — you rarely will clear more than $10-15,000 of this. One pianist we know, who earned a very respectable gross income of $77,000 one year performing almost 100 self-booked concerts (some of them school concerts linked to larger performances), realized a net income of just over $16,000 after expenses, due to the extraordinary costs involved in that particular year of travel, plus things like upkeep on his piano. (He noted that he would have earned more bagging groceries.)

During the period when a young artist is investing in her own future, though, this may be enough to get by, if supplemented by some kind of part time teaching or a day job; but in the long run, or when life, in the form of spouses or children or other interests or responsibilities, makes its presence known, it is rarely enough to sustain either body or soul.

But consider the alternative. If you want to perform enough, and are willing to put in at least a few years, it's worth a shot. It's also not entirely unpleasant; there are rewards, and from time to time it can be both challenging and actually fun to tackle and solve the problem of getting yourself some work. And as an alternative, either from the beginning or when you simply can't do it all yourself anymore, it is possible to hire and train someone to do all, or part, of the work for you. Remember though that in most cases this can be done effectively only when you already have some self-management experience, and can train the person you hire by drawing on that experience. Make sure, if you take this route, that your representative will be as effective as you would be — or more so.

Resource Section

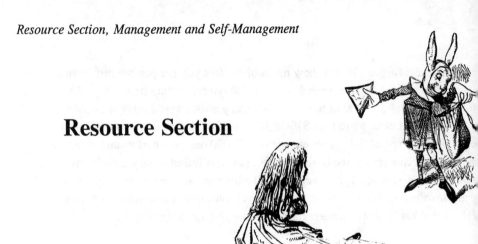

Self Management

As promised, a list of presenters who are ready and willing to present young artists. Write to them, sending biographical materials and a tape, or call, following the specific instructions below.

(All these sponsors have been contacted in 1997, so the information given is correct as of that date.)

Some Concert Presenters, New York City

American Landmark Festivals
26 Wall Street
New York, NY 10005
(212) 866-2086

Francis Heilbut arranges 200 or more concerts a year. There is payment for a few of them. Most concerts take place in buildings designated as landmarks. Mr. Heilbut also arranges some performances abroad during some seasons.

Brooklyn Public Library
Grand Army Plaza
Brooklyn, NY 11238
(718) 780-7779

JoeAnne Shapiro coordinates the programming of concerts in 59 branches, none of which has a piano at the moment. No pay, though occasionally "very nominal honoraria are paid," mostly related to transportation. These concerts are used to mainly showcase musicians from Brooklyn.

Brooklyn Public Library
Service to the Aging
2115 Ocean Avenue
Brooklyn, NY 11229
(718) 376-3577

Mario Salzano is the program coordinator of weekly and Sunday presentations at 14 branches. They pay approximately $50 for a soloist and more for groups.

The Donnell Library
20 West 53 Street
New York, NY 10019
(212) 621-0613

Cheryl Raymond coordinates this concert series. Send a letter with resume and tape by December 15th in order to be considered for the coming season. Replies may take several months as arrangements are made only through correspondence. No pay, but a program/flyer is made. Their season runs from September to June. Concerts are booked throughout the year, but well in advance of the next season. A follow-up letter might be a good idea.

Hospital Audiences Incorporated (HAI)
220 West 42 Street
New York, NY 10036
(212) 575-7681

The In-facility Performance Department at HAI arranges thousands of performances each year in a wide range of settings including hospitals, nursing homes, and physical and mental rehabilitation sites. First contact can be either by phone or by sending in a resume. A follow-up call is useful just to be sure that your resume has arrived and to request an audition; these are held throughout the year. Very few of the facilities have pianos, so performances are mainly limited to other instrumentalists. There is payment for performances. Contact the Artist Liaison, if interested.

LaGuardia Theater
LaGuardia Community College
31-10 Thomson Ave.
Long Island City, NY 11101
718-482-5151

Tom Divan, Director of the LaGuardia Theater, programs groups for educational programs geared mostly toward elementary schools, though there are some college level presentations as well. Fees vary.

New York Public Library for the Performing Arts
40 Lincoln Center Plaza
New York, NY 10023
(212) 870-1680

Allen Pally books concerts in January for the following September-June season, presenting one event every day that they are open. No pay, but no charge for a tape of the concert. Applicants must be serious musicians, as many of the other applicants come from Lincoln Center organizations.

New York Public Library
Office of Adult Services
445 5th Avenue
New York , NY 10016
(212) 340-0913

Cecil Hixon coordinates the programming of concerts throughout the branch library system. No pay, but sometimes transportation costs are paid. Some locations have pianos but most do not. A flyer is produced for each concert, concerts are also listed in their monthly events flyer.

Queensborough Public Library
89-11 Merrick Blvd.
Jamaica, NY 11432
(718) 990-0896

Doris Jones organizes the programming of a series of concerts in the library branches. The Jackson Heights Central Library and the Forest Hills branch have pianos. Honoraria are sometimes paid through grants.

King Feng, 718-990-0858, programs concerts ("Sunday Concerts at Central") at the main branch, for which a fee is paid. They have a baby grand piano which is tuned before each performance. Contact King if you are interested.

Saint Bartholemew's Church
109 East 50th Street
New York, NY 10022
(212) 378-0227

Jan Prokop (Ms.), Director of Chapel Concerts, coordinates a concert series that runs from October through March on Sundays at 2:00 PM. The chapel seats 150, and they have a grand piano. Performers split the $10 contribution charge with the church up to the first $400; after the church has cleared $200, the performer(s) keep the rest. The church will copy programs for you if you provide a master. Concerts should be one hour long (45 minutes of music). The series presents classical, jazz, cabaret and Broadway performers, including all instruments and singers. Contact Ms. Prokop in March if you are interested.

Saint Peter's Church
619 Lexington Avenue
New York, NY 10022
(212) 935-2200

Tom Schmidt coordinates a concert series that runs from September through mid-June on Sunday afternoons. No pay, but if performers choose to charge a modest admission (no more than $15) they can keep all of it. They have a seven-foot Baldwin piano. Mr. Schmidt suggests that performers who are interested call him and be prepared to send a tape. The church space is provided free, but no other services (flyers, programs, etc.) are provided. There is a $100 piano tuning fee.

Trinity Church Music Office
74 Trinity Place
New York, NY 10006
(212) 602-0768

Earle Tucker, Concert Manager, coordinates the Noonday Concert Series at Saint Paul's Chapel, a program running from September-June that presents 50 minute concerts each Monday and Thursday at 12 at Saint Paul's Chapel, Broadway & Fulton St. Attendance averages 200 per concert. Soloists are paid $250, duos $350, trios $450, quartets $500; fees for larger groups are negotiated. Resumes are accepted throughout the year. Auditions are scheduled in October and April.

Victor Kioulaphides, 212-602-9632, assists Mr. Tucker in organizing another series called Concerts To Go. This series presents performances from February-November in nursing homes, hospitals and shelters citywide. To be eligible for this program you must pass the Noonday Concert Series audition. Soloists are paid $150, duos $250, and trios $375.

Some Concert Presenters, Boston

Art Complex Museum
189 Alden Street
Duxbury, MA 02332
617-934-6634

There are 5 concerts a season, approximately one a month. Send resume, tape, and fee schedule to Charles Weyerhaeuser, P.O. Box 2814, Duxbury, MA 02331.

Candlelight Concerts
First Congregational Church
697 Main Street
Harwich, MA 02645
508-432-1053

There are 7 to 12 concerts, both classical and jazz, from June through September. A free will offering is collected, 80% of which goes to the musicians. Artists are selected by the Church's Fine Arts Committee, and materials should be sent to them.

Gallery Concert Series
Indian Hill Symphony Orchestra Series
Box 1484
Littleton, MA 01460
508-486-9524

These are two separate series. The Gallery Concert Series is chamber music; the Indian Hill Symphony Orchestra Series is orchestra with soloists. The orchestra series has 4 concerts, the chamber series 5. Contact Harry Chalmiers at the above address regarding the chamber series, and Susan Randazzo for the Indian Hill Symphony series.

King's Chapel House Noon Hour Recitals
64 Beacon Street
Boston, MA 02108
617-227-2155

This is a year round weekly concert series. They provide publicity in a monthly flyer. Contact Sheila Bosworth at the above address.

Malden Public Library Sunday Concert Series
36 Salem Street

Malden, MA 02148
617-324-0218

Concerts occur monthly, and tend to be booked well in advance, as much as eighteen months. There is no pay, but they do the publicity. Contact Dina Malgeri if interested.

United Parish Presents
United Parish
210 Harvard Street
Brookline, MA 02146
(mail inquiries only)

Concerts occur four times a year, and are held in the church parlor which holds 60 to 80 people. There is a reception afterwards. Admission is a $8.00 donation ($3.00 for seniors and students). They do the publicity. Send a resume, audition tape and projected program if interested.

Help for artists interested in school performances

Though we haven't seen this publication ourselves, it came very highly recommended, and certainly covers a very useful topic. *How to Make Money Performing in the Public Schools: The Definitive Guide to Developing, Marketing and Presenting Performances in Elementary Schools*, by David Heflick is a soft-cover book which can be obtained by writing to the author at Silcox Productions, P.O. Box 1407, Orient, WA 99160.

Regional Arts Agencies

These regional arts organizations, among others, have touring programs for individual performers and groups. Some state arts councils or other agencies have similar programs. Contact those in your area for specific information.

Arts Midwest
Hennepin Center for the Arts
528 Hennepin Avenue, Suite 310
Minneapolis, MN 55403
612-341-0755

Mid-America Arts Alliance
Exhibits USA
912 Baltimore, Suite 700
Kansas City, MO 64105
816-421-1388

Mid Atlantic Arts Foundation
23 Light Street, Suite 300
Baltimore, MD 21202
410-539-6656

Southern Arts Federation
181 14th Street, Suite 400
Atlanta, GA 30309
404-874-7244

Western States Arts Federation
P.O. Box 480765
Denver, CO 80248-0765
303-629-1166

Help with your foreign touring

Arts International
Institute of International Education
809 United Nations Plaza
New York, NY 10017-3580
212-894-5370 (phone)

This organization runs programs including grants, advocacy, exchange and information services. For musicians, available programs include grants to assist performers in participating in international festivals (the Fund for U.S. Artists) and special funds for collaborative projects with artists from specific countries. In addition, they publish numerous books which are very helpful to performers. Write to them for a list.

Sample Artist/Presenter Contract

Agreement date: January 1, 1998   Engagement date: January 1, 1999

AGREEMENT between **XYZ RECITAL SERIES** (hereunder "SPONSOR") and **JOE ARTIST** (hereunder "ARTIST").

1. SPONSOR engages ARTIST, and ARTIST agrees to perform a recital on Monday, January 1, 1999 at 8:00 p.m. in Anytown, USA for a fee of $2000.00.

2. Payment by SPONSOR of the fee of $2000.00, in the form of a company or organization check payable to "Joe Artist," is to be presented to ARTIST or mailed or delivered to ARTIST immediately following the conclusion of the performance. No deduction from the fee set forth herein shall be made by SPONSOR for performance rights fees, or for any other purpose, other than all applicable and customarily deducted taxes, without prior written consent of ARTIST.

3. SPONSOR agrees, at SPONSOR's expense, to furnish the hall for the engagement herein contracted. The hall is to be well heated and lighted, clean and in good order, with all necessary ushers, ticket collectors, licenses, and clean dressing room for ARTIST and any assisting artists provided. SPONSOR further agrees to make the hall available to ARTIST prior to the performance for rehearsal at a time previously agreed upon as acceptable to both ARTIST and SPONSOR. The house piano is to be in excellent condition and properly tuned.

4. ARTIST will furnish to SPONSOR a copy of the program to be performed. SPONSOR agrees, at SPONSOR's expense, to print and distribute a sufficient quantity of house programs in conformity with the material furnished by CAG. SPONSOR agrees to print on all programs, immediately after the musical portion, the following: "Joe Artist records for ABC Records."

5. SPONSOR agrees to arrange, at SPONSOR's expense, for a page turner to be available for the performance should ARTIST request it. ARTIST agrees to notify SPONSOR of such request at least two weeks in advance of the performance.

Sample Artist/Presenter Contract, continued

6. ARTIST agrees to provide SPONSOR with press materials and flyers in quantities ARTIST feels sufficient. SPONSOR must place the request for these materials at least five weeks prior to the date of engagement, and agrees to pay all applicable shipping charges in the event of a request for very large quantities or a rush order. SPONSOR further agrees to properly distribute and display all advertising material received and to return unused materials.

7. ARTIST shall not be under any liability for failure of ARTIST to appear or perform for any cause beyond ARTIST's control, including, but not limited to, illness or accident, regulations of public authorities, labor difficulties, civil tumult, strike, epidemic, and interruption or delay of transportation service. In the event that ARTIST defaults for reasons beyond ARTIST's control, SPONSOR will not be responsible for the payment of the fees agreed to in this contract, and ARTIST will refund any moneys already paid. Neither will ARTIST be responsible for any of SPONSOR's costs, already incurred or otherwise, for the local production and publicity of the events. Further, ARTIST and SPONSOR agree to make every effort to reschedule the events for a mutually agreeable date.

8. SPONSOR agrees to prevent the broadcast, recording, or reproduction, by radio, television, or any other device, of ARTIST's performance, or any part thereof, without the specific written consent of ARTIST. SPONSOR agrees that the engagement shall not be a joint recital, nor shall any assisting artist perform without prior consent of ARTIST.

9. This agreement shall not be binding on ARTIST until executed by ARTIST. This agreement represents the full understanding between the parties, and ARTIST shall not be bound by any terms or undertakings not contained herein. This agreement may not be assigned by SPONSOR, but shall be binding on SPONSOR and SPONSOR's personal representative and successors.

JOE ARTIST

XYZ RECITAL SERIES

DATE

DATE

VII. All of the Above: For Composers

Many ideas in this chapter came from conversations with composers Oliver Knussen and Marc Neikrug, both of whom generously spent much time with us. We talked extensively with these two because they've chosen lives which combine performance and composing in a fashion which contributes significantly to the field; the reader will come to see that this is a path we very much believe in. Also very helpful in gathering points of view for the chapter were composer and former director of the Career Planning and Placement Office at the Manhattan School of Music, Mark LaPorta; Vice President and Director of Promotions at G. Schirmer, Inc. Susan Feder; Boosey & Hawkes Director of Promotion Jennifer Bilfield; pianists and champions of new music Alan Feinberg and Ursula Oppens; and many other composers, too numerous to cite here, but to whom thanks are due.

This chapter contains much information that you would expect, and doesn't include some information that you might expect. Trying to avoid duplication, we have chosen not to include information on performing rights, for example, which are better covered by the performing rights organizations themselves, or in Meet the Composer's handbook <u>Composers in the Marketplace</u> (see the Resource Section at the end of this chapter). The same is true for contracts, commission fees and arrangements, and more. We've chosen to devote the space to topics not addressed, or not addressed in depth, by other organizations in the field.

Everything stated in the previous chapters about performers — that is, needing to understand your own musical identity, being able to communicate it to the world, creating supportive networks, etc. — is equally true for composers. But composers often have an even more difficult time of it, for a number of reasons. First, the composer not only often lacks the most basic information about career development, but has fewer resources for learning about what it entails. Second, the composer is usually in the background, rather than out there for everyone to see and admire.

A few ideas which have informed our point of view, and which you might keep in mind as you make your way through this chapter.

▶ You need to get out into the field, creating professional equity against which you can draw support and loyalty.

▶ You need to be prepared with appropriate and clear materials as soon as possible.

▶ You need to develop skills for dealing effectively with performers, colleagues in the field, and audiences.

▶ You need to support your fellow composers.

A chief problem for composers is isolation: an isolation that can cut them off from their potential audiences, supporters, collaborators, interpreters — even from composer colleagues. It can be psychologically very difficult (Oliver Knussen says, "Decide how much you want to be alone; composing is an emotion-numbingly lonely occupation. It's also extremely labor intensive, or should be."). And this isolation can, at worst, separate the composer from new and sustaining sources of musical thought and growth.

But that is a topic for another book. Our concern here is that isolation not only keeps composers hidden from view, it puts them in the position — in relation to the rest of the field — of asking for help, rather than in a relationship involving reciprocity and mutual support.

Accepting that composers need, one way or another, to be players in the game rather than onlookers on the periphery, one way is to perform, and this is the way we'll discuss first. (Further along in the chapter we'll deal with other ways of both contributing to and participating in the musical life of the community.) Through performance composers can become advocates *for themselves and for others*, find satisfying musical partners, and make important musical alliances.

Performing and Composing

We don't seem to live in a time when composers are also virtuoso performers, as in the nineteenth century. Even those composers who conduct and who are, for example, also terrific pianists — Lukas Foss, Andre Previn, and the late Leonard Bernstein come to mind — don't write primarily for themselves, or even primarily for the piano.

For a few composers, though, starting and performing in an ensemble which exclusively performs that composer's music has been the path to considerable success, and the means by which they've found their public (as Philip Glass and Steve Reich have done). An equally successful model is provided by composers who start and/or perform in chamber ensembles which play a wide variety of new music, or of both new and older music. Composer Joan Tower, for example, was pianist for many years with the Da Capo Chamber Players, for which she wrote and premiered several important works, as well as performing the works of fellow composers.

Composers can make a performance opportunity which isn't exclusively theirs, and which they haven't started, their principle compositional vehicle as well. Composer Don York, former music director for the Paul Taylor dance company, has written several orchestral works for the company, all of which have gotten significant exposure both in the company's home base and on tour.

Two of the composers interviewed for this chapter have been particularly active as performers, in different ways. Oliver Knussen has been conducting almost as long as he's been composing. Though he often conducts his own music, he has been an indefatigable champion of the music of his fellow composers. This advocacy, added to his compositional gifts and his very wide-ranging musical curiosity and knowledge, has consistently brought him the respect and attention of the field. Composer Marc Neikrug chose a life in which performance, separate for the most part from his compositional activity, was primary for a long time in terms of making a living and visibility. As half of a violin and piano duo (Neikrug performs with Pinchas Zukerman), he has had a wide experience of the field, has learned how it works and has made friends. In his own words:

"From the beginning I wanted to perform as well as compose. For a composer like me — who isn't the compositional equivalent of a 9 to 5er, and doesn't absolutely need to compose every day — this is the perfect job. I know my schedule way ahead of time, so I can plan when I can write (the minimum amount of time I need for getting back into composing, some down time, and producing some work, is three weeks). Being part of a duo was a specific choice; the enormous repertoire and the memorization required of a solo pianist would require more hours than would allow me to compose. I do some solo playing, and some conducting, but limit the amount. It's easier to go from composing to performing than the other way around, when I need time to get all the other notes out of my head before working on my own.

"There's always been an enormous pressure from outside to <u>choose</u>, to be one thing or another. I feel they're all one piece; I couldn't play the way I play if I wasn't a composer. It's probably equally true that being a performer affects the music I write; but neither is extricable from the other."

A very important note: Knussen reminds us that performing can be a way of learning, growing and maintaining an active involvement with the field *without bringing one's music before the public before it's ready*. He says:

"Many young composers are desperately anxious to be seen and recognized publicly, rather than to work hard at their musical growth. No status should be attached to being known until you are seriously convinced that the music is really ready to be heard."

Not performing ... but out in the field

A composer's living, while she's young, will almost never come primarily from composition. It probably won't come from composition even to the extent that a fledgling performer, who's free lancing and being actively entrepreneurial about creating performance opportunities for herself, will make some of her living from performing. (Royalties, rental fees, etc. for composers under fifty add up to very little money, with a few exceptions; commissions can pay very good money, but unless the composer has lined up a string of them, lasting several years, she will have to earn at least part of her living doing something else.)

However, the composer's living, if at all possible, should come from activities which teach him useful things about the field, and which create contacts with people and organizations. In general this book does not deal with vocational guidance, but we can propose some possibilities.

We've just suggested:

- developing your performing skills, and playing the music of other composers;
- learning to conduct, and conducting other peoples music as well as your own;
- starting a performing group in which you are a performer, conductor, and/or *administrator*.

We haven't discussed the last of these yet, but you can certainly start, or participate in starting, a performing ensemble or concert series without actually performing in it; all these groups need administration, and someone who's energetic, devoted and organized is beyond price. You could, moreover, be the group's in-house composer-in-residence.

By forming a local composer's alliance for example, and starting a concert series as one activity of the alliance, you could be involved with making music happen in a very important way. The example of Libby Larson and Stephen Paulus and the Minnesota Composer's Forum demonstrates how effective such organizations can become, both for the field and for those that put so much effort into them. This model is particularly useful in smaller cities where such resources for composers don't already exist.

Of course, in order to get to do any of these, you will need to follow the guidance laid out for performers in previous chapters. And it won't be easy. But it probably will be worth the effort.

Alternatively (or in addition), you could

- Work with a radio station as a programmer; or with a music festival or other performing organization in artistic administration. You'll meet lots of people, including performers, and learn a lot about reaching audiences. You can use your extensive knowledge of the repertoire (which you have, of course) to make a difference in what's being listened to, and to become an advocate for your part of the field. But be prepared to keep quiet about your own work unless asked about it.

- Work with ASCAP or BMI, or some other kind of composer's organization. These offer opportunities for very good networking, and you can develop an understanding of basic mechanisms of the business.

- Start your own publishing company or record label. This sounds very ambitious, and certainly either would take some fairly serious up-front money, but — if you can make the investment, and have the right personality — they're interesting ways of bringing the world to you, instead of the other way around.

An old friend of this author is a composer, primarily of band music. Being of an organizational turn of mind, interested in computers, and having few other options at that point in his life anyway, he bought himself a computer and the appropriate software and started to self-publish, developing a list of band directors around the country and marketing his work directly to them. He was amazingly successful on many fronts: his band music began to get known and played, he got commissions from some loyal customers after a while (including several for non-band music), he began to publish the works of other composers that interested him, and now has something of a small corner on this part of the market. The financial rewards were pretty slow in coming, but other rewards — contacts, commissions, travel, etc. — grew quite steadily. The same principle could apply to starting a record label, though the marketing would be much more difficult (not that the publishing business was easy), and the income likely to be close to non-existent, since the overhead costs can be so high. Several composers we know are recording engineers, however, and work with other composers on producing independent records for them, which is another interesting way of combining learning and getting around with income.

- Working as a critic or otherwise writing about music. This is an interesting possibility, with a distinguished history, though not one much in fashion now. We do know one or two, though, who have pursued this path. It would be good to see more active musicians involved in writing about music for the general public.

- And more and more. Internships in public relations & marketing, with an orchestra perhaps? You'll learn about how music is marketed, frightening, perhaps, but definitely interesting. An internship in development with some arts organization, not even necessarily a musical one? You will certainly learn to define and pitch a project. Also, remember that joining national composer's organizations, like the American Music Center, will keep you in touch with information about opportunities in the field and bring you together with your colleagues.

All this gets the composer "grounded," and helps him to learn the languages of other parts of the field. These ideas also represent a way of developing a place in the business in which *he can be of help to other musicians*, both performers and composers.

What about teaching?

Composers have always taught, and rightly so, both in and out of the academy. Academic jobs, though, are getting harder and harder to come by, so the university or conservatory as home base for the composer's career is an option for fewer individuals than it once was. This chapter deals principally with skills which the composer should develop and which will enhance all sorts of job opportunities — teaching included. If you love to teach, and should you find yourself with a conservatory or college teaching job (or any teaching job, for that matter), developing other sides of your professional life will not only add to your teaching effectiveness (and employability), but can help guard against a comfortable descent into the isolation which this chapter is trying to help you avoid.

Developing skills and learning about the field, early on: Perhaps while in school

Composers need to start early developing strong, supportive collegial relationships *with performers and with fellow composers*. You need to support their work while in school, and remain active as a supporter of their work when you're out. You need to develop the performance skills you will need throughout your musical life — particularly conducting, since the period in one's life when one can round up a group of musicians on a voluntary basis and convince them to let you lead them is short, and likely to be when you (and, more important, they) are younger rather than older. You need to get out and around, to hear as much as you can. And, obviously, you need to develop your own musical voice. To accomplish this, in or out of school:

Knussen: "Find some players that you genuinely get on with personally, and some you respect, start an ensemble and get them to teach you to conduct. Don't think of it as a performing ensemble, but rather as a place for everyone to try to learn things.

" My recipe for learning how to be a decent composer is to investigate as many different ways as possible of doing what interests you. Find out what you want to do, and utilize whatever you've got in your technical arsenal to achieve an end result which is the most meaningful <u>and</u> practical realization of what you want to say. Find an actual, active professional composer who has a musical life outside the university, and apprentice yourself for a bit. Offer to do odd jobs, copying or proofreading, anything that needs doing. It's an old fashioned way, but probably the best. He is more likely to talk to you about the things which actually engage him while composing, rather than give you a composition lesson. The best mentor is someone who can do something you can't, or who works in a way that you don't understand but that you respect and admire.

" Make as many contacts with as many composers of as many different backgrounds as possible. That's why a place like Tanglewood is so useful; you can learn a lot about what you want to do as a composer, through a process of elimination if nothing else, and through the cross-fertilization of ideas which can happen there. Going to a festival or studying with a particular composer for the sake of a line on your resume, isn't worth it.

" [Get to] know the literature well. Your knowledge will make you valuable as a resource for conductors, etc., and will be useful to you as composer-in-residence."

Neikrug: "You have to make composing your work, instead of cutting yourself off from the field. To do that, you must a) play something, play it as well as you can, and perform, and 2) talk, think and understand your fellow musicians. You certainly have to identify with performers; you can't presume to write a phrase of music without having played one."

"Students need to get out to hear music from outside; they need to go hear the Guarneri Quartet, and to go backstage and congratulate them, as well as the school concerts. You have to get into the field, and meet people. When I met the young composer Bright Sheng recently, he reminded me that we had met ten years earlier when he had turned pages for me at a concert at BAM, and that we had had an interesting conversation about my music. What a great way to meet lots of people that you might not meet otherwise! People can always use page turners."

A few suggestions from the publishers with whom we spoke, as to what advice they might give to young composers, particularly while in school. First, from Susan Feder of G. Schirmer.

- Cultivate performance contacts, and get good taped material.
- Understand what performers need and can do, and develop sensitivity to their needs; the clearer your performance materials, the better chance you have for a good performance.
- Learn to conduct, or to perform yourself.
- Take time to learn your craft; really learn orchestration, etc. Often less is more.

And, from a former Boosey & Hawkes vice-president.

- Take classes in notation skills and the like, things that you won't be able to get easily after you're out.
- Try to be active in the music organizations of the school — perhaps as ensemble librarian, to work with scores, parts and players.
- Start an ensemble, or a festival, in or out of school. "Bang on a Can" has been both an exciting festival in itself and a wonderful vehicle for the three composers who started it (David Lang, Michael Gordon and Julia Wolfe).

Even if it's not so early ... Some general advice

Neikrug: "I was fortunate; my father played my work, his students played my work. You will need someone of some stature to perform something, anything of yours; that gives you credibility. But you still have to hang around. Go to <u>everyone's</u> concerts, shake everyone's hand. When the time comes, they'll need a new piece — who they commission depends a lot on who pops into their head, often the last composer they spoke to. I did that for years. I never asked anyone to play a piece of mine, and never talked — on those occasions — about my music. But I was there. *Musicians are not interested in new pieces. They are interested in somebody they like. Nobody asks to hear or see some of your music when they learn you're a composer (correction: players who don't have much repertoire for their instrument or ensemble will ask); they ask after they've <u>heard</u> something.*

"When you're starting out, you can never say `no, I don't have that,' or `I can't do that.' I got my first major performance and acquired a publisher at the same time. My piano teacher was playing with an orchestra, and told the conductor about me. The conductor asked if I had written a piano concerto (I said yes though I hadn't) which I could play. He then said that if I had a publisher who would supply him with parts (I said yes, though I didn't), he would perform it. I then went to Barenreiter, and asked if they would publish [parts to] my piano concerto (!); they said yes if I had a guaranteed performance, which I told them I did. When I was at Marlboro a similar incident happened. I walked in on some percussion players who were setting up to rehearse; they asked if I had a percussion piece, because they would play it if I did. I said I would in three days."

"It's important to see your career as a long trajectory. You probably can't make most of your living from composing when you're young, but if you look at the longer view, perhaps it can be increasingly how you make your living as you go along."

Knussen: "If you're interested in writing orchestral and/or instrumental music, get yourself into as many orchestra rehearsals as possible (three times a week if you can). If you're interested in opera, write to the company's artistic administrator and ask if you can attend rehearsals.

"Don't be cowed by what everyone tells you to do. Doing other things can be helpful. Resist the temptation to write endless pièces d'occasion for money; hold out rather for working longer at a more major, more useful work."

Regarding this last issue; note that although Knussen warns against writing many pièces d'occasion, Marc Neikrug states that you should never say "no" to an opportunity when you're starting out — and many of these opportunities will likely be to write pièces d'occasion. These are very personal and equally legitimate ways of thinking about one's work, and either can be applied with wisdom to a particular phase in one's career — or to a particular composer.

It is important that composers realize that at first, at least, and perhaps in the longer run as well, they will often be writing for their friends, who will be their primary source of encouragement, inspiration and opportunities. And what their friends want may be easily programmable ten to twelve minute works. If your friends need these short pieces, don't reject writing them out of hand — unless it's absolutely the wrong thing for you musically. Only you can determine this.

Working with performers

Some kind of guidance about proper etiquette when working with performers is badly needed by many composers, certainly and most desperately by those not actually performers themselves. A few tips, from our interviewees:

Knussen: " If you're young, it's a safe bet to assume that everyone in the room knows more about what they're doing than you do. It's also safe to assume that if you've done your best with preparing materials, and if the notation of the piece is considerately done, chances are the players will be sympathetic to you. Chances are also that advice from them, if given, will be constructive. You don't waste their time, and they don't waste yours.

"Do not expect performers to like everything they're playing. You can hope that they will, but it's highly unlikely that that will be true. Do not walk in defensively or react with hostility. Accept advice graciously. If you hear a wrong note, or many, wait until the passage has been played through at least once and perhaps twice more before diplomatically pointing it out. Then point out quietly but unambiguously that you think there may be an error.

"It may be that some players detest the kind of music that you write, or generally have an attitude problem. This is not your problem. Respond quietly but unambiguously.

"Choose your words very carefully. When a trumpet player asks what kind of mute you want, don't respond, `well in the last performance the player used a blue one.' If necessary, say `I'm not sure' and ask for advice. (There's no shame in honesty!)

"Let them play. Don't fuss about minutiae. Don't say, `Yes, of course, I know that.' If there's a genuine problem, having to do with materials or something that really doesn't work, encourage the conductor or leader to leave it alone, and sort it out yourself before the next rehearsal. Less talk the better. Don't stop the conductor or leader with details during the session; keep a list and hand it to him/her in plenty of time for the next rehearsal. If you don't think this will work, transfer the items to index cards, and supplement the list handed to the conductor with placing the cards on the appropriate players stands."

Sending scores and tapes to performers

This is purely a matter of simple common sense and politeness. **Don't ever send an unsolicited score without some kind of introduction, or at least without**

some strong reason to believe that your work would be of interest to this particular performer. Include a cover letter which reminds the performer of this connection, and thanks him for his interest in your work. If you want your materials sent back, enclose a self addressed return envelope with enough postage — and don't expect things to be returned quickly, even then. People are busy. Make sure that the score you send is completely clean and legible (in these days of computer copying, no one is really willing to deal with difficult to decipher scores anymore), and that the tape is of good quality. Let the performer know what you can easily provide in addition: if you have a clean set of parts on hand, for example.

Pianist Alan Feinberg gets unsolicited scores all the time, and tries very hard to look at them all. He doesn't always succeed, and doesn't always manage to send them back. He actually has done something with unsolicited material every once in a while though, which contradicts what has been said above; he's programmed works, forwarded scores on to other artists, or gotten to know a composer's work from scores or tapes sent cold. But he's unusually conscientious about this sort of thing, and these happy results have not occurred often.

He describes a recent scenario which did turn him off, however, which might provide a cautionary tale for you. A composer came up to congratulate him after a performance, and to ask if it would be all right to send him a score, to which he replied that it would be fine. A score to a piano concerto arrived at his manager's office soon thereafter, with a cover letter which stated that this piece had the interest of a particular conductor, though it didn't mention whether the conductor was interested in Alan as well; and that there was a European recording planned, with another pianist. A few weeks later, the composer called Alan, to ask if he was interested. In regard to what performance? Evidently this composer rather expected that, if he were interested, he would make a performance happen.

The problem here is that the composer seemed to have no idea in the world what the performer's life is like. He had assumed that if Alan liked it, this piece would, or could, immediately rise to the top of Alan's "to do" list, ignoring works and composers that he's wanted to program for a long time. He assumed that finding a performance opportunity was Alan's responsibility, and that it wouldn't be too difficult: when the actuality is that there aren't that many opportunities within most performer's schedules to insert another work (or to find a concerto performance at all), that most presenters know what they want to have performed (at least generally), and there is often not much flexibility. It also assumed the wrong relationship: that is, that the composer asks for help, and the performer gives it. Had the composer had something specific to bring to the table — an actual performance or recording opportunity to offer, for example — the reaction might have been different. Without something specific, the score should have been sent purely to let Alan get acquainted with the composer's work, and the follow-up call simply a thank you for his looking at it.

Pianist Ursula Oppens adds that the reverse — that is, being offered something, but for the wrong reasons — can be a total turn-off as well. She speaks of getting a call from a composer asking if she would play a piece of his on a concert in New York. He said he had a tape which he could send her, which was quite good; when she asked why he wasn't asking the pianist on the tape to perform, he responded that she [Ursula] was more famous. This was bad. Loyalty in the field is much prized, and composers and performers develop mutually rewarding relationships which sustain them both. Stepping over loyal supporters in search of greater glory is noticed, and usually deplored.

Publishers

The role of a good publisher in a composer's life can be analogous to that of a good manager in a performer's: that is, they can do an enormous amount of administrative work for you, get your music around and played, and work with you on career development. However, it is as difficult to get a good publisher as it is for performers to get a good manager, and there is some question as to why, as well as when, you need one, given changes in the technology and finances of the publishing world over the last decade or two.

Before going into the composer's views on publishers, here are interviews with the representatives of two major, respected publishers, with the basics of the business. The author's questions are in italics.

Susan Feder, Vice President, G. Schirmer Inc.

How does a composer get on your roster?

We go to a great many concerts, and may be intrigued by someone's work that we've heard; alternatively, we may get a call from someone in the business recommending a particular composer. Some recommendations come from composers already on our list. We do listen to unsolicited submissions of scores or tapes on a regular basis, but it's rare that we find composers to add to the roster that way. When there's interest in particular composers, we go to their concerts, meet with them to get a sense of them not only as musicians but as people — as well as to learn about their career expectations and goals as well as to develop a publishing and promotional strategy. Schirmer doesn't want to take a composer on for whom we can't make a real difference in their career development.

We do look for composers with an interesting, original perspective. We recognize that we are in a multi-cultural, ethnically diverse world, and are looking for music that reflects this. We also often take into account the views of our colleagues in our sister companies around the world who can bring artistic perspective to our deliberations.

Who's `WE'?

The Editorial Committee consists of our directors of publications and rentals, members of the promotion department, and me. All form a kind of A&R *(Artists and Repertoire)* team.

What is the role the publisher plays in the life of a composer under exclusive contract?

The publisher frees composers to do what they do best: compose. The publisher protects the composer's copyrights worldwide, negotiates fees, and promotes the composer by looking for commissions, performances, recordings, and film opportunities; prepares, stores and distributes performing materials and printed publications; dispenses advice; and strategizes career development. Very much like management for performers.

We also see the publisher as an information service on behalf of the composer, providing program notes, keeping track of reviews and performances, etc. We were the first classical music publisher to develop an active presence on the Internet, so much of this information is being disseminated electronically, and to markets we might not have reached otherwise. G. Schirmer is part of the Music Sales Group, an international company with offices worldwide, so we are able to offer promotion and administration that is at once international and localized.

The printing of scores is less important than it once was; primarily it has promotional value. We do take seriously the archival importance of the printed score; in years to come, it is important that someone be able to see what the music was that Schirmer considered important at any given moment in musical history. Most printed scores of new music don't sell enough to make money; sometimes the publisher can anthologize particular works, or selections (opera arias by various composers, for example), and this may generate some income. Otherwise, income comes from rentals, performing rights, mechanical rights, synchronization, etc.

We are prepared to make an investment in our search for the next Menotti or Barber. Take John Corigliano, for example; the parts and corrections for his *First Symphony* were initially extremely expensive to produce, but there have already been nearly 200 performances, plus broadcasts and two recordings. Likewise, we devoted much time and energy to *The Ghosts of Versailles* at the time of the Met performance and revival. But the success of that piece has been enormously gratifying for all of us. So the investment has paid off.

We're increasingly interested in an exclusive relationship with our composers. Usually these are five year contracts. There are contracts which are negotiated for specific works, usually on the commercial side of the print catalog: flute music, piano music, choral octavos, etc.

What is the financial arrangement, in general?

The composer and publisher share royalties on print, rental, grand rights and performing rights income. The specific splits are affected by several factors: who is responsible for preparation of materials; the level of promotion put into a given work or composer; guarantees to print within a given period of time.

What materials should a composer have on hand?

▶ A work list, including representative works.
▶ A good demo tape, if possible. (If you have one, make sure that it has only one piece per side. Cueing a tape doesn't work! This is very important.)
▶ A CV emphasizing history of performances so we can cross-reference, or make calls, and
▶ Various narrative bios for use in programs.
▶ A CD is good if you have one, since you can cue it easily, and the quality is usually predictable.
▶ Program notes and reviews.

To what extent do you now rely on computers for printing?

We've put virtually all our new works on computer, from which we extract parts. This makes the rehearsals more effective and efficient because of the legibility and accuracy of performing materials, and revisions are easy to make.

What about composers self-publishing, using the computer? And working with a personal representative to oversee the business aspects of their careers?

It's inevitable that composers are increasingly going to use computers to copy and print their music, just as writers have gone to word processors. They will still need good editors, to ensure things like consistency, correct orthography, input on practicality and effectiveness of written choices, etc. The bookkeeping aspects of the publishing business are formidable. The licensing registration(s), fee calculation and collection, etc. are best left to professionals. Also, storage and cataloging of materials can be a major undertaking.

But, a personal representative can work with other aspects of a composer's career: speaking and teaching engagements, performance engagements, and general publicity. We also tend to make a distinction between promotion and publicity, focussing our efforts on getting the next performance rather than the next newspaper feature.

Any final words?

Music publishers tread a delicate path between art and commerce, between the traditional long-term view of developing artistic potential and profile, and the new demands brought about by changing and competitive technologies and markets. It's exciting to be exploring new international arenas for contemporary music as well as new media opportunities, and we look forward to opening these up not only for our own composers but also for contemporary music in general.

Jennifer Bilfield, Director of Promotion, Boosey & Hawkes

How does a composer get on your roster?

Composers have found their way to Boosey & Hawkes through recommendation from colleagues and other B & H composers, personal approaches to the company, and through performances of works which have piqued our interest. Since 1985, we have signed exclusive contracts with 12 composers: John Adams, Louis Andriessen, Harrison Birtwistle, Unsuk Chin, Henryk Gorecki, H.K. Gruber, David Horne, Magnus Lindberg, Steve Mackey, James MacMillan, Michael Torke, and Christopher Rouse.

Why do you take on so few composers?

The number of living composers in the Serious Music Division who have exclusive contracts with the company has been kept deliberately modest (26 in all) for several reasons. The first is the fact that it appears to be the most productive for all parties involved. Another stems from the fact that while many publishers have one office and are represented abroad by other publishers in an agency relationship, Boosey & Hawkes is an international company with offices in New York, London, Berlin, and Sydney. As such, each affiliate plays an active role in promoting/selling the composer's music once he or she joins our roster. The resources required to support a composer's music through such an international network are considerable, but often invisible to those outside the industry. For example, we negotiate contracts and commissions; license works for recordings, media uses and other rights; protect the copyright of works in tandem with the performing rights societies; provide editorial and production support for musical materials; field requests for biographies, program notes, reviews and photos; and coordinate promotional activity through industry contacts, conferences, concert travel, and printed materials. Composers who approach Boosey & Hawkes to enter into a publishing relationship cite these resources as principal attractions, along with the quality of communication between the affiliates and prestige of the catalog.

In addition to the Serious Music Division, Boosey & Hawkes works with composers through its Printed Materials Division, which has recently begun to develop exclusive relationships with composers for our choral, band and educational projects.

In short, we want to work with composers who have defined their own voice and who have a clear sense of the direction of their work and how it fits within the continuum of musical life, both past and future. If we can find music which will stay active throughout the life of the copyright, it can eventually be profitable for both the composer and company.

Is it worth sending music to a publisher?

Yes, but do approach several companies. Be sure that you know what type of music they publish and are currently considering, and why you want to work with them. Most publishers have committees that review submissions. Generally, composers are encouraged to send tapes and scores of works which represent the direction of their current writing, along with a list of performances, and forthcoming projects and performances. As mentioned above, recommendations are extremely helpful, and can often expedite the review process. I always suggest that composers add publishers to their mailing list in order to keep us apprised of upcoming performances and activities.

What is the place of print in your activities?

Each year we produce scores that are available at retail music stores. Additional scores, particularly those of very recent works, can be obtained directly from us by special order.

Many printed scores are used to enhance promotional activities, while others such as Bartok's *Concerto for Orchestra* or John Adam's *Short Ride in a Fast Machine* have strong sales, year after year, and become staples of the repertoire.

How about computers?

Computer engraved scores are now standard, and without question are expected by most performing organizations. Many composers do have access to sophisticated systems and software, and this does help to expedite revisions and corrections. Given the limited rehearsal time available to many performers, the accuracy and clarity of score and parts is paramount, and can make the pivotal difference between a passable and excellent performance.

What materials should a composer have on hand?

A good tape or CD is the most important tool a composer has in promoting his or her music — to anyone. Well-produced scores are also useful, but will generally be reviewed only after the work has been heard; they are also much more expensive than tapes for the composers to reproduce and mail. Quantities of up-to-date reviews, performance history, program notes, and resume are also important to have on hand to avoid last-minute scrambles for information.

Regardless of how a piece appears on paper, it must work in performance. The tape is *(or should be)* the next best thing to being there.

What about self-publishing?

If a composer opts for this route, she or he needs to be realistic about the amount of time self-publishing entails. A part-time assistant can provide support in copying, collating, fielding calls, billing and perhaps even in publicity, so that the composer can spend his or her time composing.

Any final words?

Perhaps the two most critical elements in a composer's career are developing craft, and building a network of musicians who are passionate advocates of his or her work. Admittedly, these facets of a composer's life are often at odds. While the act of composing is solitary and all-consuming, composers write music largely to communicate, express, incite, inspire. It should go without saying that composers should make every effort to interact with performers, although many are uncomfortable promoting their music. Ultimately, music is most eloquent, most persuasive when it is heard, performed and experienced by others. Everything else is icing on the cake.

Publishers, from the composer's point of view

Composers have much more ambivalent feelings about publishers, generally, than the other way around. The frustrations they commonly express about their publishers are strikingly similar to those expressed by performers about their managers: "Their choices are arbitrary;" "They're not knowledgeable;" "They never get me commissions or performances;" "I get them myself, and split the royalties."

These days, it's perfectly possible, with a relatively small investment, to get yourself set up with a computer, printer, and the right software, and print your own music to rent or sell to those interested. Says Oliver Knussen:

"If you are concerned about this [getting a publisher], ask yourself why, other than wanting your name in a well-known catalogue, do you want to be published? The only answer is that it is becoming a major inconvenience to deal with the demand for your work. When you do sign up, realize that you effectively lose 50% of the income from your work. Print sales royalties are negligible, but you will only get between 25% and 50% of rentals. Retainers are very unlikely anymore. Working independently, with a representative or assistant who can handle many of these aspects of your business, is a good idea. If you have stage works, or works involving text, the grand rights agreements are very complicated, probably best dealt with by a publisher, though an assistant should be able to learn how to deal with them in time."

So, just as with performers, you may well start out — and even end up — self-managing and self publishing.

Self publishing, self-management and personal representatives

If you decide to go this route, you will need to learn about copying, probably using a computer and a software program like *Score* or *Finale*; you will need to work very hard, as described above, on creating a market for your work by creating strong relationships with those who might commission or perform it; and you will need to be both organized and businesslike about fulfilling the administrative aspects of your compositional life.

In terms of working with a representative, know that there are very few representatives around who work with composers — and even fewer good ones. One path to explore might be to find someone with the skills and personal qualifications you feel you need, that complement your own strengths (and weaknesses): computer ability; good negotiating skills, to set commissioning and other fees; organizational ability; a good working relationship with many performers; above all, a strong, enthusiastic belief in your music. Even if this person has little or no experience in this line of work, it will be possible to train him to act on your behalf, perhaps at first principally secretarially, then increasingly as publisher, manager, or in as many roles as you are both comfortable.

Other important skills for composers:
Talking to audiences and writing program notes

The musical world into which most young composers are emerging is not one which comes equipped with a public eager for the composer's next contribution. Composers, like performers — perhaps even more than performers — must be prepared to convince others of the value of their work. More often than not, this will be accomplished through words and personality, even before the music gets heard. How an audience, or performer, or potential supporter, hears your work, will depend on the way the listener feels about you — and about new music in general, of course, and a variety of other factors as well. The first of these is, however, the only one under your immediate control, so use it.

The tips for performers on speaking directly to audiences in the On-Stage chapter are equally applicable to composers. Assuming that you are not performing the work yourself, the period in which you speak directly to listeners is your chance to create the atmosphere or the background against which you want the work to be heard. Something personal or anecdotal is more helpful to this end than something technical. Interesting the audience in you and your music is more engaging, and will result in the audience listening with sympathy and interest, than discussions of structure. Come up with a short list of things you might say, as you will often be called upon to briefly speak if you show up at the performance. And, of course, you should always do that if you can.

Program notes are another way of speaking to an audience. They should actually achieve something in the way of enlightenment, not substitute for listening. Avoid anything like the following (these notes have been altered only very slightly from those provided at a recent composer's concert at a major music school):

"This piece is based on principles associated with twelve tone structures but also concerns itself with the organized distribution of various levels of contrast and continuity. The rigidity of fixed interval structures did not provide internal organization for this music, but rather the mechanisms of transformation that proceed over time, the consistency between the interaction of the parts rather than the derivation of the parts themselves."

What?

This isn't useful. If the concert takes place, as this one did, in a conservatory and at a composer's concert, these notes seem to presume that only fellow composers are welcome to attend, since obviously they're the only ones who might marginally care about all that. If the piece is well written, the performance is decent and the audience is knowledgeable — as it almost certainly was in this case — the piece doesn't need this kind of annotation; one should be able to hear musical structure, generally if not specifically. If the piece isn't well written, these notes won't make it any better; if the performance isn't good, the audience won't be persuaded to make allowances because of the compelling text; if the audience isn't knowledgeable, notes like these will make them actively hostile. Notes should be a bridge to the music, and an inviting bridge at that, which at their best should make the audience want to close their programs and listen.

It would be best at this point if we could provide a really good example of a program note; we haven't done so, because really good ones are hard to find, and really good ones are often so specifically about a particular work that they might be off-putting, because the kind of work described isn't like the reader's. But we do have a few suggestions. First: since it's often very difficult to write notes about your own music, perhaps several composers could get together and write about each other's music. Since these notes would be written from the point of view of what someone sympathetic and informed actually hears, they would likely be in line with what the composer hopes the ideal listener will also hear, and possibly can point the listener in the right direction. Also, it's good to get into the habit of listening supportively to the music of colleagues, and this would help to create a formal way of doing this.

Another idea, that composers may be uncomfortable with, but that *every* listener we've spoken too really likes: state the length of the piece. This gives the first time listener a framework within which to listen, much like going into a museum and judging where to stand depending on the size of the canvas. And it is actually "hard news," so to speak, one of the things a listener simply doesn't know beforehand. A third item, if the notes are recent, or can be updated: if the work is not a new one, how does it relate to the composer's ongoing style, and how does he feel about it now. This one could be tricky, but would certainly be interesting.

Practical back-up:
Materials

In the text above we've referred to materials that the composer needs in order to be prepared when someone asks for them, as they will. The items which are absolutely indispensable are:

▶ a good demo tape, or better several, which highlight one aspect or another of your work (see Chapter II for specific advice on this);

▶ a repertoire list, including instrumentation, timings, and performance history (or combinations of these);

▶ a narrative biography;

▶ a curriculum vitae.

All should have the appropriate contact information on them, of course. See the "Materials" chapter for performers.

Additional useful items, if you can afford them or if they've somehow appeared in your musical life:

▶ a photo, so that it can be reproduced in programs or on posters;

▶ a CD;

► a promotional brochure, which combines much of the above. Many publishers put these together for their roster composers, just as a manager would for their performers.

Examples of a current repertoire list and narrative biography of Carlos Carillo, a young composer of whom we think a lot, follow.

Example 1: Narrative Biography

CARLOS CARILLO, composer
Address
Address
Phone

Carlos Carillo, composer

Born in San Juan, Puerto Rico, Carlos Carillo has been the recipient of numerous honors and award, including a Charles Ives Scholarship from the American Academy of Arts and Letters and BMI and ASCAP awards. In 1993 Mr. Carillo received the prestigious Bearns Prize in composition presented by Columbia University. A commission from the New York Youth Symphony in 1994 resulted in the composition of *The Farewells*, an orchestral work premiered in Carnegie Hall. He has received a Concert Artists Guild Fellowship for career development, and has served as composer-in-residence for that organization.

Carlos Carillo holds degrees from the Eastman School of Music and Yale University, where he has studied with Samuel Adler, Joseph Schwantner, Warren Benson and Christopher Rouse, Jacob Druckman, Roberto Sierra and Martin Bresnick. He also studied with Tania Léon at Brooklyn College while on an Exchange Program. He is currently pursuing a Ph. D. at the University of Pennsylvania, where he is a student of George Crumb.

[May 1997]

Example 2: Curriculum Vitae

CARLOS CARILLO, composer
Address
Address
Phone

Prizes and Awards

John Day Jackson Prize (Yale University)	1996
Concert Artists Guild Fellowship	1994-6
ASCAP Grant to Young Composers	1996
ASCAP Grant to Young Composers	1995
Meet the Composer Grant	1992
Charles Ives Scholarship	1995
of the American Academy of Arts & Letters	
Segundo Taller Sinfónico	1995
Orquesta Sinfónico de Puerto Rico (for *Farewells*)	
Bradley Keeler Memorial (Yale Univ.)	1995
Segundo Taller Sinfónico	1994
Orquesta Sinfónico de Puerto Rico (for *Cantares*)	
Joseph Bearns Prize, Columbia Univ.	1993
BMI Student Composers Award	1983
Edith Babcock Scholarship	1992
Eastman School of Music	

Commissions

Commission, New York Youth Symphony	1994
Concert Artists Guild(for)	(in progress)
Concert Artists Guild (for)	

Teaching Experience ?

Teaching Fellow,

Education

Ph.D. Candidate, Composition, University of Pennsylvania	present
Jay Riese, George Crumb	
M.M.., Composition, Yale University School of Music	1996
Jacob Druckman, Roberto Sierra, Martin Bresnick	
B.M., Composition, Eastman School of Music	1994
Samuel Adler, Joseph Schwantner, Warren Benson, Christopher Rouse	
Exchange Student, Brooklyn College	1988-89
Composition with Tania Léon	
Universidad de Puerto Rico (transferred)	1986-88, 89-90

Example 3: Repertoire list

CARLOS CARILLO
Orchestral and Chamber Works, 1989-96

1996: **Will the quiet time come**
Cello/Piano

Premiere: Thompson, Putz; 4/96, Stony Brook NY (Staller Center)

Como si fuera la primavera
Clarinet/Bass clarinet/Cello/Percussion

Premiere: Baeza, Hilash, Tsang, Ferrari; 4/96, Bronx, NY (NY Botanical Garden)

1995: **Ocasi el alma**
Clarinet/Cello/Piano

Premiere: Baeza, Thompson, Klibonoff; 3/96, NYC (Kosciusko Foundation)

1994: **Seufzer, Tränen, Kummer, Noth**
Violin/Viola/Cello/Piano

Premiere: Members of the New Jersey Symphony; 1/95, Newark NJ (Newark Museum)
Second performance: Koo, Espin-Guzman, Nahmer, Putz; 2/95, Yale University

The Farewells
Orchestra (2 2 3 2 - 4 4 3 1 - 3+timp/harp/piano)

Premiere: New York Youth Symphony; 11/94, Carnegie Hall, NYC

Songs of time and distance
Soprano and chamber ensemble

Premiere: Escalera, Wallace (cond.), Eastman student ensemble; 4/94, Rochester, NY

1993: **Cantares**
Orchestra (3 3 3 3 - 4 4 3 1 - 2 timp/harp/piano

Premiere: Puerto Rico Symphony, 4/94, San Juan, PR

1992: **Dos tangos y otras penas**
Saxophone Quartet

Premiere: Tower Saxophone Quartet; 2/93, Rochester NY (Kilbourn Hall)

1989: **Dias y Noches de Amor y de Guerra**
Clarinet/harpsichord

Premiere: Ross, Cameron; 4/89, Brooklyn NY (Sam Levinson Recital Hall)

Address   Phone, fax, e-mail

Resource Section

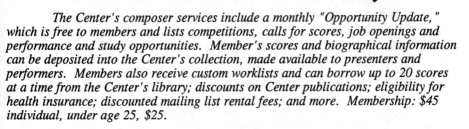

American Music Center
30 West 26th Street, Suite 1001
New York, NY 10010-2011
212-366-5260 (phone: administrative offices)
212-366-5263 (phone: library services)
212-366-5265 (fax)

*The Center's composer services include a monthly "Opportunity Update,"
which is free to members and lists competitions, calls for scores, job openings and
performance and study opportunities. Member's scores and biographical information
can be deposited into the Center's collection, made available to presenters and
performers. Members also receive custom worklists and can borrow up to 20 scores
at a time from the Center's library; discounts on Center publications; eligibility for
health insurance; discounted mailing list rental fees; and more. Membership: $45
individual, under age 25, $25.*

Meet the Composer
2112 Broadway, Suite 505
New York, NY 10023
212-787-3601

*Meet the Composer offers a wide variety of services to composers, and all
composers should become acquainted with this organization (as with the American
Music Center, above). A number of affiliates around the country makes dropping in
and getting acquainted possible for many composers.*

ASCAP

*If you are a composer, ASCAP runs a variety of programs, services and
awards which would be of interest to both members and non-members. For
information about these, or about becoming a composer member, ask for their
publication "Just the Facts". For more information about membership, or about
services to composers, call the office of Frances Richard at 212-621-6327.*

BMI

*This organization also runs a variety of programs of interest to both
emerging and established composers, including Annual Student Composers Awards,*

workshops for emerging composers of jazz musical theater, and film music, and grants to music organizations through the BMI foundation. For composer membership information, call Ralph Jackson, Senior Director of Concert Music Relations at 212-830-2537.

Volunteer Lawyers for the Arts
1 East 53rd Street, 6th Floor
New York, NY 10022
212-319-2787

Listed in the general resources section, we've included VLA here because of one of their newest publications, <u>Copyright for Musicians and Composers</u>, which is available from them for $5.95 (plus $2 s/h per book). Order by calling the number above.

The Soundart Foundation

This organization is interesting to you principally as the publisher of the Calendar for New Music, which you can advertise in if you have a concert coming up in or near New York, or can browse the advertisements both for concerts and for services to composers: copyists, recording studios, etc. A subscription is $11 a year, and issues come out monthly (student rate is $8). Write to:

The Soundart Foundation
P.O. Box 850
Philmont, NY 12565
518-672-4775

Harvestworks / Studio Pass

Harvestworks provides services to artists who use audio and digital media technology in their work. Programs include Tellus, a catalog and on-line service to distribute and publicize new work; Studio PASS, a professional audio production facility; an Artist-in-Residence program for realization of performance works using electronics, and various classes including computer music notation, audio and midi for multimedia, and more. For information:

Harvestworks
596 Broadway, Suite 602
New York, NY 11012
212-431-1130 (phone)
212-431-8473 (fax)
harvestw@panix.com
www.avsi.com/harvestworks/

VIII. Fine tuning

The following are thoughts and commentary about issues specific to singers, some advice to pianists, and a few words about teaching and performing, questions about which consistently arise in our discussions about the profession.

Singers

The world sometimes seems to be a particularly rough place for singers. There are a great many of you, and the market — yes, even for tenors — is extraordinarily competitive. As in any part of the business, there <u>are</u> opportunities, and quality, determination, collegiality, imagination and professionalism will find and make the most of them. But, it's tough.

So, what follows is advice and ideas drawn from CAG workshop sessions aimed specifically at singers, with headings as to general subject matter, followed by a few hopefully helpful tips. Though we haven't cited the sources (there are too many of them), they include singers, managers and others knowledgeable about the vocal world.

The patience factor. The first thing to remember, which is both discouraging and reassuring, is that it takes time to build a vocal career. Lots of time. One friend of ours in the vocal world suggests that it takes eight years to see if anything will happen, and another five to stabilize whatever has happened. Perhaps this doesn't sound too bad, until you measure your progress, if you're unwise enough to do this, against other people — perhaps non-musicians — who graduated from college when you did, and who after thirteen years are dealing with mid-career success, not thinking about whether to stick it out or learn computer programming. A manager we know described the career of one of his quite successful singers, one which has a very happy ending, who took sixteen years to go from small opera engagements to quite regular work at the Met. Again, this may not sound too long until you think about all the years after getting out of school, before he had those first small-ish opera roles, and before he had a manager hustling the better auditions. Modestly, add another five to ten.

Beyond la bella voce. Because the time frame is usually so long, you will have to find ways to survive in the meantime, as well as ways to honestly assess how you're doing. (This is certainly not a problem unique to singers, but the trajectory is flatter, the speed slower, in-the-field ways of getting by more scarce, and objective feedback perhaps more difficult to come by.) You may be able to slant things slightly more to your advantage, at least as far as getting some consistent work is concerned, if you have a specific interest or ability that you can be identified with: early music, new music, certain types of opera roles. Working with composers can be particularly helpful for singers: there's some work to be had, as well as opportunities for musical growth and being part of the creative process. There also are chances to get to know instrumentalists, as much new vocal music is for chamber ensemble rather than voice and piano; since singers are often somewhat isolated from the rest of the music community, this can be a very important way of meeting and working with your fellow musicians. Additionally, the better trained you are as a musician, and the more skills you develop, the more likely it is that you'll be able to take advantage of opportunities that arise, and create opportunities for yourself.

Europe or bust? Given how hard it is to make a dent in the profession, at this point the question arises as to whether to try to build a career first (that is, an opera career) in Europe. There certainly are things to be said in favor of this, though it's not the absolute requirement that it once was. Many managers like singers who've spent some time on stages in Europe, as they return with language skills, contacts, and experience. And there is work in Europe, in part because local training is very good. But sometimes coming home is hard; for several artists we know who want to sing in the U.S. and make their lives here, being out of the loop too long without local exposure can make it very difficult to return.

Management. Do you absolutely need a manager? No. Can you function without one? Yes. Can you make a serious, notable career? Ultimately, no. You can work, and you can, with a great deal of hustle, keep track of audition possibilities, particularly if you coach with someone who knows who's in town and whose schedule is what, and if you're a good networker with lots of friends looking for the same auditions. As in other parts of the business, some sponsors actually prefer not to deal with managers, and others are willing to work without them. But, most opera companies, and certainly all the major ones, won't audition artists not under management, and at some point, you need it.

But, in some ways, it may be easier (not easy, but easier) for a singer to find a manager than for an instrumentalist, for two reasons. First, because there are lots of managements, really booking agencies, specifically for singers: in fact, several non-specialized managers we know prefer to work with singers who have already been with a "singers" management first. And second, because above all managers are looking for beautiful voices, and if they fall in love with yours, that can balance out all sorts of other factors. Sometimes the factor which makes all the difference is the good overall musicianship, as noted above. The three sopranos on one management's very prestigious roster all started off playing the violin, and only came to voice later as a profession. Their good, solid musical skills and background, in addition to their vocal ability, made them more versatile, far easier to place, and therefore much more appealing to the management.

Money. A brief aside about the financial arrangements between management and singers: Commissions may be about 20% for concert fees, 10% for opera fees, but it can get very complicated; management may take a fee from gross or not; sometimes the fee is calculated on a per performance basis; and overall, which elements of the contract are subject to commission are variable. Sorry, it's not consistent. You will need to be prepared for almost anything. And the money may not be great, even for good jobs. An oratorio engagement which took place a few seasons ago, with a major orchestra got $1,500 + air fare for the young, not unknown singer they hired; the same singer received $1,000 + hotel for two Messiahs with a regional orchestra in the south. Most opera engagements underpay as well, perhaps $1,500-$2,500 per performance for mid-range companies, perhaps with transportation, perhaps with a per diem or a guest room in someone's home. One regional company paid $5,000, + $750 per show, for 6 weeks, plus air fare and housing; the manager took 10%.

Other vocal work. What other work, outside of simply temping, is there while you're working hard to develop your voice and credentials, get some exposure, and network? There is paid choral work, though it's scarce. Churches and synagogues pay very badly, generally around $70 to $85 a Sunday with one rehearsal (tenors get more): but you can meet conductors, other singers, and learn about opportunities from them. (Vocal contractors names are usually common knowledge; good sight reading is absolutely necessary. Let your friends know you can sub.) Teaching may be a good option, if you can find some steady situation, and if you're good at it. There is some commercial work, but there are very few commercials though that want a classical sound. But if you're in New York, you can go to SAG (the Screen Artists Guild) and check the boards, and keep talking to people.

And if you're in New York or another city with an active theater community, you may be able to get work in the musical theater. Know that this is still something done with varying success and very mixed reviews. Aside from the musical demands of each area, the classical field is still fairly snobbish about artists who have made their reputations doing what is considered to be commercial or pop work. But it's not impossible to cross from one to the other, as long as you keep all these factors in mind, and there's certainly great music, as well as perhaps a living, to be had by being proficient on both sides of this musical divide.

Weight. Questions about this come up frequently at our workshops, so we thought we should at least mention it. Our various experts have noted that large people need to understand that if a director has a choice between two singers, equally good, if one is noticeably too fat they will choose the other. It sounds obvious, but the question is asked, and therefore deserves a straight answer. Everyone needs to keep in shape, exercise, breathe, take care of themselves, and understand that there may be situations in which someone will lose out for only this reason.

Hints about auditions. As always, find out as much as you can about the situation and what will be expected of you, so that you can wear the right clothes, and sing the right things. What you do should fit the call, musically. For opera auditions, the first aria should be what you can sing when you roll out of bed; you must own it. Then be ready with something else, preferably four other things. Don't give the auditioner(s) a hard time, and remember that collegiality is _really_ important. Don't concern yourself with the reaction of the moment. One friend did an audition in which the listeners talked through the entire audition, but he got the job; they later told him that they were discussing where they could use him.

Another singer friend heard about auditions for the Met chorus on the day they were taking place, because he was riding home on the bus with someone who was auditioning. He walked in, auditioned, and got about $20,000 in work for the next season. Moral: be musically prepared at all times and always carry a resume and picture with you.

Assorted tips: take the ones you like.

▶ Find a teacher whose students are working.

▶ Get out of school. This doesn't mean that you shouldn't be well-educated, but rather that too many singers substitute another degree for the risks of the professional world. You can survive: there are day jobs to help you get by, and there are study grants and apprenticeship programs.

▶ Understand that there are some people who simply won't take to your voice.

▶ Learn to network! It's a very social business. Opportunities resulting from cancellations start with emergency phone calls to colleagues and friends.

► You probably need to go to New York at some point, but are you aware of the cost? Coaches, teachers, etc. are expensive. Come to New York with some salable skills, and when you're ready.

► Treat your pianists well, and listen to them. They generally know more than you do.

► Sing everything and go anywhere, if it's fun.

Pianists: Work after graduation

A few pointers, very briefly. Pianists, like singers, often seem isolated in the musical community, without the easy camaraderie of the orchestra player and the resulting connection to work opportunities. But pianists have advantages in the field, among them:

■ All those violinists and other instrumentalists need your services, and that means that there will be work for you if you're prepared for it
■ The fact that pianists are absolutely necessary for so many musical situations - from dance classes to local theater presentations
■ The fact that the piano is a popular instrument, that it has such an enormous and strong repertoire, and that so many people want to take piano lessons
■ The fact that having learned the piano (reading scores rather than parts, for example) gives you a basis for going in many directions — conducting, coaching, accompaniment, free-lancing, teaching, and more.

You also have disadvantages, in addition to the isolation mentioned above, among them:

■ Situations in which there is no piano available

- That enormous and strong repertoire, which sometimes results in less creativity in finding a niche, and pressure to achieve an extraordinarily high standard of performance in the standard literature which limits the time needed to explore.

A pianist needs, in thinking about her goals, to consider what skills and credentials will be helpful in achieving them.

If you
- improvise
- sight read
- score read
- transpose
- know the literature for a particular instrument or instruments
- can communicate verbally
- play electronic keyboards (for orchestral as well as commercial opportunities)
- handle music others can't: read figured bass, play harpsichord, read unusual notation and play complex contemporary music, etc.

or some combination of these, you can possibly work (in no particular order) as a repitateur in an opera house; as a singers' coach, or an instrumental accompanist; as a member of a chamber ensemble, new music ensemble or early music group; perform concerts which include conversation or lectures as part of the format; in commercial music; to name only a very few.

The above assumes that, even if your goal is to be a solo pianist performing standard repertoire, you need to keep busy, keep eating, and keep your name and presence out there, along the way. Since pianists may, after graduating, find the phone even more silent than their non-pianist colleagues do, think about starting your own project: forming a group, developing a special concert or in-school performance, and finding venues to it (see "Self-management"); developing a concept for a radio series, finding the funding, and bringing it to the local college or public station. What should guide you, when deciding whether to start or even take on a project, is: *If I Do This, Will I Learn Something?* If the answer is yes, do it.

Teaching and Performing

A pianist friend of ours, who teaches at a major music conservatory, was discussing his life and career. Someone to be reckoned with during his own conservatory days, he now, in addition to his teaching, performs at some music festivals (not the most high-profile ones) on a regular basis, does the occasional recording, and performs a few concerts each year. His students are gifted, and he makes a respectable living. He's not famous, but he's known in the profession, and respected. And yet he's slightly bitter, and certainly feels that he should have had more.

However, a major performing career *during the building stage* probably can't co-exist comfortably with a major teaching position. Balancing the demands of teaching — which requires lots of time for planning, being consistently, or at least predictably, available to students, staying in one place, and focusing on the requirements of others — with the demands of building a life in solo or chamber performance on a standard solo instrument — which requires being ready for anything, traveling, intensive networking and focusing to some degree on one's own musical vision — is not realistic. Our friend made a choice, and is, sadly, not comfortable with its consequences.

This is not to say that one can't both teach and perform, and do them successfully and contentedly —if your definition of success includes the kind of activity our friend finds too limited. Obviously it can be done, and it is done, all the time. And certainly senior artists, who have the stature which allows them, without risk, to set limits on either their performing or teaching as necessary, are in the enviable position of being able to have their cake and eat it too.

However, let's turn this around for a minute, and assume that the life described in the first paragraph of this section is exactly what the reader aspires to. In this case, in today's academic climate it is very much to the aspiring teacher's advantage to have significant performing credentials, often more negotiable than another degree (unless, of course, the position requires particular scholarly expertise).

Academic positions at fine music schools, more often than not, depend on the candidate's having a significant professional performing life. Such professional involvement allows the teacher to provide first hand musical knowledge and experience to their students, but also to provide the institution with connections to power and quality in the field, essential for attracting the best performing students. The better the school, the more of these kinds of connections it needs from its teachers and provides to its students. So, in this sense, balancing the two helps to get you a teaching job. It rarely works the other way around, and we have never heard of a case where an academic appointment helped to get a major performing career up and running.

Balancing both, then, requires some perspective and self-knowledge. At the same time, it requires an ability to keep motivated about your performing career; it can be all too easy to trade off the more predictable demands of the academic life, and its relative security, for the hustling one must do to stay performing. Some artists we know have postponed taking or even applying for teaching jobs until their forties, or fifties, or whenever their careers were reasonably secure (or clearly not going to go much further anyway), to insure that they didn't loose the "edge" they need to keep them in the trenches. For "edge," read not knowing where the rent is coming from, fear of having to go into another field, and just plain ambition — which can be a useful, in fact probably essential, part of getting a major career going.

A teaching job, though, can become the center of your performing life, and can allow you to become the central figure in a number of entrepreneurial projects, including establishing a concert series and hiring artists to perform in it, or forming ensembles with your colleagues and performing both at your home base and on tour. So, a teaching position can in some cases enhance, rather than limit, your options. If you do want the option of finding an academic position at some point, you can be more hireable if you develop

- Visibility in the field
- A broad range of interests
- A reputation as a teacher of master classes
- A specialty, or special relationships in the field, scholarly or otherwise.

This will all help you to attract students, which is key as far as the institution is concerned, as well as to be a good teacher. From the students' point of view, they are seeking a teacher who is inspiring, truly involved with discovering the artistic truth within each student; who has prestige, and/or power (these are different, or can be); and who can get them work, and help them to be competitive in today's world. By keeping active in both worlds, your chances of providing all of these are greatly enhanced.

A final word about teaching, what we believe a fine and an honest teacher owes to their students, and what a performing teacher is especially qualified to provide:

- Your special knowledge of and experiences in the field.
- Curiosity about the repertoire, and feedback to them as to where you believe their musical strengths lie.
- An understanding of the collegial nature of the business, and encouragement of their making alliances with other musicians.
- Emphasis on versatility as well as on skills.
- Discussion of goals. Realizing the teacher's ongoing responsibility to ask, "What will you do?" and "How can I help?"

IX. On Stage

When the Guild presents its <u>Career Moves</u> workshops, we often open them with a session on stage technique with the stage director and coach Janet Bookspan presiding. We start with this session because it's exciting and physically involving, but also because it goes right to the heart of one of the workshops' most important issues: that, no matter how well you play, it is possible to <u>prevent</u> your music from reaching others by not realizing that your audience is experiencing more than just the notes. We rely on Janet Bookspan to bring out the best each artist has to offer, with great kindness, insight, and acuity.

If we agree that the essence of successful musical performance is successful communication, we will agree that, just as it's hard to have a sensible telephone conversation on a line filled with static, it's hard for a listener to hear what you have to communicate when confronted with distractions that detract from the total experience. We've all attended concerts which we've liked a lot less than we might have because of factors not in the performer's control: the hall has been cold, the seats have been hard, the people next to us wouldn't stop unwrapping candy. Sometimes we've been able to overlook these factors, and sometimes not. Equally, if you, the performer, fail in those areas which are under your control to make your audience comfortable and confident, to include them in your musical vision rather than separate them from it, you've given yourself an additional handicap in trying to communicate with them that you may not be able to overcome.

True, some artists can transcend this problem, and we all know of cases where artists who are clearly ill-at-ease on stage become magical, once they start to play and we close our eyes. But not very many: most artists whom we enjoy going to hear put us at ease immediately, make us feel that there are great things coming, and, above all, shrink the space psychologically between the listener and the performer to almost nothing, so that we can — for a moment perhaps — see the world, musically, through another's eyes.

Specifically, this means being aware that you have a physical presence on stage which is noted by your audience, and that it is your responsibility to clear away the static, the physical debris, which comes between you and the audience's ability to hear your music. It also means that, to push the telephone analogy a bit further, that you must avoid "crossed wires"; just as your listener can't focus on what you have to say while hearing someone else's conflicting conversation, you have to be sure that you're not projecting two different messages in your performance, one in your music and the other in everything else you do on stage.

Usually, an audience will feel what you <u>seem</u> to be feeling (as distinct from what you actually are feeling), whether that is confident, relaxed, excited — or quite the opposite of these. You will have to see yourself as others do — a very, very difficult task. It also means that you may have to tackle, from time to time, outdated concert conventions, and take an active part in changing them.

We cannot touch here on any but the most general considerations about stage performance style. It is impossible to make rules like, "Smile"; "Always count to three before turning away from the audience"; "Wear velvet"; "Don't wear velvet"; "Move, and be expressive"; "Stop moving, and be less distracting." Though there are general ways of dealing with specific stage problems, this degree of personal specificity is silly, because what you do on stage must come out of the same truth which informs who and what you are as a musician. In developing your performance technique on your instrument, for example, you learn to play cleanly and accurately, usually through a set course of scales, exercises and etudes, so that you can project the overall line and structure and not have it sound like a jumble. But the *reason* you want to be able to project line and structure, in the end, is so that you can project <u>*your vision*</u> of the line and the structure, which is not anyone else's. Similarly, developing your on-stage technique is, first, a matter of developing a smoothness of presentation which clears away any distractions which come between you and your listeners; and, second, developing an on-stage technique *which is you*, part of your total communication, which enables you to be most effective at communicating your ideas.

Even the most generally applicable rules regarding performance presentation technique need hands-on work, or a very lengthy discussion beyond the scope of this chapter, or both. Therefore, our specific recommendations will be limited to directing your attention to potential trouble spots, and stating, at the end of the section, one general consideration which will inform your approach to being on stage.

First: think about all aspects of your performance, including the non-playing ones.

Just thinking about how you are going to get on and off stage, how long and whether to bow before you start and where you should look when you receive applause after you play, whom you should acknowledge and how, where you will put a handkerchief, what you're wearing, and on and on, puts you very far ahead of most emerging performers (and a whole lot of experienced ones), who just plunge on stage and hope for the best.

In thinking about these issues, watch other performers carefully. Pay attention to which performers have a performance style that seems to you to be comfortable, undistracting, elegant or casual — whatever you admire. Watch your peers perform, and think about who seems to carry things off successfully, and who instead makes the audience confused (they may not be able to tell when the pieces end, or whether and when to applaud, for example); who projects "school recital" rather than "professional performance;" who makes everyone tense, rather than expectant, by showing a contagious lack of confidence — and what might be done to improve things.

Ask people about your stage manner.

How would you describe yourself as feeling on stage, and how does that tally with how you appear to others? It's very important to see where the two views diverge, if they do, and to analyze what's creating the difference. Sometimes a very small change in one aspect of your presentation will completely alter your audience's perception, and make you more confident in the bargain.

If what you're feeling, simply, is terrified, it's probably because you're focused on the wrong aspects of what's to come or what's happened; you'll probably have to work on concentrating on positive aspects of your performance. No audience can listen positively to a performer who's obviously scared out of his wits, someone — to be more specific — who's tripped over the piano bench in getting on, fails to take a bow, never looks at the audience at all, and hides behind the music stand. See the end of this chapter for a bit more advice regarding dealing with fear, but also know that the more you have all aspects of your performance under some kind of control, the more confident and the less fearful you will be.

Look at physical mannerisms which may be getting in your way.

In these days of comparatively cheap video recorders, everyone can find someone who has one (perhaps your school videotapes performances, or could), and every performer should, at some early point, tape and watch herself perform. It may be unsettling at first, so never watch yourself directly following a performance or right before another. Prepare yourself with an arsenal of self-forgiving comments beforehand, reassuring yourself that you've certainly seen worse than what's to come, and that the audience seemed to like you so it couldn't have been as bad as you'll probably think it is, and that no one likes the way he looks on film at first anyway. And then watch, seriously and objectively. Get friends to watch with you, those who can be objective and honest when necessary, while remaining supportive.

Analyze what you see, and don't expect to change everything that you're less than satisfied with right away. Pick one or two of the most important areas to work on first — perhaps you are particularly awkward about how to get away from the piano between pieces, or how to acknowledge your accompanist. If a problem seems to be more general, an overall body tension which is getting in the way throughout, it almost certainly is affecting your performance as well, and should be dealt with without delay. There are lots of techniques that deal with tension problems for performers, and you should be able to work with someone individually or in a class on these issues.

Check whether you're reviewing your own concert for your audience while it's happening. And stop doing it.

Inexperienced performers often will send special bulletins to the audience, via grimaces, gestures or, occasionally, expletives, letting them know that they've played wrong notes, or not phrased perfectly, or whatever. This is no favor to the listeners, who might have been foolish enough to have been enjoying themselves up to that point, and certainly no favor to the player. Interestingly, the habit is probably exacerbated by long years at music school; by making faces every time you make a mistake, you're acknowledging errors and apologizing for them before your teachers, colleagues and other knowledgeable types have a chance to criticize — thereby proving that you may be incompetent, but you're no fool. Realize, therefore, that the concert hall is not the schoolroom. You're expected here to be professional, and if that means providing some of the kind of professional wizardry which makes great concerts even in the face of some wrong notes, so be it.

If concert conventions are getting between you and your audience, think about changing them.

One of the biggest, and easiest to cure, obstacles coming between an audience and a performer is a music stand. It is very important, obviously, that a performer feel confident, and if having the music there on a discreetly low and to-the-side stand will prevent panic, fine; but a music stand which you use as protective fortification between you and your audience is a no-no, as is any positioning of the stand — or of yourself — which prevents effective communication.

Even concert dress can and should be tailored to put both you and your audience in the right frame of mind. When CAG recently considered what the dress would be for a series of performances in a rather remote location that doesn't get many live concerts, we thought that really informal clothes would suit the location best. But we were wrong; in the end, we decided on formal dress. This community felt that the performance was a great occasion for them, and they wanted to dress up for the concert — and to be dressed up for. In another situation, for kids for example, a young performer might more easily get the sympathetic attention of her audience if she wears jeans.

The starting time of a performance, if it's under your control, might affect how your concert is received by its audience. So might the length of the program, or the order, or whether or not you include an intermission — or three intermissions. It should all be negotiable in the best of all possible worlds, all with the aim of engaging your listeners as positively as possible.

If you have a chamber group, discuss all aspects of your performance together, in detail.

Most of the very basic problems seen with soloists are even worse with chamber ensembles, who literally and regularly bump into each other getting on and off stage. All aspects of entrances, exits, bows, dress and even seating should be considered by the group; none are insignificant, and none are so sacred (or "traditional") that they can't be worked on and changed, if necessary.

Learn how to talk to your audience.

Most performers are never trained to speak directly to their audiences — and yet this is a skill which is increasingly required of them. Learning how to do this is a lot easier than learning how to play, so that's part of the good news. Another good part is that if you've spoken to the audience, you often will feel barriers breaking down which will help with possible performance nerves, and allow you to play better. The bad news is that this is a skill which does have to be learned, and many people who are terrific performers on their instruments aren't naturally gifted as speakers.

If you find that you can't effectively wing it, here's a technique which will help. Make a list before the performance of several ideas which you feel will interest an audience and which will illuminate some aspect of your performance: the work, your relationship to it, your relationship to this composer, etc. You don't need more than three or four thoughts, but half of them should be personal rather than historical.

An example: a young clarinetist, performing the same program at two CAG produced concerts recently, introduced performances of the Brahms Trio with the identical speech - with one exception. Before one performance, he remarked on how both Mozart and Brahms had had close friends who were clarinetists, resulting in a significant body of work for this instrument from both composers. The audience listened politely. Before the other performance, he added that he was personally very grateful that those clarinetists had been such friendly guys, because not only did he have something to play, but he would never have been invited to this very nice part of the world to play this job without them. On this occasion, the audience laughed, everyone relaxed, and he had them in the palm of his hand for the performance. They listened with greater attention because they were listening to someone they felt they knew, a little.

Anything about the performance to follow is fair game, even how you learned a difficult work, or whether you loved it immediately or grew into it. Speak briefly rather than at length, certainly at first when you're learning how to do this, but look at the audience and smile at them; you're inviting them to join you in what you feel will be an enjoyable experience, and you're using this opportunity to direct their attention to some of those aspects which are most meaningful for you.

Janet Bookspan has developed principles which are immensely helpful in the working out of a performer's own stage personality. We would not presume to try and encapsulate this accumulated wisdom in this short chapter. One particularly important idea which we certainly must repeat here, however, is that of *sharing*, a concept which goes back to the first chapter in which you were encouraged to find out what distinguishes you as an artist. When you know what you have that's special, and what it is that you want to communicate in a specific performance, you can stop worrying quite so much about PERFORMING (or AUDITIONING) and focus on SHARING: that is, on including your listeners in your musical thought.

Since sharing isn't quite as scary as performing or auditioning, by employing this concept things should improve all around, both for you and for your listeners. There is a lot of perfectly good advice around about concert terrors, ranging from the "lose your fear through repeated experience" philosophy, to some quite reasonable books on the subject, to the use of medication. The sharing concept can probably help immediately, however (unlike waiting until you've performed dozens of programs), and is certainly less potentially problematical than the pharmaceutical approach.

If at some point you find that your own ability to improve your effectiveness on stage is limited, you might think about working with a professional in this field. A few sessions can make an immense difference, and may give you the confidence you need for your total performance — freeing you to concentrate on the music, which is what all this is about.

Resource Section

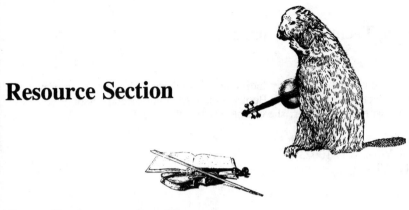

Some Resources for Singers

Should you wish to audition in Europe, specifically in Germany, there is a helpful publication entitled *Kein Angst Baby*! *a guide to German auditions in the 1990's*. It is available through the New York Opera Newsletter, P.O. Box 278, Maplewood, NJ 07040 (201-378-9549, phone; 201-378-2372 fax). When we last looked, it was $17.95.

Singers may want to know about the services of **Opera America**, which offers useful publications (including its biennial directory, *Career Guide for Singers*). Write to them or call for information:

Opera America
1156 15th Street N.W., Suite 810
Washington D.C. 20005-1704
202-293-4466
202-393-0735 (fax)
frontdesk@operaam.org (e-mail)

Stage Techniques Coach

There are undoubtedly many individuals who work with artists to improve their on-stage effectiveness, but Janet Bookspan is something special. Should you wish to discuss working with her, she can be reached at:

155 W. 68 Street, #1414
New York, NY 10023
(212) 496-0740.

X. Summing Up

    This chapter provides information on how to fit all of the above into the framework of your own musical and career growth, with particular attention to the musician still in school. It includes two subjects which didn't fit in before, but which deserve some serious attention. The first of these is about you, and your relationship to your future; the second is about all of us, and all of our futures.

It's Never Too Early To . . . A check list for the younger musician.

The very young artist doesn't need to (and probably shouldn't) try to do everything suggested for career development in the previous chapters. There are those few in the fast lane of course, for whom a great deal is generally done to push their careers forward, almost always by others: parents, teachers, managers, publicists. However, for capable, reasonably ambitious, professionally oriented younger musicians ("younger" meaning prior to emerging from the last of their formal training), here is a checklist of things which can't hurt, and almost certainly will help, to positively prepare for the future.

▶ **Get your biography and resume on a computer disk, and update the information regularly.** It's good to have this information handy and available, whether it's for the home town paper or for submitting to a competition.

▶ **Get your performances on tape.** Having good examples of your most recent playing (or your most recent piece) is very important, and since you may change dramatically with each performance when you're young, get into the habit of taping everything. It's also very important to have the opportunity to review your work for yourself, and use these performances to guide your musical direction. Even a tape made from the audience by a friend you've asked to turn the machine on and off is better than nothing — and sometimes, surprisingly, can be perfectly usable.

▶ **Develop related skills and flexibility.** Very few musicians do only one thing anymore; versatility can make the difference between frustration and excitement when you're in the early stages of your career, and employment or lack of same when you're further along. Related skills might include doubling on a second instrument; the ability to improvise, and certainly the ability to sight read well; familiarity with electronic keyboards or other instruments; knowledge of early music and performance practice; knowledge of and devotion to the works of some contemporary composers. Less obviously, speaking another language may add possible performance locales to your "places to contact" list. Some administrative experience with an arts organization might help you to organize your own concert series, or to raise the funds for it — or, at least, to find a day job in an arts related area.

▶ **Develop originality in programming.** While your teachers and your school are probably going to stress your mastery of the same literature everyone else knows, played in roughly the same program order and in roughly the same format, your own curiosity and interest in reaching out to your audiences should lead you to explore beyond this. When you fully emerge into the professional arena, you will have played your standard graduation recital — the one with the baroque work, the classic and/or romantic work, and the new(er) work, about 1½ hours worth played chronologically — for the last time, hopefully. The world has heard it from everyone else, including everyone famous, and has little interest in hearing you do it again. You could both shake things up a little, have much more fun, and get some attention, by playing something different, perhaps in a different order or format. But it may be up to you to explore what's out there; get in the habit of going to other people's concerts and spending some time in the music library.

▶ **Develop on-stage skills.** This is addressed in the previous chapter, but it's worth thinking about early on.

▶ **Start a mailing list, starting with fans and past sponsors.** There are people in your address book, including friends, relatives, contest organizers, your dentist, your travel agent, and eventually presenters, ticket buyers and industry professionals, who want to be kept up to date about your activities. The easiest way to do this is to keep this information on a computer database, so that you can update it on an ongoing basis. I'm not a fan of the annual "Dear Everyone I've Ever Known" letter, but I think that people do appreciate the occasional post card when you're on tour, or at a summer festival, or brief note (hand written or at least hand signed) when you've accomplished something special.

▶ **Look out for the right competitions and performing opportunities.** Keep a close eye on the school bulletin boards, and hang around the placement office. You need chances to try out what you're learning, and perhaps to earn some money along the way. Also, make sure that your teachers and other mentors know that you would like to hear about opportunities that come their way; often, such information is only passed on to the person who most recently reminded them to do so.

▶ **Start to build relationships with other musicians.** This sounds absolutely obvious, but it's worth stating, since some musicians — notably composers, singers and pianists — tend to work in isolation more than others, and since even players of orchestral instruments may find themselves with a fairly musically limited circle of musical acquaintances: the students in their teacher's studio, for example. Most of the successful (meaning pretty continuously working) musicians we know still get much of their work, and even musical ideas, from the strong relationships formed while they were students. The broader these relationships the more interesting your musical life can be. Performers should be actively seeking out composers whose work they enjoy; singers should read chamber music with instrumentalists, and vice versa; pianists should do as much accompanying as they can reasonably fit in, in many disciplines. (How else can a pianist really learn to play Schubert, but by working with singers, for example? And then, there is always the accompanying work that may pay the rent ... .) It's important to periodically move out of the musical surroundings of your own school into another place, where you can come into contact with a new set of musicians and musical ideas. Summer festivals may be an ideal venue where you can broaden your artistic horizons, and there are as many different kinds of these as there are different kinds of musicians.

Most important, earlier I've mentioned getting into the habit of going to other people's concerts. It's all too common while in school to find that your time doesn't allow you to go to any but the most essential — perhaps required — events. Make the time: this is an essential part of your education as a student, a responsibility as a good colleague, and a potential delight as an artist interested in learning more about repertoire and your fellow musicians. Also, who will attend your concerts, if you don't attend those of others?

▶ **Become knowledgeable about your field.** Read the newspapers: the "think" pieces, not just the reviews. Read the specialty magazines, like *Chamber Music*, or *American Record Guide*, or your instrument specific publications. You will find out about your discipline, your colleagues, about the musical environment, and about how you can contribute as well as what opportunities there are for you.

What not to leave school without

Many musicians find themselves in post-graduation befuddlement, wondering what all those years, and many thousands of dollars, amount to, in the face of an uncertain future and very difficult job market. Rather than confront this for the first time as one is about to leave the academy, it's useful to think, upon entering it, what you don't want to leave without. My own list would include at least four items, the first of which is absolutely obvious:

▶ **A great education.** You should emerge from music school with the musical and technical skills (both on and off your instrument), historical perspective and breadth of knowledge of the repertoire, to allow you to hold your own with the best young artists out there. It is clear that the degrees that you acquire will be very important (sometimes essential) if your future plans include teaching within the academy; however, for purposes of this topic, degrees are secondary to educational content.

▶ **Advice and direction: true-life adventures.** One important aspect of a good music school is that it is where a great many knowledgeable, often perceptive, sometimes insightful and almost always opinionated musicians are gathered in one place. Honest opinions and feedback are very hard to come by in this business, but even harder once one has lost an institutionally mandated claim on these people's time and attention. Even while you have it, it is very hard to get your teachers or other mentors to give you their real opinions about your current work, your progress and your future; they will be afraid of hurting your feelings, or over praising and therefore "spoiling" you in some way, or encouraging you to do something which may prove to be wrong, or not encouraging you to do something which would have been right. Nevertheless, you have to armor yourself with the knowledge that any opinion about you can be wrong or right, and with the grains of salt which allow you not to be overly impressed by praise or discouraged by its opposite, and find <u>benign</u> ways to get people you respect to tell you, and to really hear, what they have to say.

You need this feedback because, certainly when you're young, you need more than your own ears to find out what your musical strengths are, the areas that need improvement, and how you fit in to the larger music community — that is, outside your school or department. **Ask advice.** It is more likely that someone will tell you that you might be stronger in different repertoire, or that you need to reinforce certain musical or technical areas, than that they will simply tell you that you're terrible, or wonderful. And this advice, when multiplied by a number of sources, can be immensely focusing and helpful.

Every musician needs to grow up with musical heroes, and with stories of adventures, good and bad, in the field. These can help you determine both who you want to be, and what kind of life you want to have. Stories are a serious part of your musical education, and you shouldn't leave school without a lot of them.

▶ **An edge.** By the time you graduate — certainly from graduate education, but hopefully well before that — you will have acquired a knowledge of your own particular musical interests and strengths, and the skills to back them up, that will enable you to have a fighting chance out there in the world. School is an excellent place to affordably (given that you, or someone on your behalf, is already paying large sums for tuition) arm yourself with these skills and pursue your interests. Some possibilities are listed in the previous section, under "Related Skills and Flexibility."

▶ **Connections, and as a result, credibility.** You shouldn't emerge from school without someone — or, preferably, many someones — who will be willing to make a phone call for you: to make an introduction, to get you past the tape round of an orchestra audition, to hook you up with someone who might be a musical partner. These people are the ones who will call because they believe in you, not because they are obligated to, as these are the recommendations which will carry some weight out in the world. They can include friends and colleagues as well as teachers; therefore, you should remember that you may be called upon to do as much for them, and that you should be more than willing to do so.

Providing all this should be included in the school's own, albeit unwritten, goals; however, getting this will be your responsibility: it is, in the end, your life and your career. There will be many items you can add to the above list, but thinking about what school can provide should begin with the question,

What do I need to succeed at my goals, that I could, or should, be developing while at school?

Is this all there is?

Allen Hughes, when speaking at our workshops, likes to relate a story about interviewing a young violinist a number of years ago. This young woman had the career which many of the readers of this book probably dream about; the 100 or so ideal engagements a year, playing in the world's finest halls and with the world's finest orchestras; a top manager; very good fees; the respect of the music community. And yet, she felt that her life had simply become a series of hotel rooms, and trying to remember whether she'd packed the hair dryer and what concerto she was performing that night. Though she still liked the actual playing, she was so unhappy with the life that it entailed that it was unclear how long her love of it would last. Her main reaction was, "There must be more to life than this."

A successful solo or chamber career is maintained not simply by an ability to keep playing well, but by a great tolerance for conditions that would not be tolerable for many of us. You have to like, or at least not mind, being on the road: living out of suitcases, rarely being home and maintaining a comparatively sketchy family life. You must be able to remain capable of smiling at those who are putting you up, picking you up at terminals, or entertaining you at a pre- or post-concert party, when you'd far rather be watching TV in your hotel room. And you must be able to concentrate and prepare for performance after long airplane flights or dealing with lost luggage. And on and on.

These conditions are worst, perhaps, during the period in which the career is taking off but not yet in the superstar league — which is, after all, the place where most quite successful careers stay. Though your income at that point may be very good, it has to be very good indeed to alleviate, on a regular basis, all the problems alluded to above. One of the artists interviewed about self-management said, "You have to want [a career] a lot to stand all the rejection you'll face..." We would amend that by adding, "and the life that comes with success, should you achieve it."

It is wise, therefore, to think about whether having this kind of career is worth the effort you'll put into getting it. There are many possible career configurations, based, for example, on a regional orientation, on using the university as a base, on developing a musical specialty for which there is a particular, but possibly limited, demand, even on developing a career in another field and performing on a limited basis. As you move along in your career, it is important to reflect regularly (and objectively, if you can) on where you want to go at a given point, and what the achievement of your goals will entail: on how realistic you are about achieving these goals, and what alternatives to your goals might be possible, would make you happy, and keep you in the field. You don't need to re-evaluate constantly, but you should do so periodically.

The Artist's Responsibility

It is a cliche of the music business these days that we're losing audiences: that the educated European immigrants who sustained the growth of many of the nation's musical organizations and events are dying off or moving to retirement communities, and that they've been replaced by a generation for whom the neglect of serious music education and changes in society's cultural values has resulted in an overall lack of interest in the kind of music most of you perform.

The situation isn't quite that simple, however. There are in fact a great many people listening to classical music, though the percentage, rather than the real numbers, who listen to it in concert halls may be shrinking. They're listening to it in different ways. They're listening to recordings, which get better all the time. They may be listening to the radio, and sometimes watching musical performances on television. And they're still coming out to hear live music, perhaps most enthusiastically at the summer festivals or the highest profile events.

But the fact remains that for the performer seeking a career it is more and more important to take some responsibility for there being the possibility of careers for anyone at all in the future — that is, for there being an audience. You must actively be concerned with issues that for earlier generations, perhaps, could remain peripheral to their main performing activities, including education and even concert format; you must develop a unique and personal commitment to the future, not just the present or past, of your field.

Music, to be successful, must be participatory. The listener must feel some point of identification with the performance and/or the performer, to feel that for a time she is transported to another viewpoint, is experiencing the excitement of a new discovery or the replaying of a familiar and loved scenario. You must make sure this happens by shrinking the space between you and your listener (alluded to in the previous chapter) — which you achieve, first, by making sure that there is nothing in your musical or non-musical technique preventing your message from being heard, and then by being as truthful, focused and wonderful in your performance as it is possible to be.

It is nonetheless possible for your audience to be unable to really hear you for reasons that go beyond the scope of any individual recital. Unfamiliarity with the music, the people performing it and the situation in which it's performed is, sadly, the rule rather than the exception for most people these days. Therefore, a commitment to music education in the broadest sense must be part of your concerns as an artist. By this we don't mean telling people who Beethoven was, interesting as that might be: but, rather, to try to widen the circle of friends, to include more people in the family, the knowing and knowledgeable; to increase the number of those who aren't frightened by the concert hall or by music they haven't heard before; and to enlighten those who think that classical musicians are some strange breed, quite apart from normal humanity.

This may mean working on in-school performances, cultivating such opportunities and welcoming these engagements. It may also mean developing part of your performance which includes talking to the audience before the concert — or during it, if the situation is casual enough. It certainly means looking carefully at all aspects of performance, from finding people to bring into the halls and figuring out how to reach them to rethinking exactly what a concert is, what a concert hall is and when performances should be held. If you are producing your own concerts — if you have a chamber group that produces a series, for example — all these areas are directly in your control, and can be creatively explored for new solutions.

Whatever you do, though, should come out of your own experience as an artist, why you love music and why you want to share your music with others. You must learn to communicate why it's all worthwhile, and why it's even worth special effort. In articulating this to your public, you will first have to understand it yourself. Posing the question, and answering it with truth and with care, should remind you of the value of all that you are trying to achieve.

XI. General Resources

Non-Profit Status

"Non-profit" (also called "not-for-profit") groups can receive contributions which are tax-deductible to the donor, and they are exempt from paying federal taxes (and certain state and city taxes as well). In order to be granted such status, the group has formally been incorporated as a not-for-profit corporation, and has been granted legal tax-exemption usually under section 501(C)(3) of the Internal Revenue Service code (there are other non-profit classifications for religious and educational organizations).

Being non-profit doesn't mean that no one makes any money; it means that money received by the group is used for fees, salaries, program expenses, administrative costs and the like, and not as profit to be distributed among principals of the organization (as profits might be among the shareholders or partners of a for-profit corporation, for example).

It is useful to have such status if your group does a significant amount of self-produced activity: puts on an annual concert series, organizes its own tours without fees or at fees which don't cover the expenses, commissions works, produces recordings, and more. However, it is something of a hassle to get, and, like any incorporation, there is a lot of formal organizing, paperwork and form-filing that will have to be complied with on a regular basis.

Volunteer Lawyers for the Arts (see below) can help you to understand the whole process, decide whether it would be important for you to have, and either do the legal work on your behalf or refer you to a lawyer who will.

If you go this route, you'll need some assistance in learning about the strange and constantly changing world of grants and funding. You can start by heading for your most local arts council, whether that's on the community, county, city or state level. They should be able to direct you to other sources of information, and to tell you what sort of groundwork you need to do before being of interest to funders.

There are lots of books on the subject, but talking to those who've done it, as well as to the funders themselves, is probably the best way to learn.

Volunteer Lawyers for the Arts
1 East 53rd Street, 6th Floor
New York, NY 10022
212-319-2787

Founded in 1969, VLA was the first legal aid organization in the U.S. dedicated to providing free arts-related legal assistance to artists and arts organizations in all creative fields. It provides artists and arts organizations with limited pro bono legal advice, and helps to find further legal representation on arts related issues at affordable rates. Call to ask about eligibility for a free one hour consultation for individual artists or arts organizations. VLA also offers clinics, conferences and workshops on a variety of arts-related legal issues, has a speakers bureau, and operates a legal hotline for any artist or arts organization which needs quick answers to arts related legal questions. The hotline number is: 212-319-2910.

VLA publications include All You Need to Know About the Music Business; The Musicians Business and Legal Guide; The Artist's Tax Guide and Financial Planner; How to Form Your Own New York Corporation; and many other useful books. Write to the above address for a complete listing and for prices, or call the publications department at the above number, extension 25.

Other help with the non-profit world, once you're in it:

If you would like to do some of your research about non-profits, grants, and various other ways that the arts and the rest of the world interact, try:

Americans for the Arts
1 East 53rd Street
New York, NY 10022
212-223-2787

This organization both sells books for artists and arts organizations and maintains a library. Write for their publications catalog, which has lots of interesting items in it. ACA also keeps lists of grants and competitions.

Individual artists assistance, various:

New York Foundation for the Arts
155 6th Avenue, 14th Floor
New York, NY 10013
212-366-6900

NYFA is generally a very good, informed source of information about programs and assistance for individual artists. It can act as a non-profit conduit for individual artists' projects; has a very useful quarterly newsletter, FYI (though it's much more oriented to visual arts than music, and more to composers than performers even within the music field); administers a program of individual artist fellowships (again, for composers); runs a revolving loan program and a management services program for non-profit organizations.

Astral Artistic Services
230 South Broad Street, 3rd Floor
Philadelphia, PA 19102
215-735-6999 (phone)
215-735-6856 (fax)

This organization was formed as a "pre-management resource center, providing ongoing assistance and advice free of charge [except for a nominal non-refundable application fee] to classical instrumentalists, singers, conductors and composers who are residing in the U.S." Certainly worth the application fee, if you can use any of the services which Astral provides: assistance with preparation of pr materials, grant applications and the like, advice on presentation and repertoire, translations, and more. Astral's president, Vera Wilson, formerly was executive director of the Astral Foundation, which worked extensively with emerging artists.

National Foundation for Advancement in the Arts (NFAA)
Astral Career Grants
305-377-1147
Wendy Page Wheeler

No relationship to the previous Astral, these modest grants are awarded to meet expenses related to activities that will directly further an artists career. Examples of needs that qualify would be costs of travel to an audition, or repair of an instrument; examples of needs that would not qualify are medical expenses or general living support. The program is open to pianists, singers and composers, American citizens or full-time residents, and applicants must not be full-time students. Up to $250 grants are awarded at meetings held four times a year; no more than one grant a year can be given to one artist. Write for an application form.

Unions and Professional associations:

Here are the addresses of the two major musicians' unions:

American Federation of Musicians (AF of M)
1501 Broadway, Suite 600
New York, NY 10036
212-869-1330

American Guild of Musical Artists (AGMA)
1727 Broadway
New York, NY 10019   .
212-265-3687

Both of these organizations issue publications including important information about the field. The former has many more instrumentalists, the latter more singers, among its members. Union membership is required for much of the regular and free-lance work in most cities. Contact the above offices for the addresses and phone numbers of the local in your city, or look in the phone book.

There are several professional associations, organized by discipline, which serve as lobbyists for that part of the field and clearinghouses for information, and offer services of particular value to their constituencies. There is an Early Music America, several new music associations, and more. One example, of a particularly successful and useful professional association:

Chamber Music America
305 Seventh Avenue
New York, NY 10001
212-242-2022 (phone)
212-242-7955 (fax)

CMA administers a number of grant programs for chamber groups, including one that helps ensembles establish residencies and one to commission chamber works. CMA produces an annual conference, runs workshops on career development and other important issues, offers technical assistance to its membership and publishes a newsletter, CMA Matters, a magazine, "Chamber Music," and other publications relevant to the field of chamber music and chamber music education.

A professional association of a different kind:

College Music Society
202 West Spruce Street

Missoula, MT 59802
406-721-9616 (phone)
406-721-9419 (fax)

This organization offers several services of interest to musicians working within the academic community. Its members may attend conferences around the country, and may obtain special publications of interest to specific areas of the field — women's music, world music, etc. Both members and non-members may subscribe to a bi-monthly listing of music faculty openings nationwide.

Also, the CMS mailing lists are the most complete of any in this area of the field. Which leads to the question:

Looking for Mailing Lists?

Computers for the Arts
375 Riverside Drive, Apt. 10E
New York, NY 10025
212-316-3953

This group rents computerized mailing lists, including lists of audiences sorted by musical interests, presenters, radio, press, record companies, opera companies and symphony orchestras. Generally, list rental (including the actual printed labels) costs $.08 each, and the lists range from about 50 to about 2,500, depending on how they're sorted. (They will also computerize your mailing list, and print lists in various formats.)

If you're doing a mailing using this or any other computerized list, try to check on how often it is updated. It's sometimes very difficult to keep lists from these organizations current, since returned mail coming from a rented list goes back to the organization doing the event, not to the one holding the list. For a large scale, blanket mailing it's probably not too important if a few duds sneak in; but if you are trying to really reach a special constituency, perhaps you want to develop your own cleaner list over time.

In addition to well-known sources of lists for musicians like this one, think creatively about where your constituency might overlap with another, though perhaps less obviously. For example, if you do cutting-edge music, perhaps a group which has mailing lists of people who go to cutting-edge dance would be more useful to you than a standard music list. In this case, it might be of interest to you to join an organization like:

Dance Theatre Workshop
219 W. 19th Street
New York, NY 10011
212-691-6500

Their members include composers as well as dancers, choreographers, and others, and members can get the benefits of bulk mail services, discounts on ads in the major newspapers, listings of rehearsal spaces, and an updated, interdisciplinary national press list. **Note also**: *this organization runs seminars on taxes every spring, open to non-members as well as members.*

Be creative about finding out who and where your potential audience is, and how to get to them.

Some Final Resource Suggestions: Survival

Health Insurance

It would be wonderful to believe that by the time this book has been out for a short while this will be a non-issue, a universal health care package of some kind having been adopted nationally. Probably that won't be the case, and we will still have to muddle through for a while. There is a recent publication which should be helpful: Health Insurance, A Guide for Artists, Consultants, Entrepreneurs, and Other Self-Employed, by Lenore Janecek. It also covers retirement planning and things like that. It's available from ACA books, listed above, and costs 15.95 per copy, plus $4 postage.

Credit Union

Artists Community Federal Credit Union
155 Avenue of the Americas, 14th Floor
New York, NY 10013-1507
212-366-5669 (phone)
212-366-1778 (fax)

This organization provides services that often are difficult for musicians to come by: loans for artistic purposes, lines of credit, and no-fee savings accounts and IRAs. It is a national organization. The one time membership fee is only $10; call to learn how to join.

Day Jobs

Sometimes it does become necessary to support oneself by working a regular job, and earning a regular paycheck. It might be nice, though, to use your musical skills while doing this. Two publications which might help you to think about the

various possibilities in the field other than playing or composing:

Careers in Music is a pamphlet issued by the Music Educators National Conference, and available from them — free — by writing to the organization at 1902 Association Drive, Reston, VA 22091, or calling 703-860-4000. Though very brief, it covers a lot of possibilities, and includes a list of sources to go to for further information. We particularly like the fact that the handy chart which is included lists approximate earnings, qualifications and skills required, recommended training, and opportunities for employment.

Your Own Way in Music: A Career and Resource Guide, by Nancy Usher, **St. Martins Press**. Vocational guidance. The most interesting parts of this book are the "case histories," which describe how highly trained musicians can be happy and fulfilled in various non-performance (and performance) jobs in the field. Ms. Usher covers arts administration, acoustics, instrument making, free-lancing, academic positions, music therapy, Alexander technique teaching, copying, music production in all sorts of areas ... soup to nuts, in fact.

If you've decided to find a job in arts administration, there are several publications to which you can subscribe which may help you to find one:

Artsearch
Theatre Communications Group, Inc.
355 Lexington Avenue
New York, NY 10017-0217
212-697-5230 (phone)
212-983-4847 (fax)
tcg@tmn.com

You can subscribe by mail or e-mail. Fax or e-mail for subscription rates.
Another possibility:

ArtJob
Western States Arts Federation
236 Montezuma Avenue
Santa Fe, NM 87501-2641
505-986-8939 (phone)
505-983-3732 (fax)
artjob@rt66.com

Topic and Resource Index

NOTES

ANNUALLY UPDATED!

CONCERT ARTISTS GUILD'S

GUIDE TO COMPETITIONS

New Editions Released Every Septmeber!

Published since 1987 and updated annually, the *Guide* serves as a
fundamental reference work for individual performers, music libraries,
career development offices, and teachers. A copy of the *Guide* is the
essential resource for anyone seeking up-to-date, detailed information about
competitions worldwide.

Each entry contains important information about:
> *Prizes, Contact information, Age requirements, Deadlines,*
> *Application fees, Comments, ...and other essential information.*

ORDER FORM

MAIL this form with payment to:
> CONCERT ARTISTS GUILD PUBLICATIONS
> 850 Seventh Avenue, Suite 1205
> New York, NY 10019

- Checks should be made payable to Concert Artists Guild.
- Please allow 2-3 weeks for delivery.
- Call for information on multiple copy discounts.

✂ -

_____ *Making Music in Looking Glass Land*, $17.95

_____ *Guide to Competitions*, $17.95

_____ Please add $4.00 for the first book and $1.50 for each
additional book for postage

_____ New York State residents must add sales tax for each
book ordered ($1.48 per book)

_____ **Total Enclosed**

NAME

ADDRESS

CITY/STATE/ZIP   **TELEPHONE (DAY)**

ELLEN HIGHSTEIN

As Executive Director of Concert Artists Guild from 1986-1997, Ellen Highstein initiated and established a program of national concert presentations, a west coast office and music festival, a national program of radio residencies and broadcasts, the widely presented career development workshops, and a publications division, among other programs. She has overseen the growth of the Guild's full service management to one of the nation's foremost non-profit managements, and the Guild's annual international competition to one of the largest and most respected in the country. Through the *Career Moves* workshops, she has been a frequent speaker on career development issues at colleges, conservatories and music centers throughout the country.

Prior to joining the Guild, Ms. Highstein was a music program officer at the New York State Council on the Arts, and continues to serve as a consultant for many government agencies and foundations. As a writer, she has contributed articles to various magazines including *Chamber Music* magazine as well as to the *American Grove's*, and has collaborated on a workbook in theory for the Manhattan School of Music Preparatory Division.

Ms. Highstein holds degrees in composition from The Juilliard School and in education from New York University, has studied at the Paris Conservatory, and has trained and performed in piano, voice and conducting. She has been on the music department faculty of Brooklyn College Conservatory, and on the pre-college faculties of The Juilliard School and the Manhattan School of Music.

Ms. Highstein was appointed Director, Tanglewood Music Center in November, 1997.

CONCERT ARTISTS GUILD

Concert Artists Guild is devoted to the career development of the emerging classical musician. Since 1951, the Guild has advanced the careers of over 500 instrumentalists, singers, and ensembles from around the world. The Guild's programs include the annual international competition, the artist management program, radio residencies, commissions, fellowships, career development workshops, and publications. For information on Concert Artists Guild's programs, please write to: 850 Seventh Ave., Suite 1205, New York, NY 10019, or call: (212) 333-5200.